Key Issues in
Bilingualism and
Bilingual Education

Multilingual Matters

Bilingualism: Basic Principles (Second edition)
HUGO BAETENS BEARDSMORE
Bilingual Children: Guidance for the Family
GEORGE SAUNDERS
Conflict and Language Planning in Quebec
RICHARD Y. BOURHIS (ed.)
Bilingualism and Special Education
JIM CUMMINS
Bilingualism or Not: The Education of Minorities
TOVE SKUTNABB-KANGAS
Language Proficiency Assessment (Four volumes)
CHARLENE RIVERA (ed.)
The Education of Linguistic and Cultural Minorities in the OECD Countries
STACY CHURCHILL
Learner Language and Language Learning
CLAUS FAERCH, KIRSTEN HAASTRUP AND ROBERT PHILLIPSON
Bilingual and Multicultural Education: Canadian Perspectives
STAN SHAPSON AND VINCENT D'OYLEY (eds.)
Language Acquisition of a Bilingual Child
ALVINO FANTINI
Modelling and Assessing Second Language Acquisition
KENNETH HYLTENSTAM AND MANFRED PIENEMANN (eds.)
Aspects of Bilingualism in Wales
COLIN BAKER
Minority Education and Ethnic Survival
MICHAEL BYRAM
Age in Second Language Acquisition
BIRGIT HARLEY
Language in a Black Community
VIV EDWARDS
Language and Education in Multilingual Settings
BERNARD SPOLSKY (ed.)
Code-Mixing and Code Choice: A Hong Kong Case Study
JOHN GIBBONS
The Interdisciplinary Study of Urban Bilingualism in Brussels
ELS WITTE and HUGO BAETENS BEARDSMORE (eds.)
Raising Children Bilingually: The Pre-School Years
LENORE ARNBERG
Introspection in Second Language Research
CLAUS FAERCH and GABRIELE KASPER (eds.)
The Use of Welsh: A Contribution to Sociolinguistics
MARTIN BALL (ed.)
3rd Int'l Conference on Minority Languages: Celtic Papers
G. MAC EOIN, A. AHLQVIST & D. O HAODHA (eds)
Sign & School
JIM KYLE (ed.)
The Open Door
FINBARRÉ FITZPATRICK

Please contact us for the latest book information:
Multilingual Matters, Bank House, 8a Hill Road,
Clevedon, Avon BS21 7HH, England.

MULTILINGUAL MATTERS 35
Series Editor: Derrick Sharp

BE

Key Issues in Bilingualism and Bilingual Education

Colin Baker

MULTILINGUAL MATTERS LTD
Clevedon · Philadelphia

Library of Congress Cataloguing-in-Publication Data

Baker, Colin, 1949—
   Key issues in bilingualism and bilingual education/Colin Baker.
      p.   cm. — (Multilingual matters; 35)
   Bibliography: p.
   Includes index.
   ISBN 0-905028-95-3. ISBN 0-905028-94-5 (pbk.)
   1. Bilingualism. 2. Education, Bilingual. I. Title.
II. Series.
P115.B34 1988
404'.2—dc19   87-22682   CIP

British Library Cataloguing in Publication Data

Baker, Colin, 1949—
   Key issues in bilingualism and bilingual
   education.—(Multilingual matters; 35).
   1. Education, Bilingual
   I. Title II. Series
   371.97   C3715

   ISBN 0-905028-95-3
   ISBN 0-905028-94-5 Pbk

Multilingual Matters Ltd,
Bank House, 8a Hill Road,   and   242 Cherry Street
Clevedon, Avon BS21 7HH,   Philadelphia
England.   PA 19106-1906, USA

Typeset by Photo-Graphics, Honiton, Devon
Reprinted 1990 by Short Run Press Ltd, Exeter, U.K.

Contents

Acknowledgements

The origins of the book go back to undergraduate days. A first taste and appetiser for the subject of bilingualism and bilingual education was given by some understanding and colourful lecturers, W. R. Jones, Professor Roger Webster, Dr Bryn Davies and Dr Ivor Leng in particular. At the same time, a young enthusiastic lecturer in social psychology, Alun Waddon, inspired my generation and future generations with the excitement and importance of his subject. With the same enthusiasm he read parts of the draft of this book and proved beyond doubt, who can still inspire, motivate and teach.

The passage of the book owes much to Derrick Sharp. He encouraged its production and then provided expert, detailed and sympathetic comments on the whole of the draft. His friendly, sensitive and perceptive approach has been both motivational and a true learning experience. I suspect the British Diplomatic Service should have secured his services after "retirement", but bilingualism has been the winner. Diolch Derrick.

In revising the first draft, I have been fortunate to be surrounded by an abundance of helpful and encouraging colleagues. Professor Iolo Williams gave generously of his advice, making useful and detailed comments, and giving the support, encouragement and backing that is so valuable from the Head of a busy Department. Professor Phillip Williams' expertise on intelligence, cognitive development and motivation was invaluable. To have someone of his experience and knowledge of psychology along the corridor is both re-assuring and of great help. He never failed to show interest in the passage of the book. Dr B. L. Davies, a model tutor from undergraduate days, read the whole of the first draft, spotted my weaknesses, and was, as always, generous with his time and comments. He provided a translation service with care and skill, and because of his modesty, will never know the debt I owe him. Sidney Whitaker demonstrated with gentility and care how a trilingualist is superior to a monolingual in the skill of writing. Máirtín Ó Fathaigh of the University College, Cork in Ireland kindly agreed to read and comment on parts of the draft and to share his knowledge and understanding of Irish bilingualism and Irish bilingual education. To all these colleagues, my sincere thanks.

Where mistakes and wrong interpretations have been made, they are all mine.

There are a second group of people who were not requested to read the draft, but create the environment to write about bilingualism and bilingual education, and provide the tacit, subtle knowledge about bilingual matters that is an important addition to reading and research. There are too many people to mention by name, however, I wish to acknowledge the warm friendship of my Welsh-speaking colleagues in the School of Education and in the rest of the Faculty of Arts. Glyn, Delyth and Elen teach across the dinner table and amidst the happy noise of home. Having an extended family of bilinguals is a rich source of stimulation. They answer endless questions with love and humour. Geraint ap Iorwerth kindly provided the graphics in Chapter 7, just one of his many talents.

I am fortunate in knowing two of the most cheerful of word processors: Beryl Hughes and Dilys Parry. They type and edit without complaint and with much skill. Their readiness to help is only matched by their sense of fun. The sound of laughter is a daily tonic.

My greatest debt is to my wife and three bilingual children. They rarely complained when writing has taken preference over wallpapering and mountain walks. All four provide a daily example of how to speak two languages with consummate ease and effortless efficiency. To Anwen, Sara, Rhodri and Arwel this book is lovingly dedicated.

Introduction

The book centres around three questions that all those interested in bilingualism and bilingual education seem to ask, be they parents, teachers, administrators, students or lecturers. These three questions will be phrased slightly differently by different people, but are:

1. Will children suffer if they become bilingual?

The first question is usually asked in this negatively loaded fashion. The majority of the population seem to expect children to suffer rather than benefit from speaking two languages. The implied effects are often "on the brain", on the intelligence or in the process of thinking. The expectation seems to be that facility in two languages leads to less room for other skills such as mathematical, musical, scientific or creative skills, and that the two languages will be half developed in comparison with the monolingual's one well developed language.

2. Will children suffer from education which uses two languages?

The second question is also usually asked in a negative vein. Learning through the child's second language, or using both languages in the curriculum, is often expected to result in lower overall performance at school. Full attainment in maths, science, history and geography, for example, may be at risk in bilingual education according to many a parent, teacher and politician. The expectation is often that children cannot cope with the demands of schooling through a second language or through two languages.

3. Isn't the "right" attitude and motivation, and not compulsion and conformity, vital in becoming bilingual and in bilingual education?

In many countries, bilingual education or monolingual education, bilingualism or monolingualism are imposed, provided under pressure or sometimes enforced. Having the freedom to decide for oneself or one's children is more rare. Hence the third question concerns inner motives and attitudes, as well as the kind of supportive or unsupportive environment surrounding the individual, that affects the development or otherwise of bilingualism and bilingual education.

The three questions are examined from educational and psychological perspectives. Each question is examined by two chapters. Question 1 is engaged by Chapters 1 and 2 which focus on intelligence, cognitive development and bilingualism. Question 2 is addressed in Chapters 3 and 4 which examine bilingual education in the USA and Canada, England and Wales, Ireland and Scotland. Question 3 is the foundation for Chapters 5 and 6 which examine research on attitudes, motivation and bilingualism. The three questions are brought together in the final chapter which, through various theories of bilingualism and bilingual education, attempts to integrate and summarize the current answers to these questions.

The book attempts to avoid giving over-simplistic answers or banal generalizations. Like doubting Thomas, we always need to ask for the proof. There is always the need to delve into the limitations and assumptions of research and researchers, and then, with the evidence available, to make as fair and as balanced a verdict as is possible. Where there is a lack of evidence, the preference has been to reserve judgement rather than give an unsupported verdict.

To be academically acceptable and publicly informative is a difficult, even impossible task. Yet building a bridge between data and dispute, research and reform, publications and practice is important. The book seeks to inform the debate, make reform more rational, and stimulate better practice.

1 Bilingualism and Intelligence

Introduction

Bilingualism is to intelligence as food is to human fitness. The relationship between the two is both central and controversial. Central, in that the disadvantages or advantages of being bilingual have been historically measured by reference to intelligence. Controversial, in that both terms are difficult to define, elusive to measure and evoke passions and prejudices.

For the parent or teacher, the relationship is important and simple. In learning or speaking two languages, will the child become less intelligent, more intelligent, or will bilingualism have no effect one way or the other? The justification for bilingual education is partly built on the resolution of the intelligence issue. If a child benefits cognitively from being bilingual, then bilingual education becomes justifiable. If there are deficits in being bilingual, support for such education may be more difficult to find.

The controversies

A simple statement about bilingualism and intelligence is as impossible as is prescribing one simple food for human survival. To state simply that bilingualism has a beneficial or detrimental effect on intelligence is to be naive and simplistic. To understand the relationship between the two, the problems involved in the definition and measurement of intelligence and bilingualism must be first understood.

Bilingualism

The problem of the definition of bilingualism

To suggest to parents and teachers that being a bilingual person is beneficial in terms of intelligence would, among other concerns, require "being bilingual" to be unambiguous. Unfortunately, deciding exactly who is or is not bilingual is problematic (Mackey, 1962; Skutnabb-Kangas, 1981; Baker, 1985).

The initial issue is that of dimensions. To be called bilingual, is it necessary to show literacy as well as oracy in two languages? Mackey (1962) suggests four basic language skills: listening, reading, speaking and writing. These skills can be further subdivided. For example, in speaking two languages, people may differ in terms of extent of vocabulary, correctness of grammar and pronunciation. As defined by Mackey (1962), there are at least 20 dimensions of language skill in each language. People have varying skills in listening, speaking, reading and writing a language. Within those four skills there are sub-skills in vocabulary, grammar, pronunciation, meanings and style.

Take a hypothetical case. A pupil may be able to understand spoken English and Welsh, speak English fluently but Welsh only haltingly, read in Welsh with a reading age of six and in English with a reading age of eight, write poorly in English and not at all in Welsh. Is that pupil bilingual?

If we add to the many dimensions of language skill, the *context* or domain of language usage, defining who is or is not bilingual becomes even more difficult. While someone may have ability in two languages, one language may be restricted to the home. Each language may be used in a narrow or broad range of contexts. The context or domain of language usage defines when each language is spoken, to whom, where and why (Fishman, 1965).

Given the great number of dimensions of skill in each language and the great range of different contexts where a language may or may not be used, it becomes apparent that a simple categorization of who is or who is not bilingual is almost impossible. Between the notions of complete bilingualism and complete monolingualism there are not only different shades of grey, but different shades of a great range of different colours. Deciding which colours must be included in definition and measurement and the strengths of the shades of colour is a near impossible task. There are no definitive cut-off points to distinguish the bilingual from the monolingual.

The measurement of bilingualism

If defining who is or is not bilingual is fraught with problems, how have studies relating bilingualism and intelligence gathered together their research sample? What populations do the samples represent? How many children or adults were selected and how were they categorized in terms of language usage or ability?

The key question is that of generalization. If the sample is biased towards certain types of bilinguals (e.g. those with great skill on many dimensions who are bilingual in many varying contexts), then the results may have very limited validity and applicability. As will be seen later in the chapter, controversy has particularly surrounded the use in research of balanced bilinguals, this group sometimes being thought of as being representative of bilinguals. Balanced bilinguals may be said to have approximately equal skills in both languages. This does not imply that their language skills are at a high level or that they are very able bilinguals. Rather, it implies that in terms of the reception and production of oral and literary language skills, a person has almost equal competence. While in theory, the less gifted and the more gifted bilinguals may be included as "balanced bilinguals", MacNab (1979) has suggested that, in practice, restricting the choice of bilinguals to balanced bilinguals in research has led to the selection of a special and non-representative group. Cummins (1976) has disputed this, believing that use of balanced bilinguals induces only the slightest of biases in the research.

Nevertheless, as Cummins (1976) notes, much of the recent research has centred on samples of balanced bilinguals. The use of balanced bilinguals partly evades the difficulty of defining who is or is not bilingual, given the large number of dimensions upon which language skills can be scaled. Children who are dominant in one language, but who may be regarded as bilinguals, tend to be excluded from research because of their imbalance in language skills.

Intelligence

Almost all research which has examined the relationship between bilingualism and intelligence fails to indicate that intelligence is an area of great controversy in psychology and sociology, genetics and semantics. Indeed, it is the contention of this chapter that the most severe limitation and criticism of the bilingualism and intelligence research lies in the problems of defining and measuring intelligence and in using IQ tests. The value and relevance of this research has to be judged from a critical appreciation of the intelligence controversies. Four issues will be briefly raised.

The definition of intelligence

To define the height or weight of a person is relatively straightforward. Both can be defined and measured with accuracy and agreement. Weighing scales and a tape measure allow such measurement to be viewed. To ask to view the intelligence of a person would be to invite much mirth. Intelligence cannot be directly observed. It has to be inferred from behaviour. Such inference with be based either on intelligent acts (e.g. reaching the moon) or on mental processes that promote such acts (e.g. being clever, talented).

If attempts are made to define intelligence by behavioural acts, the immediate issue is "who judges?" The expert thief cracks the security system of a bank vault. To thieves that may be highly intelligent behaviour; to many police, very unintelligent because of the consequences if the criminal is caught and sentenced. As a footballer, was Pele intelligent? As a financier, was Paul Getty very intelligent? Could Don Juan as a lover be described ·as intelligent? Is there social intelligence, motoring intelligence, musical intelligence? Is intelligence the same as wisdom or political acuteness? Clearly to label such acts as more or less intelligent requires a subjective judgement which is culturally and sub-culturally relative. It reflects a judgement as to who or what is of more worth (Mercer, 1978/79).

It may be argued that intelligent behavioural acts have a common denominator. Underlying each intelligent act is the same or similar mental processes, e.g. reasoning ability, logical thinking, problem solving. This raises the issue of the structure of intelligence. Is intelligence basically one mental process, one overall ability? Alternatively, is intelligence an umbrella term representing a number of separate factors, linked in a hierarchy or in a relational network without hierarchy? Or is human intelligence best conceived in terms of an information-processing approach which examines the mechanisms of intelligent functioning, the strategies of intelligent performance and the mental representations of such functioning and strategies? (Sternberg, 1985).

The structure of intelligence

To understand the bilingualism and intelligence research, it is important at least to understand two extremes. The one extreme is monism, which argues that intelligence is a unitary trait, and the other extreme is pluralism, which argues that there is a group of independent traits of intelligence. The research examined in this chapter mostly focuses on a psychometric concept of intelligence which insists that intelligence is hierarchical and is ultimately composed of one or two factors. The second chapter will examine a broader concept of intelligence and cognition that implies a multi-factored, multi-dimensional representation and moves towards the recent information-processing approach to human abilities.

At one extreme of the psychometric concept of intelligence is Spearman's (1927) belief that there exists one basic, general factor of intelligence, labelled "g". From a variety of pencil and paper tests where usually only one correct answer is possible, the Spearman school, through the use of a statistical categorizing tool called factor analysis, purported to show that the test items all measured, to a greater or lesser extent, the general factor "g". Bilingual research has tended to follow later theorists who separated "g" into two parts, verbal and non-verbal intelligence. Such research, up to approximately the 1960s, assumed this narrow view of the structure of intelligence. W. R. Jones (1966), for example, was a strong supporter of the "g" factor.

At the other extreme of the psychometric concept of intelligence is Guilford's (1982) 150 factor model of intelligence. Guilford argued that all mental tasks involve operations, products and content. He lists *five operations*: cognition, memory, divergent production, convergent production and evaluation; *six products*: units, classes, relations, systems, transformations and implications; and *five* types of *content*: visual, auditory, symbolic, semantic and behavioural. The model may be thought of in three-dimensional or cubic terms, such that there are 5 × 6 × 5 = 150 different mental abilities. Guilford claims to have demonstrated the testable existence of 105 of the 150 factors. Another multi-factor view of intelligence comes from H. Gardner (1983) whose list includes linguistic intelligence, musical intelligence, logical–mathematical intelligence, spatial intelligence, bodily-kinesthetic intelligence and personal intelligence. This popular view, and the multi-factor tradition is critically considered by Sternberg (1983).

Although bilingualism and intelligence research since the 1960s has centred on a variety of theories of cognition and intelligence, Guilford's (1982) theory suggests a different research avenue. A multi-factored model raises the question "on which factors are bilinguals different from unilinguals?" Research on bilingualism and the "g" factor invokes a simple black and white answer. Research on bilingualism and multi-factored intelligence requests a profile of a variety of colours and shades. Of Guilford's (1982) 150 factors, are bilinguals relatively strong on some factors, weak on others, no different from monolinguals on the remaining factors? Future research may answer this question.

The IQ test

If the precise definition of intelligence is impossible and if the structure of intelligence is described in a variety of forms (e.g. Thurstone, 1938; Cattell, 1971; Guilford, 1982; H. Gardner, 1983) with little agreement, it can be seen immediately that use of IQ tests in bilingualism and intelligence research is contentious.

One issue regarding the IQ test may best be viewed in terms of the Hebb–Vernon model of intelligence (P. Vernon, 1979). The model has three parts: Intelligence A, which measures inborn potential, impossible to measure accurately and unambiguously; Intelligence B, which is intelligent behaviour, a product of hereditary and environmental influences; and Intelligence C which is measured intelligence (IQ). Intelligence C is a small, and very unrepresentative sample of Intelligence B. Thus the operational definition of "intelligence is that which is measured by IQ tests" is immediately seen to be narrowly circular.

Simply stated, in much of the bilingualism and intelligence research, it is IQ and not intelligence that has been measured. IQ tests usually require one correct answer to a question. Are all abilities measurable in this form? IQ tests generally require pencil and paper. Is intelligence represented fairly by such a task? Caution is needed in assuming that such bilingual research concerns intelligence. In truth, it concerns IQ tests and not intelligence.

There exist a varity of other criticisms of the use of the IQ test (Sternberg, 1985). Some of these concern pedagogic uses and effects from usage of the test (e.g. self-fulfilling prophecy, discrimination against black and other minority groups, effects of coaching and streaming on IQ scores and a mutually reinforcing effect with a convergent school curriculum). As Cummins (1984a) has shown, IQ tests have been used as diagnostic and predictive instruments in a biased manner against minority group bilinguals. Important as these criticisms are, they are not of central concern to the issue of the relationship between bilingualism and intelligence.

Further specific criticisms of the IQ test will be examined later in the chapter. What needs to be noticed is that IQ tests have been, and mostly still are, regarded by parents and teachers as not only measuring intelligence, but also as being powerfully predictive of future attainment and achievement at school and beyond. IQ tests purport to measure intelligence. Intelligence is a highly prized possession in a competitive meritocratic society. Thus, if bilingualism promotes more or less intelligence, IQ tests may themselves gain in importance. IQ tests may take on extra value as they appear to monitor the relationship between bilingualism and ability, performance and "success".

IQ tests have gained their status from being seen as the best single predictor of academic achievement throughout the whole educational system. As Mercer (1978/79) and Cummins (1984a) note, this has undesirable effects on the curriculum and on maintaining dominant groups in society. However, for the purposes of this chapter the implication is different. Given the predictive power of the IQ test, a positive or negative relationship between bilingualism and IQ appears crucial. If bilingualism is associated with lower IQ, the message for parents and teachers would appear to be to avoid bilingualism if greater school achievement is desired. If bilingualism is associated with a higher IQ, the message changes. Fostering bilingualism at home and at school would appear to increase the chances of academic success with positive employment and status consequences following that success.

Whether there is a direct link between bilingualism and academic achievement will be examined in Chapters 3 and 4. The link between bilingualism and achievement through IQ tests is indirect and uncertain in terms of a causal chain (i.e. A related to B; B related to C; but A not necessarily related to C). More importantly, a relationship does not imply cause.

The problem with the common view is not that IQ tests fail to predict academic achievement with moderate power. Rather, the problem is that IQ tests have partly supported the kind of achievement that favours majority, white, middle class groups (Cummins, 1984a). IQ tests have tended to reflect and reinforce mainstream culture, the educational status quo and a curriculum where convergent thinking skills are highly valued. IQ tests are related to intelligent behaviour at school partly because of a joint narrow view of intelligence as well as extraneous factors such as the self-fulfilling prophecy (Evans & Waites, 1981). Given a more multicultural, creative and progressive curriculum, IQ tests may have a much lower predictive power.

Heredity and environment

The greatest controversy concerning intelligence lies in the extent to which intelligence derives from genetic or hereditary influences. Some of the early Welsh IQ and bilingualism researchers implicitly believed in the genetic standpoint which states that approximately 70% to 80% of variability in IQ scores is due to genetic endowment. W. R. Jones (1966) for example, supported the relatively greater emphasis on hereditary factors and dismissed educational sociologists who claimed that intelligence is largely an acquired characteristic.

One difference between the hereditarian and environmentalist cases lies in the extent to which "intelligence" can be modified by experience. For the former, "intelligence" is relatively static, less modifiable by family, education and culture. For the environmentalist, intellectual capacity is derived relatively more from environmental determinants, is more pliant and modifiable.

The environmentalist view may be more attractive for those scholars who argue for the positive benefits of bilingualism (see Chapter 2). If "intelligence" is mostly inherited and capable of but little positive change, then learning two languages for the sake of improved intellectual functioning appears of little worth. If on the other hand intellectual capacity is capable of considerable environmental influence, and if bilingualism improves intellectual abilities, then the environmentalist standpoint favours bilingualism. The tacit assumption of recent research on bilingualism and cognitive functioning is of the plasticity of human "intelligence". While the standpoint of researchers on the heredity–environment issue is rarely spelt out, and while such researchers should not be termed "environmentalists", the assumptions underlying such research would appear to have changed considerably. The hereditarian assumptions of W. R. Jones (1966), for example, have given way to implicit assumptions that are more environmentalist in nature.

It may be that the interaction between genetic endowment and environment is so complex, variable, additive, cumulative and detailed that no general statement precisely fixing their relative contributions is possible. Nevertheless, researchers differ in their tacit beliefs about heredity and environment, which may affect in a latent and unconscious manner the orientation and conclusions of the research.

Summary

So far the chapter has attempted to highlight the underlying issues and controversies in the bilingualism and intelligence research. Such research needs to be critically examined with such issues in mind. Who is or is not bilingual is difficult to define and measure. In practice, arbitrary cut-off points are set to define a group of bilinguals for research purposes. Much of the research restricts its sample to balanced bilinguals. This may be a special group of bilinguals, thus restricting generalization of results.

Research on bilingualism and intelligence has used IQ tests. Almost all of this research tends to ignore the controversies surrounding the term "intelligence" and the use of IQ tests. Defining intelligence is subjective, value laden and culturally relative. Defining intelligence as that which is measured by IQ tests is precise but narrow, operationally neat but dangerously myopic. IQ tests tend to assume a one- or two-component view of intelligence. In contrast, some authors represent intelligence in multifactor terms. IQ tests tend to relate to a narrow, middle class, white, Western view of intelligence and generate fierce debates about the genetical or environmental origins of intelligence. IQ tests tend to propagate the wrong idea that intelligence can be measured, that people have a certain amount of it in the brain, that people can be ranked on it, that it is constant over many years and that it determines how people think and act.

Research on bilingualism and intelligence tends to assume that each entity is definable and measurable. Rather, each entity is contentious and problematic in conception, definition and measurement. A proper understanding of the research requires the constant awareness of such debates and dangers.

Research findings

Introduction

The history of research which has examined a link between bilingualism and intelligence falls into three overlapping periods. These will be termed:
1. the Period of Detrimental Effects
2. the Period of Neutral Effects
3. the Period of Additive Effects.

The period of detrimental effects

Overview

From the early nineteenth century to approximately the 1960s, the common belief among educational researchers and writers was that bilingualism had a detrimental effect on intelligence. Laurie (1890:15) in lectures at Cambridge University suggested that

"If it were possible for a child to live in two languages at once equally well, so much the worse. His intellectual and spiritual growth would not thereby be doubled, but halved. Unity of mind and character would have great difficulty in asserting itself in such circumstances".

One hundred years after the lectures were given, many people's "commonsense" view of bilingualism and intelligence is little different. Many still believe that a facility in two languages reduces the amount of room or power available for other intellectual pursuits. Indeed, early research tended to confirm that view. As three comprehensive reviews of these early studies show, the superiority of monolinguals over bilinguals was seemingly international (Darcy, 1953; Jensen, 1962; Peal & Lambert, 1962). What is interesting is the two focal geographical areas of this early research. In the USA, Jewish, Spanish, Mexican, Italian, German, Polish, Chinese, Japanese and Bohemian bilinguals were usually, but with some exceptions, shown to have a lower verbal (and occasionally lower non-verbal) IQ score than monoglot Americans. In Wales, the research of D. J. Saer (1922, 1923), Frank Smith (1923), Ethel Barke (1933), Barke & Parry-Williams (1938) and W. R. Jones (1959) also pointed to bilingual Welsh/English speakers having poorer performance on verbal IQ tests than monolingual English speakers. On the surface, the agreement of United States and Welsh research suggests that in a minority language situation, bilingualism is detrimental to "intelligence". It is tempting to link the United States' assimilationist melting-pot policy with the possible desirability of monolingualism. While it would be wrong to assume that the intentions and motives of such USA researchers explain the results, it appears that the melting-pot ideal was well served by such "detrimental" findings.

In Wales there appears to have been a difference between research results and researchers' personal values. The Welsh language was on the decline during the period between the World Wars (Baker, 1985). Its status decreased and Welsh language education was often lowly regarded. In this respect, the trend towards anglicization was supported by the "detrimental" findings. In certain areas of IQ research the motives and expectations of the researchers have affected findings. The case of Sir Cyril Burt's faking and altering IQ findings is a demonstration of personal motives and needs interfering with objectivity (Hearnshaw, 1979).

Did the Welsh researchers seek and prefer a "detrimental" result? The evidence suggests the contrary. Saer, Smith & Hughes (1924) were positive that Welsh should be used as a medium of instruction up to approximately nine years of age with those for whom Welsh was the mother tongue. Welsh language education was also seen as an important vehicle for Welsh children to understand and maintain Welsh cultural forms. While it is fashionable to see the ideological assumptions of researchers channelling and affecting research, this is not necessarily the case in the early Welsh research.

How valid was this early research? From early North American and Welsh research is it fair to conclude that bilingualism has a detrimental effect on "intelligence"? In order to explain the limitations of the early research, an example will be given as an introduction.

The research of D. J. Saer

D. J. Saer (1923), a headmaster at Aberystwyth in mid-Wales, researched on a large sample of 1,400 children aged 7 to 14 from rural and non-rural backgrounds. Such non-rural backgrounds comprise small towns and cities, which Saer (1923) termed urban areas. These are not urban areas in the modern sense. The 1916 Stanford–Binet Scale, plus tests taken from the 1911 Binet Scale and Cyril Burt's English version of the Binet Scale not in the 1916 Stanford–Binet Scale, were used to measure "intelligence". For Welsh language speakers, these tests were translated into Welsh. Results for four language groups were as follows:

	Average IQ
Urban bilinguals	100
Urban monoglot English speakers	99
Rural bilinguals	86
Rural monoglot English speakers	96

While no real difference was found between urban monoglot and urban bilinguals, in rural areas monoglot English speakers were regarded as of superior "intelligence" to rural bilinguals (Saer, 1923). On a Rhythm test, bilinguals were found to be two years behind monoglots. From this investigation, Saer concluded that bilinguals were mentally confused and at a disadvantage compared with monoglots.

Two of Saer's other researches extended this conclusion. First, Saer showed that amongst 939 students at the University College of Wales, Aberystwyth, rural monoglots had a superior IQ to rural bilinguals, "suggesting that this difference in mental ability as revealed by intelligence tests is of a permanent nature, since it persists in students throughout their University career" (Saer *et al.*, 1924:53). Saer's belief was that the detrimental effect was longitudinal, even irrevocable. Second, Saer believed that bilingualism affected the brain. Testing 960 children's "dextrality" (e.g. the ability to show their right hand or point to their left ear) and finding monoglots superior, the conclusion was reached that a confusion had been carried over from the brain area concerned with language to related specialized areas (Saer, Smith & Hughes, 1924).

A critique of the early research

Much of the early research into bilingualism and IQ is invalid by present standards because of deficiencies in testing, experimental design, statistical analysis and sampling. These deficiencies will be briefly considered.

Language of the IQ test

It is clearly desirable to test bilinguals in their preferred language. Welsh speakers, for example, need to be tested in Welsh. In early research (e.g. Smith, 1923) this was not always the case. As Arnberg (1981) has considered, the majority of verbal IQ tests were administered in the bilingual's weaker language. Therefore, in much world-wide research, bilinguals were at a disadvantage and were likely to show lower IQ than was possible, due to the language of testing.

Standardization of the IQ test

When IQ tests have been available in both languages, the minority language version is often a translation from the majority language. It is likely that two sources of invalidity occur in translation. First, the difficulty level and subtle meanings of questions may alter slightly in a verbal IQ test. Second, and related to this, the cultural content of verbal and non-verbal tests may be less appropriate for minority groups (Cummins, 1984a). Take an example. In the Wechsler Intelligence Scale for Children, the question is asked "Who discovered America?" For English and American children, Columbus and Ericson are acceptable. North Wales children are taught that Madoc, Prince of Gwynedd, discovered America in the twelfth century. And what answer is allowed for American Indian children, indigenous to the country? (P. Williams, 1984.) However good the translation, the difficulty level and validity of the items may change from one language to another.

Validity of the IQ test

As Peal & Lambert (1962) show in their review of research, a great variety of tests purporting to measure IQ have been used. The Stanford–Binet Scale, Pinter Tests, WISC, Otis IQ Test, Goodenough Draw a Man Test, Spearman Visual Perception Test, Burt's Northumberland Standardized Test of General Intelligence, Mental Survey Test of SCRE, Cattell's Non-Verbal Scale, Jenkin's Scale of Non-verbal Mental Ability, Moray House Intelligence Test, Raven's Progressive Matrices, NFER Non-verbal Test No. 2, Daniels' Figure Reading Test, Dawson Mental Tests, Ohio State University Intelligence Test, USA National Intelligence Test (Scale A), Haggerty Intelligence Tests, Arthur Point Performance Scale, Atkins Test, Henmon–Nelson Tests of Mental Ability, Terman–McNemar Mental Ability Test, Army Alpha Test and the Army Beta Test are just some of the measures authors have used to measure IQ. Do they all measure the same entity? Do any or all of them measure "intelligence"? A sceptical note must be sounded.

Statistical significance

Should the average scores between monoglot and bilingual groups differ, it is customary to apply a test of statistical significance to establish whether the difference in scores is real or due to chance factors. Thus W. R. Jones' (1966) re-analysis of D. J. Saer's University research showed that Saer's conclusion was invalid. No statistically significant difference was found between monoglot and bilingual students from rural or urban areas. It therefore follows that Saers' belief in the permanent nature of mental confusion was not supported by his data.

Classification of bilinguals

As has been seen, it is impossible to provide a simple and unambiguous classification of subjects into a bilingual grouping. For each research, two questions must be answered: (1) "On what dimensions were the group called bilinguals more or less competent in their two languages (e.g. reading, writing, speaking, listening)?"; (2) "What was their degree of fluency in each language?" Simple classification into bilinguals and monoglots makes unrealistically simplistic Mackey's (1962) model of the four basic receptive and productive skills each having sub-skills of vocabulary, grammar, pronunciation, meanings and style.

Sampling and generalization

As with all research, the findings are restricted to the population of whom the sample is an exact miniature. Thus research using groups not selected randomly from a population, who were merely convenient for research, may say nothing about people other than those in that group. Research on 10-year-olds may not strictly be generalized to any other age group. Findings in Wales may not be generalized to Canada, the USA or the rest of Britain and Europe. There is a tendency in bilingual research to generalize too freely across countries and continents. A mountain of advice and conclusions seems often to be generated from a molehill of research.

Comparability of groups

To compare a group of bilinguals with a group of monoglots on IQ requires these groups to be equal in all other respects. For example, if the monoglot group were from the upper middle class and the bilinguals were from the lower working class, an unfair comparison would result. To conclude that monoglots were of higher IQ would be wrong. The result may be explained by a difference in socio-economic status, rather than, or as well as, by differences in language abilities.

It is therefore necessary to ensure that the bilingual and monoglot groups are equal; that is, matched on variables that could affect the comparison. Apart from socio-economic class, the minimal variables that should normally be controlled include: gender (girls may be more advanced in language development than boys), age, and type of school attended (e.g. designated bilingual school, submersion or immersion).

There are two possible ways of attempting to control for alternative explanations. First, subjects can be matched. For every pupil in the bilingual group, there is an identical monoglot pupil in terms of social class, gender, age and type of school attended. Identical matching is difficult to achieve and may result in the subjects in the research not being a true sample of the population of bilinguals or monoglots whom they represent. Excluded by the matching process may be some influential (e.g. "high" IQ) pupils. Second, control may be exerted statistically through the technique of analysis of co-variance. This technique allows for initial differences between monoglot and bilingual groups to exist (e.g. in social class and age) and then controls for them in the computational stage. A critique of this technique may be found in Lambourne & Wheldall (1979).

In most "detrimental effects" research, matching subjects or the control of intervening variables is noticeably absent. Such research is therefore invalid.

Majority or minority language

As Swain & Cummins (1979) note, negative findings are often associated with minority language groups. Do feelings of inferiority and lower status attached to minority language usage affect IQ? Lambert's (1977) consideration of subtractive forms of bilingualism (as opposed to additive bilingualism) suggests that low prestige bilingualism may be a context for a variety of negative effects. This is again a problem of generalization. Results from one language context may be different from results from contrastive contexts.

Conclusion

In this section concerning "detrimental effects" of bilingualism on IQ, the theme has been that research up to, very approximately, 1960 showed that bilinguals were inferior on verbal IQ. These early researches tended to share methodological weaknesses. While not all the research has all the weaknesses, researches containing one or more of these weaknesses have to be either very tentatively and critically accepted or even dismissed. Singly and cumulatively, the early research on bilingualism and IQ has too many limitations and methodological errors for its conclusion of detrimental effects to be acceptable.

The period of neutral effects

Research which reports neutral effects is not numerous and was of interest for only a short period. However, its importance lies in its illumination of the inadequacies of the early research. In time span, the neutral research overlaps with the periods of detrimental and additive effects. Due to lack of statistical sophistication, this research must also be viewed critically.

One important example of the "neutral effects" research is by W. R. Jones (1959). Some two and a half thousand children of ages 10 and 11 in the research initially showed the typical relationship between language and measured intelligence: monoglots superior to bilinguals (Jones, 1955). A re-analysis by W. R. Jones (1959) of these data showed that the earlier conclusion was unwarranted. After categorizing the children into twelve parental occupation groups, Jones found a decided and statistically significant tendency for the bilinguals to be relatively over-represented in the manual groups, especially agricultural workers, and for monoglots to be relatively over-represented in the non-manual groups. While the statistical procedures used in the re-analysis (analysis of variance) did not directly examine whether any difference between bilingual and monoglot groups remains after socio-economic class is taken into account, Jones (1959) was nevertheless willing to amend his earlier conclusion. After the re-analysis, he concluded that:

1. Monoglots and bilinguals did not differ significantly in non-verbal IQ when parental occupation was taken into account
2. Occupational differences may largely account for previous research which reported the inferiority of bilinguals on non-verbal IQ
3. Bilingualism is not necessarily a source of intellectual disadvantage.

In the USA, similar results to Jones' (1959) had been found. As Peal & Lambert (1962) demonstrate in their review, some of these studies attempted to control for sex, age and social class differences. For example, Pintner & Arsenian (1937) found a zero correlation between verbal and non-verbal IQ and Yiddish–English bilingualism. The most recent investigation in Wales also found neutral effects on children's development when gender, age, socio-economic background, rural–urban background and parents' education were taken into account (Dodson, 1981).

The period of additive effects

A major turning point in the IQ and bilingualism issue was reached in 1962. Peal & Lambert's (1962) research on the issue was a major step forward in the history of bilingual research. There are three reasons for the importance of the research. First, the research was methodologically more advanced, with a more sophisticated statistical analysis. Second, partly because the research has been regarded as an improvement on previous studies, its finding that bilingualism may have positive outcomes has been widely quoted to support bilingual policies in a variety of institutional and geographical settings. Third, it laid the foundation for further research to seek positive consequences of bilingualism, not in terms of the narrow concept of IQ, but in terms of a wider view of cognitive abilities (see Chapter 2).

Peal & Lambert's (1962) sample of children comprised 164 10-year-olds from six middle-class French schools in Montreal with a gender ratio of six boys to every four girls. The original sample of 364 children was narrowed down to 164 children by four measures of bilingualism. Only balanced bilinguals and monoglots were included. Thus some 55% of the original sample were excluded from the selected research sample. Among the 46 variables on which data was gathered, 18 variables measured IQ. An initial analysis revealed that the bilingual and monoglot groups differed on socio-economic class and school grade. The first analysis showed that the bilingual group was of a statistically significant higher socio-economic rating (on a 7-point scale) than the monoglot group, and was similarly more advanced in school grade. The authors then further reduced the sample to 110 children so that there would be equal numbers of bilinguals and monolinguals in each of the seven socio-economic classes. Having adjusted for socio-economic differences by exclusion of subjects, a statistically significant difference between the two groups on school grade still existed.

Of the 18 variables measuring IQ, 15 variables showed bilinguals to have a statistically significant higher IQ than monolinguals. On only three variables was there no difference, these being the Space, Perception and Number components of the Primary Mental Abilities Test. The significant 15 variables included verbal and non-verbal aspects of IQ. Separate factor analyses of monoglots and bilinguals revealed a difference in factor structure. The authors suggest that this implied a difference in the structure of the intellect, with bilinguals having a more diversified intelligence.

As will be seen later when the research is critically assessed, the findings are not necessarily so clear-cut and valid. However, the historical importance probably lies more in the authors' discussions of the findings. In an interpretation of the positive relationship of IQ to bilingualism, Peal & Lambert (1962) provided an appetizer, stimulant and menu for future research. Being bilingual, they argued, may give:

1. greater mental flexibility
2. the ability to think more abstractly, less concretely, more independently of words, resulting in superiority in concept formation
3. a more enriched bicultural environment which benefits IQ
4. positive transfer between languages benefiting verbal IQ.

The research has aroused controversy. The controversy has been concerned not so much with disputing that bilingualism can under certain circumstances be cognitively beneficial, but with the methodological weakness of the research. Principally there are four objections to the research.

1. The results depend on 110 children, 10 years of age and of middle class, Montreal extraction. This is not a sample of any defined population. The original sample of 364 children did not appear to be representative of any defined population. The selected 110 were even less representative. Therefore, strictly, the results cannot be generalized to any children other than the 110. Although most researchers tacitly assume that their results are likely to be generalizable to similar children across cultures, across ages, across social classes, such generalizations are statistically indefensible. On grounds other than statistics, such generalizations tend to rely less on logic and more on hope and faith.

2. The bilingual children selected were balanced bilinguals. Logically the results cannot be generalized to non-balanced bilinguals, who are perhaps the majority of bilinguals. Balanced bilinguals may be a special group with their own characteristics in terms of motivation, aptitude for languages, cognitive abilities and attitudes. Was their higher IQ due to factors such as these rather than to owning and operating in two languages? MacNab (1979) has argued that such samples may be self-selecting or parent-selecting in that the desire for bilingualism is not a "normal" customary behaviour. Special children with exceptional parents may generate unusual results. It is a pity that Peal & Lambert (1962) did not use the excluded 254 children as further comparison groups. Although not specifically criticizing Peal & Lambert's (1962) research, Martin-Jones & Romaine (1986) make an important point about the notion of balanced bilinguals. The term is distinct from, and not to be considered interchangeable with, complete or full bilingualism. In much of the research on bilingualism, the notion of "balanced bilingualism" has, however, functioned as an implicit synonym for "good" or "complete" bilingualism and has been used as a yardstick against which other kinds of bilingualism have been measured and stigmatized as "inadequate" and/or "underdeveloped" (p. 33).

3. The association between IQ and bilingualism does not imply causation. The results are correlational. Statistical correlations do not, in themselves, provide evidence of the order of cause and effect. The design of the research is cross-sectional and associational. A preferred design is longitudinal where, by random assignment to treatment and control groups, cause and effect may be better, though imperfectly, studied. The research suggests that IQ and bilingualism are linked. This does not allow a conclusion that bilingualism in itself affects IQ or that higher IQ promotes bilingualism. The relationship may even be spurious.

Peal & Lambert (1962) themselves are aware of the alternatives of causation. Does the ownership of two languages lead to a greater IQ?

Alternatively, does the possession of a higher IQ lead to becoming bilingual more easily (Lambert & Anisfeld, 1969)? There is also a third part to the "chicken and egg" game. It may be that there is a mutually reciprocating relationship between bilingualism and IQ. One is simultaneously the cause and effect of the other. That is, there is mutual interaction and stimulation between dual language and cognitive abilities.

4. Peal & Lambert (1962) initially found a difference in socio-economic class between their bilingual and monolingual groups, favouring the bilinguals. By exclusion of children, the two groups were said to have been equated. Such equating relied on the difference in the means and variance of the two groups being statistically insignificant, a technique sometimes less exact than matched pairs. As several authors have noted, socio-economic class does not control for differences in a child's home environment (Cummins, 1976, 1984a; MacNab, 1979). Matching or equating children on parental occupation relies on the assumption that this measure adequately sums up relevant environmental background differences between the groups. Indeed, more research is needed to explore precisely what socio-economic class means in a bicultural and cross-cultural sense. Parental occupation is likely to summarize such differences inadequately. The results may, however, be explainable, in part or in whole, by differences in environmental background rather than in the possession of one or two languages.

An example will illustrate. Two children of the same sex and age living in the same village may have fathers who work side by side as underground miners. One family regularly attends Welsh chapel, eisteddfodau, and competes in penillion singing and poetry competitions at local and national eisteddfodau. The miner and his wife send their bilingual child to a designated bilingual secondary school. The culture of the second family concerns bingo, the Club, discos and pigeon racing. Their monolingual child attends a non-Welsh speaking school. For the quantitative researcher, the children are matched on socio-economic class. In reality the differences are great. Thus it may not be the first child's bilingualism that is connected with higher "IQ". Rather it may be the social and cultural milieu *per se*.

One piece of research alone rarely or never proves a point. Thus Peal & Lambert's (1962) study is more important in that it signalled and promoted a change in the debate; less important in its precise results because of methodological weaknesses. However, the results cannot be dismissed completely because, as will be examined in Chapter 2, they are in keeping with much research since 1962.

If Peal & Lambert's (1962) study heralded a new era of research, it also marked the end of the old era. Research after 1962 has tended to move away from the "monistic" notion of IQ to the "pluralistic" notion of a multi-component view of intelligence and cognition. Although there are researches after 1962 which examine the relationship between IQ and bilingualism (e.g. Cummins & Gulutsan, 1974; Barrik & Swain, 1976; Skutnabb-Kangas & Toukomaa, 1976; Hakuta, 1986), the mainstream activity has examined intelligence in terms of a multi-factored structure. One catalyst was Peal & Lambert's (1962) discussion of their results. Such discussion ranges more widely than the results strictly warrant, but may be an essential ingredient in the nourishment of future research.

Summary and conclusions

Research on bilingualism and IQ has developed through three broad and overlapping periods. The early research tended to report negative consequences of bilingualism. Verbal IQ in particular, but also occasionally non-verbal IQ, was found to be lower amongst bilinguals than monolinguals. The early research, however, contained a number of flaws. Lack of sophistication in the choice, use and analysis of IQ tests, inadequate sampling techniques and lack of control over important variables limit the validity of almost all the early research in an individual and cumulative sense. The second, interim period was brief and may have been largely restricted in its influence to Wales and the rest of Britain. W. R. Jones (1959) argued that if social class was allowed for, bilingualism had no positive or detrimental effect on non-verbal IQ. In Wales in the early 1960s, the academic view was of the neutrality of bilingualism in cognitive functioning. The third period commenced with Peal & Lambert's (1962) famous research. Important historically, but in retrospect marred by methodological deficiencies, it marked the beginning of a stream of researches in the 1970s which attempted to show the positive consequences of bilingualism. These will be considered in the next chapter. Peal & Lambert's (1962) research marks the start of the belief amongst many researchers that bilingualism can enhance cognitive functioning.

The conclusion of this first chapter has to be critical and cautious. To define and categorize who is bilingual or not is fraught with problems. With different dimensions of language skills and sub-skills, there is the danger of a research sample being too specialized (e.g. balanced bilinguals) or vaguely defined. To use measures of intelligence is to enter an arena of even greater controversy. The impossibility of an agreed definition, the proliferation of a variety of structures and models of intelligence, the great scepticism concerning the validity of IQ tests, and the furious debate about the genetic or environmental origin of intelligence, all cause the bilingualism and intelligence issue to be a minefield.

The passionate desire felt by many parents and teachers for a clear-cut statement about the relationship between intelligence and bilingualism is matched only by the difficulty, even impossibility, of basing a valid statement upon the results of published research. The question is crucial; the answer can only be cautious.

2 Bilingualism and Cognitive Functioning

Introduction

In 1914, at the outset of the First World War, a progressive North Wales educationalist by the name of James Williams undertook an interesting comparative examination of bilingualism in Belgium and Wales. In his report of 1915, Williams spelt out the implications of his research for Wales. One conclusion he reached was that "the learning of Welsh by English children within the borders of Wales in the habit forming epoch between six and twelve years of age is an intellectual advantage" (p. 104).

During the last seventy years, researchers, educators, teachers and parents have not all shared his belief. Yet as this chapter will examine, James Williams' (1915) comment appears prophetic and valid. Since Peal & Lambert's (1962) research, the research issue has been "On what products and processes are bilinguals superior to monolinguals?" The question has been phrased positively, with the expectation of positive consequences of bilingualism.

This chapter will illustrate the different dimensions upon which bilinguals appear to have advantages. Following discussion of recent research, the limitations and implications of such findings will be critically examined.

Divergent and creative thinking

In the first chapter, it was shown that a restricted view of the structure of IQ was assumed in most of the early research. The IQ tests used in such research required one correct answer to each question. This has often been termed "convergent thinking". The child or adult has to converge onto a single, acceptable answer. Guilford's (1982) model has one element termed "divergent thinking". Divergent thinking is, in process and product, a more creative, imaginative, open-ended and free-thinking skill. Instead of finding one correct answer, the pupil is given a set time to produce a variety of answers, most of which are likely to be valid answers.

For example, divergent thought may be tapped by asking, "How many interesting and unusual uses can you think of for tin cans?" "Animal feeder, hair roller, hole for golf green, tie together and put board on top for a raft" are all possible and correct answers. A pupil has to diverge and find as many answers as possible.

In the tradition of British research (e.g. Hudson, 1966) divergent thinking is often measured by the absolute number of sensible answers given to such a question as "how many uses can you think of for a brick?" In the North American tradition, divergent thinking concerns not only total numbers of responses, but also their variety, originality and elaborateness. An example will demonstrate. Imagine that in response to the "Uses of Tin Cans" question a pupil gives six answers:

1. Animal bed
2. Animal cage
3. Insect house
4. Hole for golf green
5. Hair roller
6. Tie together and put board on top for a raft.

In the North American tradition, the answers would be scored on four dimensions. The pupil's *fluency* score will be 6. Then by reference to Torrance's (1974a) manual, it is possible to derive scores for the *flexibility*, *originality* and *elaboration* of the responses. For flexibility, Torrance lists 28 different categories into which almost all responses fall. For example, listed categories include Animal shelter, Art Use, Tools and Weapons. A person's *flexibility* score is the number of different categories into which answers can be placed. Thus animal bed, animal cage and insect house all fall into one category and earn one point. Answers four, five and six above, fall into three different categories. For *originality*, reference to the Test Manual provides a score of 0, 1 or 2 for the originality of some 180 responses. A score of 1 on originality means that Torrance (1974a) found the answer to occur in less than 20% of the population. A score of 2 means that the answer is rare, occurring less than 5% of the time. "Insect house" would be scored 0 on originality; hair roller and hole for golf green both score 2. *Elaboration* refers to the extra detail which elaborates over and above that which is necessary to communicate a basic idea. Thus "Animal house" has no elaboration and scores 0; "tie together and put board on top for a raft" elaborates twice on the "raft" idea and obtains an elaboration score of 2 (Torrance, 1974a). The average 11-year-old obtains a "Use of Tin Cans" score of 20 on fluency, 7 on flexibility and 11 on originality (Torrance, 1974b).

Creativity tests also contain figural (non-verbal) tests. For example, a sheet with 40 blank circles is provided. The person being tested is asked to make as many different and unusual pictures as possible. Answers are similarly scored in terms of Fluency, Flexibility, Originality and Elaboration. Whether the verbal or figural tests measure a concept of creativity that can be widely accepted is as problematic as the definition and measurement of intelligence. Although there is a difference between British and North American operational definitions and measurement of divergent thinking, it seems safer to use the term divergent thinking than creativity for both methods of scoring the same questions.

Bilingualism and divergent thinking

On what basis might a hypothesis be made suggesting that bilinguals have superior divergent thinking abilities? Does the ownership of a dual language system increase fluency, flexibility, originality or elaboration of thought? Does having double or more words for the one object allow a person to have more freedom of variation in thought, even perceiving reality in two more or less distinct forms? For example, a bilingual person in Wales may not only have two words "music/cerddoriaeth" but a variety of different perceptions, conceptions and emotions attached to each word. Does the bicultural attachment to bilingualism allow a wider context in thinking?

A variety of research has compared bilinguals and unilinguals on a variety of measures of divergent thinking (Anisfeld, 1964; Gowan & Torrance, 1965; Torrance et al., 1970; Bruck, Lambert & Tucker, 1976; Scott, 1973; Carringer, 1974; Cummins & Gulutsan, 1974; Landry, 1974; Cummins, 1975; Cummins, 1977a; Noble & Dalton, 1976). The research is international and cross-cultural: Ireland, Canada, Singapore, Mexico, USA but not Britain. A majority of research findings suggests that bilinguals are superior to monolinguals on divergent thinking tests. Two examples will illustrate.

First, analysis of data from the St Lambert Project (see Chapter 4) revealed that children from monolingual homes receiving bilingual education were superior to control groups on divergent thinking (Bruck et *al.*, 1976; Scott, 1973). Controlling for differences between the experimental and control groups for IQ and social class by analysis of co-variance, Scott (1973) found that skills in the second language at age 9 were better predicted by divergent thinking than by IQ. Perhaps the most interesting facet of this research is Scott's (1973) discussion of the cause–effect relationship. Do bilingualism and bilingual education cause relatively superior divergent thinking skills? Or does the possession of divergent thinking skills promote bilingualism? Scott (1973) argues for a two-way causal relationship. Bilingualism is both the promoter of, and is promoted by, divergent thinking skills.

Second, the research of Cummins and co-workers provides an important clue as to a key variable in the bilingualism–divergent thinking relationship. An early finding was that balanced bilinguals, when matched on sex, age and socio-economic class with a monolingual group, performed better on verbal originality but not on fluency or flexibility (Cummins & Gulutsan, 1974). Later Cummins (1975, 1977a) found that balanced bilinguals (N = 12) were superior to non-balanced bilinguals (N = 11) on the fluency and flexibility scales of verbal divergence, and marginally on originality. In this research the unilingual group (N = 12) scored at a similar level to the balanced group on verbal fluency and flexibility but substantially higher than the non-balanced group. On originality, unilinguals scored at a similar level to the non-balanced bilinguals, and substantially lower than the balanced group. Probably due to the small numbers involved, the results did not quite attain customary levels of statistical significance.

That there are differences between matched groups of balanced bilinguals and non-balanced bilinguals suggests that bilingualism itself may not be unrestrictedly connected to superior divergent thinking skills. More specifically, Cummins (1977a:10) suggests that

> "there may be a threshold level of linguistic competence which a bilingual child must attain both in order to avoid cognitive deficits and allow the potentially beneficial aspects of becoming bilingual to influence his cognitive growth".

The seemingly contradictory results of Cummins are thus explained by a threshold. Once a child has obtained a certain level of competence in his or her second language, positive cognitive consequences can result.

However, competence in a second language may, in certain contexts, not only fail to give benefits, but may have negative, detractive cognitive consequences. For example, an English-speaking pupil receiving compulsory but minimal tuition and education in Welsh may suffer cognitively.

Benefits may accrue when such a pupil's Welsh language competence is fairly similar to their English language skills. That is the theory. The threshold theory will be further examined in Chapter 7.

Although the weight of the evidence suggests that balanced bilinguals have superior divergent thinking skills compared with less balanced bilinguals and monolinguals, some caution must be taken in making too firm a conclusion. All the researches on this topic have methodological limitations and deficiencies. In order to ensure a balanced judgement, these problems need to be taken into account. The five major problems are listed below:

1. Some studies fail to control adequately for differences between bilingual and monolingual groups (e.g. Carringer, 1974; Cummins & Gulutsan, 1974; Torrance *et al.*, 1970; Landry, 1974; Noble & Dalton, 1976). A difference in age between the two groups in Noble & Dalton's (1976) research may explain their positive results. Carringer (1974) does not indicate whether or not his groups were matched on socio-economic background or IQ. Both these variables may explain his results instead of, or in addition to, bilingualism.

2. Some studies have such small samples that attempts at generalization must be very restricted. Thus Carringer's (1974) bilinguals numbered 24, Noble & Dalton's (1976) bilinguals totalled two groups of 19 and 29 respectively, and Cummins (1975, 1977a) used 12 balanced bilinguals and 11 non-balanced bilinguals. Given the millions of bilinguals in the world, such small numbers are unlikely to be very representative.

3. Some studies fail to define or describe the level or degree of bilingualism in their sample. Torrance *et al.* (1970) and Gowan & Torrance (1965) fail to assess the level of second language competence of their unilingual samples. Landry (1974) provides no details about second language competence of their "bilingual" sample. As Cummins (1977a) has shown, the extent of such competence is an important intermediary variable.

4. Not all studies find a positive relationship between bilingualism and divergent thinking. Cummins (1978d) notes that superior divergent thinking was not consistently observed among pupils in the St Lambert project. Anisfeld (1964), for example, found no difference between bilinguals and monolinguals on measures of divergent thinking. Cummins & Gulutsan (1974) found differences on only one of their five measures of divergent thinking.

5. Use of analysis of co-variance to control for extraneous variables violates the assumptions of the technique (Lambourne & Wheldall, 1979). Scott (1973) and Cummins (1977a) both use this technique with a non-randomly selected sample in a quasi-experimental design. The technique is not theoretically applicable when there is the absence of random sample selection.

Given these methodological restrictions on the research, what conclusion can be reached? Because of deficiencies, should all the research be dismissed and an open verdict be returned? When the variety of research into the cognitive consequences of bilingualism has been discussed, at the end of the chapter some "macro" limitations will need to be added to the "micro" limitations given above. However, very tentatively, the verdict seems marginally to be in favour of a positive link. In an additive context, balanced and competent bilinguals tend to exhibit relatively better scores on divergent thinking tests.

Bilingualism and an analytic orientation to language

The research on bilingualism and divergent thinking tentatively suggests that bilinguals may have some advantage over comparable monolinguals. This link may suggest that ownership of two languages allows some advantages in the way language relates to thinking. A bilingual may be more free and open, flexible and original particularly in meanings attached to words. Is a bilingual person less bound by words, more elastic in thinking?

Leopold's (1939–1949) famous case study of the German–English development of his daughter, Hildegard, noted the looseness of the link between word and meaning apparently due to bilingualism. Favourite stories were not repeated with stereotyped wording; vocabulary substitutions were made freely in memorized songs and rhymes. Word sound and word meaning were separated. The name of an object or concept was separated from the object or concept itself. Leopold's study cannot be generalized to other bilingual children. One case proves nothing. However, it provided the early pieces of research in this area with an hypothesis.

Ianco-Worrall (1972) tested the sound and meaning separation hypothesis on 30 Afrikaans–English bilinguals aged 4 to 9. The bilingual group was matched with two groups of monolinguals on IQ, age, sex, school grade and social class. In the first experiment, a typical question was "I have three words: CAP, CAN and HAT. Which is more like CAP, CAN or HAT?" Choosing CAN might suggest a child's choice was governed by word sound. Choosing HAT might suggest that choice was based on word meaning. Her results showed that in 7- to 9-year-olds, there was little difference between bilinguals and monolinguals. Both groups responded by choosing word meaning. However with 4- to 6-year-olds, Ianco-Worrall (1972) found that bilinguals tended to respond to meaning, unilinguals to word sound. Her conclusion was that bilinguals "reach a stage of semantic development, as measured by our test, some 2–3 years earlier than their unilingual peers" (p. 1398).

In a second experiment, the line of questioning followed Vygotsky (1962). The children were asked three types of question. Examples of the three types of question are:

1. Why is a cow called a cow?
2. Suppose you were making up names for things, could you then call a cow "dog" and a dog "cow"?
3. Let us call a dog "cow". Does this "cow" have horns? Does this "cow" give milk?

On the first type of question, no difference was found between bilinguals and monolinguals. On the second type of question, proportionately more unilinguals than bilinguals replied that names could not be interchanged. This difference was marginally statistically significant at 4 to 6 years, and statistically significant for 7- to 9-year-olds. On the third type of question, no difference between bilinguals and unilinguals was found with either age group.

Ianco-Worrall's (1972) experiment was one of the first to examine possible metalinguistic advantages for bilinguals. "Metalinguistic" concerns the ability to get above or outside language, being aware of language forms and properties. The experiment, however, is not unambiguous. An alternative explanation is that bilinguals were superior on the second question of the second experiment due to their being more aware of what was the "wanted" answer. In the way the second question is phrased, there is a subtle hint. The question is asked positively, making it a leading question. It may be better to "suppose" than "fail to suppose". The possibility that bilinguals can be more responsive to cues, more sensitive to feedback, will be examined later. Another ambiguity is whether, on the evidence of the first experiment, bilinguals have a temporary, short-term gain. Do unilinguals catch up later such that initial differences are soon equalized? Is there any long-term advantage from an early short-term gain?

Cummins (1978a & b) extended Ianco-Worrall's experiment, investigating children's metalinguistic abilities with an Irish–English bilingual sample from Dublin. The children numbered 53 bilinguals and 53 monolinguals matched on verbal IQ, socio-economic class, sex and age. Groups of 8/9 year olds and 11/12 year olds were tested. One test was similar to that of Ianco-Worrall (1972). Children were asked "Suppose you were making up names for things, could you call the sun 'moon' and the moon 'the sun'?" The method, called the Arbitrariness of Language Task, differed from Ianco-Worrall (1972) in that the children had to give reasons to support and justify their answers. With both age groups, Cummins (1978a & b) found that bilinguals were more aware of the arbitrary nature of names than unilinguals. A significantly higher percentage of bilinguals gave answers such as "You could change the names because it doesn't matter what things are called", compared with monolinguals. An example of responses by the majority of unilinguals was, "they are their right names so you can't change them".

Cummins (1978a & b) used the same group of children for a second test. Using coloured counters, the children were asked eleven questions such as "The counter in my hand is yellow and it is not green". Answers could be true, false, or can't tell. Sometimes the counters were visible, other times hidden in the experimenter's hand. The test focused on a child's being able to detect contradictions and tautologies in language. While each question was analysed separately for the two different age groups, and while not all individual question comparisons were statistically significant, overall, bilinguals tended to answer more questions correctly. Bilinguals appeared to be more analytical of the language of the questions. They appeared to have more flexibility and emancipation in separating words and meanings. In an extended attempt at replication of these results with Ukrainian–English fluent bilingual and non-fluent bilingual groups, Cummins (1978a & b) found that fluent bilinguals were at an advantage on their ability to analyse language rather than on just an awareness of language. On being assessed on their sensitivity to different kinds of ambiguous sentence (e.g. "The eating of the chicken was sloppy") with the ambiguity lying in the eater, fluent bilinguals were ahead of non-fluent bilinguals.

For Ben-Zeev (1977a & b) the greater ability of bilinguals to analyse language stems from the necessity of resolving interference between two languages. An example of interference would be a Welsh-speaking child saying in English "Listen, I am siarading to you" ("siarad" is Welsh for "speak"). Ben-Zeev's (1977a) research was conducted on middle-class Hebrew–English bilinguals from Israel and the USA, aged 5 to 8. The two matched comparison groups were Hebrew and English monolinguals.

One test used by Ben-Zeev was the Symbol Substitution Test, where a child was expected to substitute one word for another (e.g. "macaroni" for "I" as in "Macaroni am warm"). To answer correctly, a child must be able to resist the interference of word substitution, to ignore word meaning and also sentence framing (e.g. avoid saying "*I* am warm" and "Macaroni *is* warm"). A harder example was substituting "clean" for "into" as in "The doll is going clean the house". Bilinguals were found to be superior in symbol substitution not only with regard to meaning but also with regard to the grammatical rules of sentence construction. Having experienced two language systems with two different rules of construction, the bilinguals appeared to be more flexible and analytical in language. The alternative explanation, that bilinguals were able to ignore the usual syntax rules because they have not mastered such rules and were therefore not impeded by them, was unsupported in other tests. The preferred explanation is in terms of the bilingual having to deal with the potential interference between two languages. More processing effort or incipient contrastive linguistics may give increased linguistic sensitivity to bilinguals.

The evidence that bilinguals have some advantages in terms of analytical orientation to their languages seems fairly strong (Swain & Cummins, 1979; Ben-Zeev, 1984; Cummins, 1984b; Bain & Yu, 1980; Arnberg, 1981; Rueda, 1983; Hakuta, 1986). Vygotsky (1962:110) suggested that bilingualism enables a child "to see his language as one particular system among many, to view its phenomena under more general categories, and this leads to awareness of his linguistic operations".

The suggestion of Vygotsky (1962) seems confirmed. Yet, in addition to some "macro" criticism of such research (see later), various constraints must be placed on the generalization of the findings. Research has tended to focus on middle-class subjects. The effects may be less powerful with working-class children, as Ben-Zeev's (1977b) research suggests. The subjects also tend to be children, and young children in particular. While early beneficial effects may be cumulative and additive, research has generally failed to examine age-bound effects. The context of the research has mostly been in "additive" contexts rather than "subtractive" settings. Would the findings generalize to Wales, where one language is a minority language, with varying status according to geographical area? What degree of fluency in the two languages is required for such analytical language abilities to blossom? Is it only balanced bilinguals to whom such benefits accrue? Does bilingualism cause such analytic benefits? Or is the cause the other way round? Does the ability to be analytic of language cause increased fluency in two languages? Do only the more able bilingual children receive benefits, or are they shared by less able bilinguals? Since most studies use balanced bilinguals, is overall high ability confounded with bilingual ability? For example, McLaughlin (1984) suggests that a bilingual child's advantage comes from sensitivity to the formal aspects of language, rather than from owning more general cognitive abilities. This is further problematic in that language and thought have a complex and contentious relationship (e.g. compare the theories of Piaget and Vygotsky). Finally, are the tests valid? Do the tests used by the researchers measure with reliability the construct they are said to measure? Are the verbal labels given to the results (e.g. greater cognitive flexibility, analytical orientation to language) true and accurate in describing test results? Do authors tend to interpret more widely than their results strictly allow, or is the discussion an intelligent and sensible explanation of a wider concept represented in miniature in test questions? Questions have to be posed rather than answers given, due to the primitive stage of such research. Such questions set a research agenda.

Piaget and bilingualism

With Piaget and the possible cognitive advantages of bilingualism there is a paradox. While Vygotsky (1962) saw language as central to cognitive development, for Piaget (1955) language is far less central. For Piaget, a child's language is determined by, rather than a determinant of, cognitive operations. The paradox is that research has used Piagetian cognitive tests to examine the possible advantages of bilingualism. While various authors (Chávez, 1980; Kessler & Quinn, 1982; MacNamara, 1970; Cummins, 1976) have discussed the theoretical possibilities in the relationship between bilingualism and Piagetian developmental theories, this section will focus on research findings.

In one of the early researches, Feldman & Shen (1971) used 15 Spanish–English bilingual children and 15 unmatched monolingual children from the Head Start programme. On one test, the 4- to 6-year-olds were tested for "object constancy". For example, a cup was crushed and then placed with a cup identical to the original. Each child was asked to select the object as initially shown; 95% of the bilinguals' answers were correct compared with 84% of monolinguals, a statistically significant difference. Liedtke & Nelson (1968) hypothesized that the two "worlds" of experience of bilinguals would create a difference in responding to Piagetian tests when compared with the one "world" experience of monolinguals. Using six tests of linear measurement from Piaget (1952), Liedtke & Nelson (1968) compared 50 bilinguals and 50 monolinguals matched on sex, age, IQ and socio-economic status. The bilinguals were found to be ahead on concept formation. They were more advanced on the concept of conservation (e.g. of the length of plasticine when changed from a ball to a "worm") and on the concept of measurement. The authors explain their findings through the possible different social interaction and social environment of bilinguals, rather than through the ability to analyse language which in turn accelerates concept formation. The bilingual may have two cultural worlds and additional experiences due to operating in two languages. For Liedtke & Nelson (1968) it is the additive social and cultural experience that benefits concept formation. Both the Feldman & Shen (1971) and the Liedtke & Nelson (1968) research suffer from the absence of precise details of the language proficiency of their bilingual and monolingual groups. The former research created a bilingual group on the basis of "several simple Spanish questions and (the ability) to speak Spanish at home" (p. 236). The latter research assigned pupils to a bilingual group solely on the basis of teacher observation. Neither way of creating a bilingual and monolingual group is satisfactory or valid.

However, two further researches, better controlled, lend support to Feldman & Shen (1971) and Liedtke & Nelson (1968). Duncan & De Avila (1979) compared five groups on neo-Piagetian tests of conservation of identity, number, length, substance and distance. The order of best performance was: Proficient Bilinguals, Monolinguals, Limited Bilinguals, Partial Bilinguals and Late Language Learners. The difference between Proficient Bilinguals and Monolinguals was statistically significant. Ben-Zeev (1977b) tested children on Piagetian classification and reclassification tests. An example of the stimuli in such a test is given in the diagram opposite. Sorting objects into correct groups was required, taking into account shape, colour and size. A child may be asked to sort outside circles from outside squares, thus ignoring colour and inside shape. Then red objects may be requested to be separated from white objects, thus ignoring a previous classification.

Although the results were mostly only marginally statistically significant, the trends were in favour of bilinguals. Bilinguals tended to give more classifications, were less inconsistent across the tests and gave more attention to detail.

In Ben-Zeev's research (1977b), it was found that on these Piagetian tests, bilinguals were more responsive to perceptual "hints" than monolinguals. Bilinguals picked up clues quicker, and once given feedback, corrected their mistakes faster than monolinguals. This leads directly to the next section, where communicative sensitivity is examined.

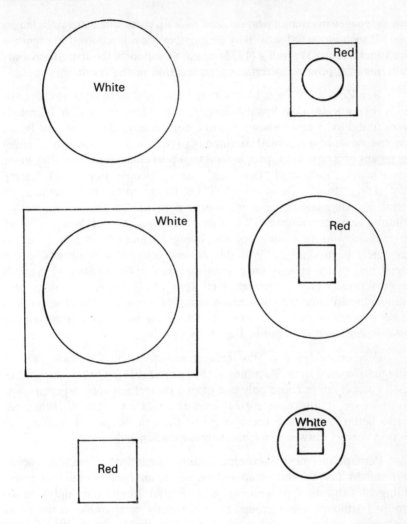

Communicative sensitivity

In discussing Ianco-Worrall's (1972) research, it was suggested that bilingual children may be more sensitive to cues in the way a question is phrased. Bilinguals may have extra demands placed upon them by speaking two languages. They have to be aware of which language fits which interpersonal communication, attempt to avoid interference between their two languages in communication, and pick up clues when to switch languages. If such increased sensitivity exists, does it evidence itself in cognitive outcomes? Ianco-Worrall's (1972) research supports the hypothesis only in terms of a *post hoc* alternative explanation of the results.

Ben-Zeev's (1977a & b) researches may appear to support the sensitivity hypothesis. Her Spanish–English and Hebrew–English bilinguals were found to be more susceptible to a nonsense word illusion test. When a nonsense word is repeated continuously (twice a second for two minutes) by means of a tape loop, people tend to report changes in what they hear. For example, instead of "fline" and "tress", people may report hearing "fly" and "stress". Ben-Zeev (1977a & b) interprets these findings in terms of bilinguals being more sensitive to the content of the verbal stimulus than monolinguals. When the researcher asked if there really had been changes in the stimulus or not, bilinguals more often said there had *not* really been changes. Was this an indication of a sensitivity to the social hint that they may have been mistaken in their answers? As with Ianco-Worrall's (1972) research, Ben-Zeev's (1977b) evidence of greater bilingual sensitivity rests on interpretation of a result rather than on an a priori hypothesis and direct examination of the hypothesis, although the issue is discussed in detail in Ben-Zeev (1977b).

Further evidence of the greater sensitivity to feedback cues of bilinguals comes from Cummins & Mulcahy (1978). On an ambiguities test, when children chose only one of two correct answers, a prompt was given to see if the other correct answer could be obtained. Bilinguals made better use of the prompts given than monolinguals, finding the second correct answer more often than monolinguals.

Perhaps the most interesting finding comes from Genesee, Tucker & Lambert (1975) who compared pupils in an Early Total Immersion Bilingual Education programme with Partial Immersion and Control groups. Although these groups are not strictly comparable to the usual comparison of balanced bilinguals and monolinguals, the results are very revealing.

In the research, pupils aged 5 to 8 were required to explain a board and dice game to two listeners, one blindfolded, the other not. The listeners were classmates, not allowed to ask questions and after the explanation, tried to play the game with the explainer. The Total Immersion group was found to be the most sensitive to the needs of listeners. It was this group who gave more information to the blindfolded than to the sighted listener compared with the Control group. The authors conclude that Total Immersion children "may have been better able than the control children to take the role of others experiencing communicational difficulties, to perceive their needs, and consequently to respond appropriately to these needs" (p. 1013). In short, the possibility is that bilingual children may show increased social sensitivity in situations requiring verbal communication.

A related but different approach to the sensitivity hypothesis derives from the research of Bain (1975). His tests consists of 24 black and white reproductions of famous portraits. Each portrait is said to express the emotion of love, surprise, fear, anger or contempt. Forty-two bilinguals aged 10 to 12 and a comparable group of monolinguals differed in their sensitivity to emotional expressions. Bilinguals were significantly better at the task than monolinguals. According to Bain (1975), a bilingual can better locate the appropriate feeling due to a more complexly organized language system. Bilinguals may be better able to use their more enhanced symbolic background to separate out one kind of emotion from another. While not doubting a relationship between language and analysing emotional experience, as tantalizing as is Bain's research, the explanation of the result remains speculative.

Skutnabb-Kangas (1981) and Ben-Zeev (1977b) have further speculated on the sensitivity hypothesis. Skutnabb-Kangas (1981) argues that sensitivity to non-verbal communication (e.g. the ability to interpret facial expressions, gestures, intonation, varying situations) is related to overall social sensitivity, and explained by it. In order to know when to switch languages, a bilingual needs to pick up cues and vary behaviour accordingly. Very small changes in situation may give the clue to switch languages. The bilingual, she argues, must therefore pay attention to the fine details of each social situation and react appropriately (Skutnabb-Kangas, 1981). Ben-Zeev (1977b) suggests that such sensitivity stems from constant scanning to see if the language is correct or incorrect. Children who experience some minor interference between languages may be more sensitive to feedback cues, verbal and non-verbal. Such cues may indicate when, for example, a Welsh word has crept into a sentence in English. Ben-Zeev (1977b) argues that the motivation for such sensitivity is two-fold: cognitive and emotional. The cognitive motivation exists in the need to keep two languages separate. Accommodation of two systems requires sensitivity to their separateness. The emotional motivation exists in the need to avoid anxiety. Anxiety may be generated by loss of status or ridicule when there is interference between languages (Ben-Zeev, 1977b).

The evidence for the increased sensitivity of bilinguals is far from strong. Research on this topic has not been sequentially developed and is operationally diverse. The theory and discussion of the issue far exceeds the amount of supportive or confirmatory research. Yet the issue is important and intriguing. It moves questions about bilingualism on from cognition to interpersonal relationships, from skills of the mind to social skills. This may be an important area for future research to explore in more depth and breadth.

The cognitive style of field dependence–independence and bilingualism

Cognitive style refers to an individual's method of thinking (e.g. in sorting information, remembering, transforming and using information). One well researched dimension of cognitive style along which people vary is field dependence–field independence (Witkin *et al.*, 1971). An example from one of Witkin *et al.*'s (1971) tests will help describe the dimension. In the Embedded Figures Test, a child has to draw in the left hand figure over the right hand figure. Can the child recognise the cuboid in the right hand figure?

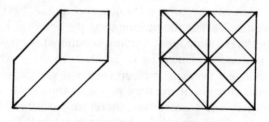

Children who are field independent will tend to be able to see the object separate from the other lines in the right hand figure. Those field dependent will tend not to be able to separate out the cuboid figure from the background. Simply stated, some people tend to see in wholes, others in parts. Witkin *et al.* (1962) found that as children grow to maturity they become more field independent. While field dependence–independence may appear as a perceptual ability, Witkin and his co-workers regard it as a general ability to overcome embedded contexts, and this dimension relates particularly to problem solving ability and ease of cognitive restructuring that occurs in cognitive development. Thus field independent individuals tend to achieve higher academically than those field dependent.

One early study which examined whether bilinguals have a particular cognitive style compared with monolinguals was conducted in Switzerland by Balkan (1970). French–English balanced bilinguals aged 11 to 17 were matched with monolinguals on IQ, and compared on an adaptation of the Embedded Figures Test. Balkan (1970) found that bilinguals were more field independent and that those who learnt their second language before the age of 4 tended to be more field independent than late learners (who had learnt their second language between 4 and 8 years). In the Canadian St Lambert Project (see Chapter 4), at 12–13 years of age, pupils in a bilingual education programme were superior to the control groups on the Embedded Figures Test (Bruck et al., 1976). Although the comparison groups were different from Balkan (1970), the St Lambert research provides some confirmation of bilingualism being linked to greater field independence. However, Genesee & Hamayan (1980) found that those more field independent learnt a second language better. This pinpoints the question of the direction of the cause–effect relationship that will be examined in more detail at the end of the chapter. Does field independence cause bilingualism to occur more easily? Does bilingualism cause field independence? Or is one both the cause and the effect of the other?

Apart from the Swiss and Canadian research, one further piece of evidence comes from English–Spanish bilinguals in the USA (Duncan & De Avila, 1979). Using the Children's Embedded Figures Test, the descending order of scores on field independence was:

1. Proficient Bilinguals
2. Partial Bilinguals, Monolinguals and Limited Bilinguals
3. Late Language Learners.

The authors conclude that proficient bilinguals may have advantages in cognitive clarity and in analytical functioning. There is also evidence here for the threshold theory, to be examined in Chapter 7.

Explanations of findings

Cummins (1976) suggests three hypotheses to explain why there may be a beneficial link between bilingualism and divergent thinking, an analytical orientation towards languages, Piagetian conceptual development, communicative sensitivity and field independence. The hypotheses provide both an attempted integration of the findings and an explanation. Further theoretical perspectives will be considered in Chapter 7.

The *first* explanation is that bilinguals have a wider and more varied range of experiences than monolinguals due to operating in two languages and possibly two cultures. The shades of meaning peculiar to one language, the stream of experience embodied in a particular language, the cultural values and modes embedded in a language, are increased for those with two languages. Although not doubling the richness of experience, there may be potential gains for the bilingual child and adult. Cummins' (1976) conclusion about this explanation is still true over a decade later. "It has not been demonstrated that bilinguals are exposed to a wider range of social or cultural stimulation than unilinguals or that, even if they were, this would accelerate their rate of cognitive growth" (p. 30). The research evidence to test the validity of the hypothesis could be difficult to gather. Nevertheless, the hypothesis is still an interesting speculation.

The *second* explanation concerns a switching mechanism. Because bilingual children have to switch from one language to another, they may be more flexible in thought. Also, two languages provide two different perspectives, possibly providing some flexibility and originality in thinking. Morrison (1958) relates the story of an 11-year-old Gaelic–English bilingual taking an IQ test. On being asked which language he thought in when taking the test, the lad answered: "Please sir, I tried it in English first, then I tried in the Gaelic to see if it would be easier; but it wasn't, so I went back to the English" (p. 288). Neufeld (1974) has been critical of this hypothesis, suggesting that monolinguals also have to switch from one register to another. Cummins & Gulutsan (1974), using the Russian psychologist Uznadze's Laptic Illusion Test, found no empirical support for this hypothesis. So while Peal & Lambert (1962) and the divergent thinking research both suggest an explanation in terms of switching, research has not directly supported the possibility.

The *third* explanation is termed the process of objectification (Cummins & Gulutsan, 1974). A bilingual may be involved in the process of comparing and contrasting two languages: for example, comparing nuances of meaning, attending to different grammatical forms. Bilinguals may be constantly vigilant over their language, inspecting it, resolving interference between languages. Varying language rules may be sought out, word sound and word meaning may be differentiated. Cummins (1976) suggests that cognitive development is promoted by this linguistic explanation, and is compatible with both Piagetian and Vygotskian theory. This, as has been noted in the chapter, is an explanation given by a number of authors for their research, and seems relatively well supported.

Critique

In comparison with the IQ–bilingualism research, studies examining the cognitive advantages of bilingualism have tended to be much more sophisticated in terms of the control of variables and in their analyses. However, these studies need to be critically assessed in terms of certain "macro" criticisms. Not all the research reported in this chapter is faulty in design, procedure or analysis. However, a number of studies have limitations and weaknesses that, while possibly not invalidating the overall finding of cognitive benefits attached to bilingualism, do cast doubts on their individual validity. These need to be briefly mentioned.

Matching groups

Despite the well-publicized criticisms of the IQ–bilingualism research, some studies have made the same mistakes in experimental design as did the early IQ studies. One common fault is failing to match bilingual and monolingual groups adequately on variables that may explain the results: socio-economic class, age, gender, IQ for example. The critique of the divergent thinking results illustrates this problem. A second common and related fault (e.g. Duncan & De Avila, 1979) is research which does not give full and precise details of how variables were controlled or how groups were matched.

Even when groups are matched on IQ and socio-economic class, there still remains the question of whether the groups are equivalent on other variables which could (alternatively to bilingualism) explain the result (MacNab, 1979; McLaughlin, 1984). Differences between the bilingual and monolingual groups on factors such as motivation, parental attitude, school experience and culture might be the causal factor rather than, or in addition to, bilingualism. McLaughlin (1984) suggests an alternative approach. A longitudinal study would examine the effects of bilingualism over the passage of time. The design could be as follows:

A: *Pre-test*

Group 1 ⎱ Matched on relevant variables including the cogni-
Group 2 ⎰ tive variables in question

B: *Treatment*

Group 1 — Monolingual experience
Group 2 — Bilingual experience

C: *Post-test*

Group 1 ⎱ Measured on the cognitive variables to see if
Group 2 ⎰ change has occurred from pre-test to post-test.

Rather than comparing monolingual and bilingual groups at one point in time, this longitudinal design examines the effect of bilingualism over an extended period of time. Using this kind of design, Lambert & Tucker (1972) found no difference on measures of creative thinking over time between bilinguals and monoglots.

Are the positive results from the cross-sectional research an artefact of research design? This is unlikely, but it points to the necessity of future longitudinal research.

The nature of the groups

MacNab (1979) has argued that in relevant research, the bilingual group is not really representative. Apart from the issue of research tending to use balanced bilinguals (see Chapter 1), MacNab (1979) also suggests that bilinguals are a special, idiosyncratic group. Learning a second language and being involved in its culture requires a person very different from someone who, in similar circumstances, prefers to stay unilingual. Bilinguals are not a random selection of the population. Rather, they are a biased selection. The parents of bilingual children may have different parent–child interaction patterns compared with unilinguals, and this in turn has cognitive consequences.

Parents who want their children to be bicultural and bilingual may emphasize divergent thinking and rational thinking or accelerate and emphasize language skills. Thus individual attitudes and motivations, child rearing practices and family environment may be the causal factor in cognitive benefits rather than bilingualism. MacNab (1979) argues that children who became bilingual "tend to come from homes where there is an open cognitive ambiance and where there is encouragement of learning in general and language learning in particular" (p. 251).

The nature of the relationship

A chicken and egg problem exists with bilingualism and cognitive development. Almost all the research reviewed in this chapter assumes that bilingualism causes cognitive benefits. The opposite causal pattern is possible, as is a mutually reciprocating interaction between the two. Those who have cognitive "advantages" may be the ones who become bilingual, especially balanced bilinguals. The associational design of almost all the research studies cannot indicate the direction of cause and effect. Mac-

Nab's (1979) analysis of Scott's (1973) data and that of Barrik & Swain (1976) leads him to conclude that "there is no evidence in the literature that becoming bilingual leads to cognitive enhancement" and secondly, that "any causal link is more apt to run from cognitive abilities towards enhanced language learning" (pp. 250 and 251). This would seem somewhat over-cautious, if not a little unfair. A more level judgement might be that the process of language learning and cognitive development work hand in hand. One will both stimulate and be stimulated by the other. A simplistic cause–effect pattern seems unreal in the continuous process of interactions between language and cognition. Recent advances in statistical analysis (e.g. path analysis, structural equation modelling) which can examine various causal models including interactive effects, plus the use of longitudinal designs, should help shed future light on this chicken and egg issue. Thus Hakuta (1986), using a causal model, found that bilingualism positively affected non-verbal IQ, rather than the reverse. More research of this type is needed.

Ability effects

Is it the case that only the more able children who become bilingual will experience cognitive advantages? MacNab (1979) has suggested that research (e.g. Cummins & Gulutsan, 1974) has centred on more able children, due to ensuring that bilinguals are balanced bilinguals. While research does tend to centre on middle-class children of above average ability, Rueda's (1983) research suggests that the link may be found in less able children. Using children of well below average IQ (51–69 IQ points), Rueda (1983) compared bilinguals and unilinguals on three tests: a Meaning and Reference Task which examines the stability and meaning of words (e.g. an imaginary animal called a "flump" who dies); the Arbitrariness of Language Task (see above, p. 29); and the Non-Physical Nature of Words Task (e.g. does the word "bird" have feathers?). On each of the three tasks, the low IQ bilinguals tended to score significantly higher than the unilinguals. Although Rueda (1983) found no difference on a Piagetian conservation test, this research, which needs replication, hints that the bilingualism–cognitive advantages link may not be specific to high or average ability children.

Replication of the research

Three issues need to be mentioned about replication. First, of the studies available, the great majority find a positive relationship between bilingualism and cognitive abilities. Are these studies a representative sample of all studies carried out on the topic? As Rosenthal (1984:125) notes, "the probability of publication is increased by the statistical significance of the results so that published studies may not be representative of the studies conducted". This is not a problem peculiar to bilingualism. Educational and psychological research in general tends to fall within the same criticism. When results are different from previous research, does the author attempt to publish, will a journal carry a discrepant finding, will the author forget and bury the research?

Second, all research needs replication. Such replication should be with different ages, different ethnic groups, different socio-economic and ability samples. The research on bilingualism and cognitive abilities is conspicuous not only for its lack of replications, but also for its non-sequential, arbitrary, unconnected development. Possibly because of a variety of available cognitive measures and partly because of the lack of a clear theoretical starting point that integrates languages and cognitive development, research has developed in a piecemeal and disparate fashion. Little reference exists in the literature to the information-processing approach to human abilities. Such an approach provides a theoretical basis and a methodology different from the psychometric tradition which has dominated bilingual research.

Third, irrespective of the subject of the research, one must always take into account the hopes and ideology of the researcher. Rosenthal (1966) has shown how experimenters' expectations can affect the results of human and animal studies. As Wagner (1980:35) suggests, these findings "seem to fit a picture of bilingual 'advantage' — a view which conforms to the ideological desires of many concerned with problems of bilingual education and particularly with those combating anti-bilingual/anti-ethnic prejudice". Hakuta (1986:43), like Wagner (1980), poses a question about the influence of researcher ideology on results: "a full account of the relationship between bilingualism and intelligence, of why negative effects suddenly turned into positive effects, will have to examine the motivations of the researcher as well as more traditional considerations at the level of methodology". To what extent have the studies been designed to increase the chances of a positive result for bilingualism? Have the ideological assumptions about bilingualism of positivist authors crept unintentionally into their research and affected both results and interpretations? Siguán & Mackey (1987:125) are sure of their answer, arguing that each research worker has

"personal motives which will affect the path he follows in his study and the ease with which he will accept or reject certain conclusions.

The personal involvement of the researcher is more clearly percep- tible in the human than in the natural sciences, and it is particularly obvious in the study of bilingualism and bilingual education".

As Hearnshaw's (1979) biography of Sir Cyril Burt reveals, superficially rigorous research can hide a myriad of faults and sins. It would be a brave researcher and editor to publish, in the last decades of the twentieth century, research showing that bilingualism has detrimental cognitive effects.

Length of benefits

If it is assumed that there are positive cognitive advantages linked with bilingualism, it is important to ask whether these are temporary or cumulative and everlasting. Research studies tend to use children aged 4 to 17. What happens in the twenties or middle age or older age? Does bilingualism accelerate cognitive growth in the early years, with monoglots catching up in later years? Balkan (1970) and Ben-Zeev (1977b) have suggested that such cognitive advantages are predominant in younger rather than older children. Arnberg (1981) disagrees and argues that cognitive development is additive and that the further the child moves towards balanced bilingualism, the more cognitive advantages can be realized.

It is possible that certain advantages (e.g. greater awareness of language, separation of word sound from word meaning, Piagetian concept development) will be temporary. Age and experience may eventually even out the bilingual and monolingual. However, with the ideas of cognitive style (e.g. divergent thinking, field independence) and communicative sensitivity, may go relatively more stable and lasting effects. While humans are ever open to change and development, research on extended age links between bilingualism and cognitive style and communicative sensitivity, may reveal some interesting results.

Conclusion

Two extreme conclusions may both be untenable. First, to conclude without a doubt that bilingualism gives cognitive advantages fails to take due cognizance of the weight of the criticisms and limitations given throughout the chapter. Second, to conclude that such criticisms are so damaging as to suggest all the research is invalid, fails to acknowledge that the judgement of the great majority of researchers tends to be positive. While individual pieces of research are sometimes weak and with limitations, cumulatively the verdict seems to favour a bilingualism–cognitive advantages link. There is insufficient evidence to satisfy the sceptic, but what evidence there is leads in the direction of supporting believers in bilingualism. A conclusion also needs to be made about the extent of any advantages. Are such advantages great? Do they foster accelerated educational progress? In this respect, a conclusion must be cautious. It seems unlikely that the advantages are great when related to everyday functioning. Such advantages may give a head start, or make a small difference in the classroom. It would be wrong to exaggerate claims on present evidence. Nevertheless, a verdict marginally in favour of some advantages seems appropriate. James Williams (1915) concluded as such after viewing bilingualism in Belgium. The research evidence from the USA, Israel and Canada supports Williams' hunch seventy years later. While it may take another seven decades to produce more conclusive, well replicated and better synthesized research, for supporters of bilingualism the signs are positive.

3 Bilingual Education in Britain and Ireland

Introduction

Much research on bilingual education has led to little public enlightenment about bilingual schooling. Despite considerable research from North America and Europe, prejudice, innuendo and guesswork often form the basis of public pronouncement.

The neutral person will ask whether bilingual schooling has a positive or detrimental effect on pupils. The number of people who believe the answer to be positive appears to be greatly outweighed by those who are convinced of negative outcomes. Whether the school teaches through a minority home language (e.g. Spanish in the USA), through an indigenous heritage, minority language (e.g. Welsh, Irish and Gaelic in Britain) or through a prestigious second language (French in Canada), politicians, parents and professional educators too often pontificate without reference to the increasing amount of serious research that seeks to provide some kind of empirically tested answer.

Education has historically been mostly monolingual. In Wales, for example, state-financed education was mostly through English until recent decades, even in areas where the great majority of the population spoke Welsh as their first, and sometimes only language. The melting-pot policy of assimilating a variety of peoples and tongues in the USA has traditionally assumed that English must be the medium of school instruction sooner or later.

Since education has traditionally been monolingual, with a few exceptions, parents and teachers may naturally be concerned about the provision and occasional enforcement of bilingual education. How can it be that at the tender age of 4 or 5, when anxieties may exist within the child about breaking from the home, a child in Wales or Canada may be dropped in at the deep end, having to swim immediately in a second language? Full immersion or ducking and drowning? How can it be that

a child from a minority language home in the USA or England is sometimes taught in both the home and the majority language in the elementary
or primary school? Doesn't this lead to inequality of opportunity in the
employment market where the English language has greater economic
currency value? Do such children suffer in the academic stakes, failing to
achieve examination success and university education because of being
held back by their home language being used in school? Bilingual education or belligerent and betraying enfeeblement?

The next two chapters attempt to answer the kind of basic questions
that parents and teachers ask, and administrators and politicians should
ask, about bilingual education. Is bilingual education for good or for bad,
for richer or for poorer? This chapter examines reports and research from
Ireland, Wales and England. What is the Celtic and English experience?
The following chapter considers research from Canada and the USA,
from where much recent and more technically proficient studies have
come.

Before consideration of the research, some definition and classification of bilingual education needs to be provided. The research does not
deal with the same context or same type of schooling even though it is
subsumed under the title of bilingual education. There are considerable
variations in bilingual education and these need to be kept in mind when
drawing conclusions.

Types of bilingual education

A variety of different typologies of bilingual education exist. John
Edwards (1984a), in defining bilingual education as "education in which
two languages are used within the school" (p. 185) suggested that amongst
the many variations are two major models. First there is *transitional
bilingual education*, where the plan is to phase out one language as the
mainstream or majority language develops. Second, there exists *maintenance or enrichment bilingual education* where two languages are kept
throughout all or most of schooling. In *transitional* bilingual education,
the child's first language is only an interim medium for school instruction,
hence such education tends to be compensatory in nature. The aim is
fluency in the majority language. Examples are to be found in the USA
and Europe where language "deficiencies" of minority group children are
"cured" so they can continue to be educated in English or another majority
language. In *maintenance* education, both languages may be used in
school, the aim being to ensure the child has good facility in both langu-

ages. Examples are to be found in Canada and Wales, where English speakers are taught French or Welsh to enable them to be fully bilingual. Transitional programmes are often concerned with assimilation; maintenance programmes with pluralism, enrichment, language restoration and biculturalism.

Another useful distinction comes from Gaarder (1976) who considered *élitist bilingualism* compared with *folk bilingualism*. *Élitist bilingualism* often serves the interests of the dominant power group and upper class membership. A knowledge of two languages may have high cultural and economic value, allowing access to privileged groups or high status positions and power. An English speaker learning French or Welsh, a Japanese student learning English may be experiencing bilingual education with élitist goals. Élitist bilingualism derives from choice. *Folk bilingualism* is often by necessity or compulsion. A person may become bilingual in order to survive. Immigrants may need to learn the majority language to gain access to employment. Bilingualism may be imposed by those politically dominant. The distinction between folk and élitist bilingualism is important because it highlights the motives of children during and upon entry to bilingual schooling. The success and failure of bilingual education programmes is partially dependent on the motives and commitments of pupils, their parents and sub-culture. For one child, the motive may be to achieve high status in society. For another child, the motive may be for security and survival. For one, full commitment to bilingualism may be induced through prospective economic and social rewards. For another, commitment may be lacking due to the imposition of bilingualism and where there are no or few perceived useful advantages of bilingualism. The role of attitudes and motivation in bilingual education is considered in Chapters 5 and 6.

A distinction between *immersion* and *submersion* bilingual education contains a graphic analogy with the swimming pool. Rather than a quick dip into a second language (e.g. teaching German as a second language in British comprehensive schools), submersion contains the idea of a non-swimmer being thrown in at the deep end. A submersion programme means pupils being forbidden to use their home language, with all the curriculum being experienced in a second language. Being thrown in at the deep end also extends to the idea that a pupil will be amongst fluent swimmers. A child may be placed in a class with native speakers, and have to try to adopt their language.

Immersion bilingual education paints a picture of moving gradually from the shallow to the deep end. Pupils are allowed to splash about in their home language while being taught the skills of swimming. Soon they move into deeper and deeper water, eventually acquiring the four basic strokes and skills to swim unaided in either language (listening, speaking, reading and writing). In an immersion programme, pupils are homogeneous in their initial level in the second language. The class contains non-swimmers and not a mixture of learners and experts. Children are allowed to use their home language until confidence grows and until they naturally start to switch to the second language with their bilingual teachers. "The practice in the first and second years of the programme is to expose children to a large amount of second language use (by the teacher), but to let them talk among themselves and to the teacher in their home language" (Swain & Lapkin, 1982:5). Successful immersion bilingual education means ideally that a student can dive into either language pool and mix with either language group.

There are a variety of other typologies (see Trueba, 1979). The most elaborate of these is by William Mackey (1970), which culminates in 90 different types of bilingual schooling. Mackey (1970) plots variations in home language, school curriculum, community and national context and the status of the languages. This extensive typology, while important to linguists and theorists, does not seem to have helped empirical research to formulate hypotheses, nor does it appear to be a natural way of reflecting the key issues of bilingual education. Concerns raised by parents and politicians, academics and administrators are often to be found in the distinctions between transitional and enrichment, folk and élitist, and submersion and immersion bilingual education. Research has provided some important evidence on each of these concerns. Reports and research from Ireland, England and Wales will now be examined for such concerns.

Bilingual education and Ireland

Historical perspective

Some 130 years ago, an Irish Schools' Inspector wrote of the disastrous effect of educational policy on the Irish language. In the Gaeltacht (Irish-speaking) areas "where all social communication is carried on in Irish and where, in short, few or none of the adult population know a word of English, the language of the National Schools, the books, the teaching, etc., are entirely English" (quoted in Ó Buachalla, 1984:76). Transitional education at its worst. The Inspector forecast that the children of such children would in nine cases out of ten speak English only.

In 1878, a foot in the door was obtained by the Society for the Preservation of the Irish Language. Irish was allowed as an extra subject outside regular school hours. The allowance was made reluctantly, with Irish being seen as a non-essential subject. The Commissioners of National Education asserted in 1884 that they had "reached a limit to the steps which in the public interest, could be wisely taken in respect of the cultivation of the Irish language in the primary schools" (quoted in Ó Buachalla, 1984:78).

The nineteenth-century shift in language in Ireland from Irish to English was caused in part by educational policy, provision and practice. Irish culture also suffered. Pupils' knowledge of their own country, its traditions, music, history and geography was kept minimal. The inevitable reaction was symbolized by the activities of the Gaelic League who launched campaigns in the early years of the twentieth century to reverse the language and cultural trends. The Gaelic League campaigned not only for Irish to be a proper school subject, but also for Irish to be the language for instruction where the home language was Irish. In 1904, a Bilingual Programme was introduced as a result of much pressure and provided a syllabus for each primary school year in Irish and English. This represented a significant mark in the Irish language movement.

Between 1900 and 1921, the number of schools teaching Irish increased dramatically from 100 to close to 2,000. Thus by 1921 when the Irish Free State was founded, a quarter of national schools taught Irish, with 240 schools being Irish-medium schools.

With the advent of the Irish Free State, "truly national" Irish education became policy. The Irish language, its history, culture and traditions were given a significant place in the curriculum of schools. The National Programmes of 1922 and 1926 were particularly influential in promoting Irish in the primary sector. The high point was reached in the 1940s when Irish was taught in all schools and was used as a medium of instruction in 12% of primary and 28% of secondary schools (Ó Buachalla, 1984). The campaign for the inclusion of Irish as a matriculation subject for university entrance may at least partly account for the increase in pupils taking Irish in secondary schools.

Growth was joined by doubt. Teachers began to have misgivings about the educational benefit of teaching Irish. A survey by the Irish National Teachers Organization reported, in 1941, a strong rejection by its members of the official language policy. Many parents joined teachers and requested instruction through English with the teaching and writing in Irish to be ignored or postponed until self-expression in English was sufficiently developed. Movements against compulsory Irish in schools were founded, stressing equality of opportunity, the importance of science, major European modern languages, practical subjects and modern curriculum. In 1975, the CILAR (Committee on Irish Language Attitudes Research) Report (see Chapter 5), found that many parents were dissatisfied with the way Irish was taught in schools and opposed Government policies involving compulsion. Majority verdicts were returned on children doing better at school if taught through English rather than Irish and children failing their examinations because they were taught through Irish. In 1960 there were 420 Irish medium primary schools; by 1979 this had dropped to 160, all but 23 of these in the Gaeltacht. A similar movement occurred at the secondary school level. Economic and political factors account for much of the post-war decline, but educational policy both reflects and in its turn became a determinant of language shift. Thus Séamus Ó Buachalla (1984) concludes: "There is ample evidence to indicate that the Irish language within the school system is in a weak condition; its status is no better now than it was in the early years of the century" (p. 90). Part of the blame is given to the absence of early systematic research on bilingual educational policy.

This brief historical perspective illustrates two related points. First, minority languages in schools can be like the tide, ebbing and flowing, with action and reaction. The negative discriminatory policy of the late nineteenth century provoked counter-measures which themselves provoked some negative reactions. As will be considered later, very recent developments indicate some more positive movements in bilingual schooling in Ireland. Second, *compulsion* in learning Irish following the foundation of the Irish Free State in 1921 did little to further the minority language cause. Conformity can exist without conviction. To be taught Irish is not to become Irish. Being made able to speak a language does not, *ipso facto*, lead to speaking that language. Potential is not the same as production. Conformity to school objectives is easily thwarted by the later freedom of choice in medium of communication and mode of culture. Compulsion may so easily result in rejection. All minority languages have something important to learn from the history of the Irish language.

MacNamara's (1966) research

One piece of research has, until recently, dominated the evaluation of bilingual education in Ireland. Father John MacNamara commenced his research in the early 1960s. He stated two objectives: "to discover the effect on arithmetical attainment of teaching arithmetic through the medium of Irish to children from English speaking homes" and "to discover the effect of the entire programme for reviving Irish in national schools on the level of English attainment" (1966:6). The research followed in the wake of controversial statements by Father O'Doherty, Professor of Logic and Psychology at University College, Dublin. O'Doherty (1958a and b) had criticized Irish educational policy regarding its aims of Irish language teaching. He argued that, due to the restorationist policy, Irish children became retarded by 1 to $1\frac{1}{2}$ years and there was clinical evidence of much emotional disturbance in such young people. Emigration and general dissatisfaction were two further outcomes of the language policy. Research evidence to support O'Doherty's views was lacking until MacNamara (1966) provided his analysis.

MacNamara's sample comprised 119 schools and 1,084 children, each being given tests of non-verbal IQ, Irish, English, Problem and Mechanical Arithmetic and a measure of socio-economic status. Irish and English versions of the arithmetic and non-verbal IQ tests were used. The statistical procedures used for analysis, multiple regression analysis and analysis of co-variance, were relatively novel and sophisticated in bilingual research of the 1960s. A virtue of the research is its technical sophistication in the use of multivariate statistical analysis.

When allowances were made for differences in non-verbal IQ, socio-economic background and "teaching skill", children from English-speaking districts who were taught all subjects in Irish were behind on problem arithmetic by about 11 months, but not behind on mechanical arithmetic. MacNamara (1966:103) stated that it is "probable that the use of Irish in teaching problem arithmetic hinders the progress of English-speaking children". The evaluation of Irish bilingual education was seen to be negative as a consequence.

Cummins (1977b), in a critical review of MacNamara's research, disputes this finding. He argues that problem arithmetic success involves language skills as well as arithmetical skills. The problem arithmetic questions require the analysis of language before computational activity. The children who were weakest at this test, those from English districts being taught through the medium of Irish, were given the Irish version of the test. Cummins argues that had such children been given the test in English (their home and stronger language), their performance may have improved. He supports this by reference to the lack of difference on the mechanical reading test. Cummins (1977b:125) concludes that "MacNamara's findings may amount to nothing more than that children tested through their weaker language perform more poorly than children tested through their stronger language".

MacNamara (1966) did attempt to control for this potential effect by pre-testing the Irish and English versions of the problem arithmetic test with two random groups of 48 pupils. While MacNamara was able to show that the two versions were of a similar order of difficulty, Cummins' (1977b) critical review notes that these 96 pupils were not similar to the pupils in the main research, with differences on the urban/rural dimension, likely parental attitudes to Irish medium schooling and the use of Irish at home. Thus the pre-testing was achieved with children of higher socio-economic status, whose parents were more likely to be Irish-speaking and have pro-Irish attitudes. Such children were likely to have greater competency in Irish, and thus fewer problems with the language of testing. Hence the pre-testing was invalid, and the Irish problem arithmetic test may not have been of equal difficulty compared with the English medium test.

Cummins (1977b) does seem to be correct in doubting the validity of the pre-testing as being appropriate to the main research group. MacNamara had failed to show incontrovertibly that the problem arithmetic test was equal for the Irish and English versions. However, Cummins' (1977b) critique does not allow a conclusion that those undergoing "immersion" Irish schooling were equal in performance to other groups. The conclusion that there were no detrimental effects resulting from Irish language "immersion" education is untenable. An open verdict is the more sensible conclusion. Immersion education may have led to negative effects with problem arithmetic, or the language of the problem arithmetic test in Irish may have caused the negative result, or both could be operative with the test partially but not fully causing the negative effect. Another alternative is that other variables not entered into the research account for the detrimental effect. That is, factors other than immersion education may provide the explanation. MacNamara (1966:74) himself gives a clue as to other possible influencing factors:

"In rural areas and country towns (that is, in all but four of the 119 schools) few parents had a choice of schools for their children. And even where there was a choice, it is likely to be decided on grounds other than teaching medium".

The parents of children in these immersion schools would have tended to hold neutral or negative attitudes towards Irish and Irish language education. Parental attitude may thus be an important factor to take into account in the evaluation of the success or otherwise of bilingual education. However, Cummins (1977c), using a small sample, did not find this to be the case.

On the more positive side, MacNamara (1966) found that the immersion group performed at the same level in English reading comprehension as did children taught through English. Thus Irish immersion appeared to have no detrimental effects on the majority language. Such a result tends to be contrary to MacNamara's (1966) own explanation of the overall results in terms of a balance effect. He argued that language learning is like a balance. The heavier one side becomes, the lighter must be the other side. An increase in second language skills means a decrease in first language skills. The balance theory is examined in more detail in Chapter 7.

Cummins' (1978c:277) concluding comment on MacNamara's (1966) research is both perceptive and fair.

"When one considers the unfavourable context (in comparison with North American immersion programs) in which Irish immersion programs operated (e.g. low prestige, low-utility language, non-supportive parental attitudes) what is surprising is that there is so little evidence of negative academic effects!".

Cummins' research (1977c)

When at the Educational Research Centre, St. Patrick's College, Dublin, Cummins compared the Irish and English reading achievement of pupils in Irish medium and English medium schools. The sample of children was from Dublin; 91 standard 3 children from three Irish medium schools, and 76 children from two English medium schools.

Analysis of English reading scores showed no difference between the Irish and English medium schools. Thus Irish immersion experience appeared to have no detrimental effects on progress in the majority language. The Irish immersion children also exhibited higher Irish reading scores, a result not found by MacNamara (1966).

Cummins' (1977c) research is small-scale, lacking in the matching of groups and precise control of alternative explanatory variables such as IQ and social class, and tends to use middle-class pupils and not a general population sample. Given these limitations, the study shows that such Irish immersion education may not be a negative influence on specific academic skills.

Harris' research (1984)

John Harris' (1984) research was basically concerned not so much with evaluating the effectiveness of Irish immersion education but with a survey of the degree of competency in Irish of a large sample of pupils. Such a survey required the construction and use of criterion referenced tests rather than the usual norm referenced tests. Such criterion referenced tests attempt to assess the degree of skill of a child in a specific curriculum area. For example, a criterion referenced listening test will contain a large number of graded items. The aim of the test will be to determine precisely what listening skills a pupil has and has not mastered. A criterion referenced test provides a profile of a child's skills in a certain curriculum area. A norm referenced test essentially compares a pupil with national averages. For example, a norm referenced reading test may provide a reading age for a child. In theory, a criterion referenced test does not provide evidence as to the progress of children compared with their peers throughout the country, whereas a norm referenced test does not provide evidence as to the progress of children in mastery of a skill. The former concerns a comparison of self with skill level; the latter concerns a comparison of self with others. In practice, one test may achieve both comparisons.

The survey included three types of school: English medium schools, Irish immersion schools and schools in the official Gaeltacht (Irish-speaking) areas of the country. The samples were large and randomly selected, children being tested for specific listening and speaking skills.

Large differences were found in mastery of Irish between the three types of school when using 2nd grade pupils. Table 1 summarizes the findings.

TABLE 1   *Average Percentage of 2nd Grade Pupils attaining Mastery of Five Listening and Five Speaking Objectives*

Objectives	English medium schools %	Irish immersion schools %	Gaeltacht schools %
Listening to Irish	36	89	61
Speaking Irish	26	79	55

Immersion schools contained children who had developed communicative skills in the minority language in advance of those from designated Irish areas and strikingly more than those who spent about 5 hours per week in English medium schools learning Irish. Or should mastery of objectives in immersion schools have been even better?

Two pieces of evidence suggested that children from English only homes were benefiting from the immersion experience. First, such children's mastery of objectives was not too different from that of 2nd grade children from bilingual homes in the same school, as Table 2 reveals.

TABLE 2

Objectives	Home Language	
	English %	English and Irish %
Mastery in Listening to Irish	84	95
Mastery in Speaking Irish	74	85
(Average)	(79)	(90)

Second, children from monoglot English homes carried achievement in spoken Irish beyond the level reached by pupils from bilingual homes in English medium schools. The former group had a mastery average of 79% (see Table 2); the latter group obtained 69% average mastery. Harris (1984:131) reports that this position

"is summarised very neatly by the finding of the second grade survey that if 'English only' pupils in ordinary schools are taken as the standard of comparison, the increase in performance due to attendance at an all-Irish school is greater than the increase in performance due to having 'English and Irish' as home languages but attending an ordinary school".

While social class and ability factors are not controlled in the comparisons, Harris (1984) is convinced from the data that there is "considerable scope for improving achievement by the further development of all-Irish education" (p. 133). Care is needed in interpreting Harris' data, as differences and performance that appear to favour immersion schooling may be due to such children having relatively higher IQ or socio-economic class. Factors other than immersion schooling may explain the positive results.

A move towards more Irish immersion education derives support from recent institutional and attitudinal sources. An increase in the number of Irish pre-school play groups (naionrai) has recently occurred. In 1975 there were 28 naionrai. By 1985 this had increased to more than 150 such groups (Curriculum and Examinations Board, 1985). Between 1977 and 1982, the number of Irish immersion primary schools outside the Gaeltacht increased from 22 to 40. Since 1983 an average of six new Irish immersion schools has opened annually (Curriculum and Examinations Board, 1985). The early growth in such schools occurred in and around the capital city of Dublin. Recent growth has also been in provincial areas: Cork, Limerick, Galway, Carlow, Dungarvan, Castlebar, Navan, Drogheda, Dundalk and Youghal. As in Wales, *parents* are often important initiators of such provision. This recent growth in Irish immersion schools shows a reversal of the trend away from minority language education that occurred in recent decades. These newer immersion schools may provide a better basis for Irish language restoration than in the past. Commitment tends to be replacing enforced conformity. As Cummins (1978c:280) noted,

"a necessary condition for an increase in the number of immersion schools is a reversal of the belief held by the majority of the population that children doing subjects through the medium of Irish perform less well than children taught through English. The recent Irish and North American research provides support for a reversal of that belief."

Such a reversal is indicated in a recent attitude study (Ó Riagáin and Ó Gliasáin, 1984). Between 1973 and 1983, significant changes were found in response to the following statements:

	1973 % Agree	1983 % Agree
Many children fail their exams because of Irish	77	40
Children doing subjects through Irish don't do aswell at school as those doing them through English	60	44

The movement is clear. Attitudes to Irish in education are apparently becoming less negative, although this movement may be partly due to compulsory Irish, for examination purposes, being removed in 1973. Yet there was no change in the same survey with regard to preference for bilingual education. Some three-quarters of the population wanted Irish taught as a subject only, and only about a fifth wanted some form of bilingual education. This reveals that change towards bilingual education is, and sometimes needs to be, slow and careful. Convictions, unlike conformity, rarely occur instantaneously.

Bilingual education in Scotland

Of the major Celtic languages still alive in Britain and Ireland, Gaelic in Scotland is the weakest. In the 1981 Irish Census, 31.6% of the population reported themselves as Irish speakers, although the Census question was limited and has been criticized. In the 1981 UK Census, 19.0% of people in Wales regarded themselves as Welsh-speaking. The same UK Census revealed that only 1.6% of the population in Scotland spoke Gaelic, some 79,307 people. Close to four out of every ten speakers of Gaelic did not read or write in Gaelic. The Gaelic speakers tend to be dispersed, with the main concentration being located in the Western Isles, Skye and Lochalsh. Glasgow contains about nine thousand Gaelic speakers and Edinburgh some three and a half thousand.

Around the turn of the twentieth century, close to 5% of the population in Scotland spoke Gaelic, numbering a little under 250,000. "From the end of the nineteenth century Gaelic faced its most serious challenge — the use of the State's schools to eradicate what one Inspector called 'the Gaelic nuisance'" (Stephens, 1976:63). The 1872 Education Act for Scotland made no reference to Gaelic, and under the Act, Gaelic was actively discouraged in schools. Stephens (1976) argues that the school system in Scotland was a major agent in the decline of Gaelic, by English dominating as the medium of instruction, by creating negative attitudes to Gaelic, by the replacement of Gaelic culture by, for example, English historical perspectives, and by encouraging gifted children to leave heartland areas and become assimilated into anglicized culture.

It is not surprising, therefore, that bilingual education in Scotland is comparatively undeveloped and lacking in research. Discussions of the language and recent developments may be found in Stephens (1976), Withers (1984), N. Grant (1984) and MacKinnon (1984a & b). Two points need mentioning. First, despite the low incidence of Gaelic in Scotland, there have been positive educational moves that are innovatory and may both reflect, and contribute to, a small change in the status of Gaelic.

Second, MacKinnon (1986) found within the 1981 Census data small increases in the number of young people speaking Gaelic. Thus, there is some evidence that Gaelic is not a forgotten nor a dying cause.

Until recently, it was taken for granted in Scotland that not to be taught through English constituted a major disadvantage and handicap (Grant, 1984). Since the 1950s there has been a small change amongst a minority of the population whose interest and concern have been shown in four different ways. *First*, pressure groups committed to the continuation of the language have voiced the need for bilingual education, namely An Comann Gaidhealch (Highland Association), Comann Foghlam na Gaidhlig (Gaelic Education Association) and Comann nan Sgoiltean Araich (Gaelic Playgroups Association). Typical demands are for full bilingual education in the Gaidhealtachd (Gaelic speaking heartland areas), opportunities for children and adults throughout Scotland to learn Gaelic, and bilingual schooling in anglicized areas where parents demand it (Grant, 1984).

Second, Gaelic can be taken as a language in all secondary schools in the Western Region, with partial and selective provision in Argyll, Central Region, Glasgow and Edinburgh. Gaelic medium teaching is relatively rare, and tends to be confined to the Western Isles and the Isle of Skye (Grant, 1984). However, interest has recently developed in the Highlands, Glasgow and Argyll for the provision of such schooling in anglicized areas. This interest stems partly from recent voluntary initiatives by parents to set up Gaelic pre-school playgroups similar to the more well established movements in Ireland and Wales.

Third, since 1975, a Bilingual Education Project has used Gaelic as a medium for all primary school general education and has been located in the Western Isles (Murray & Morrison, 1984). The Project started in some 20 primary schools. In 1982, the Western Isles Authority took over the Project and continued the development of bilingual education in primary schools within their own authority resources. The Project has facilitated the production and use of modern Gaelic resource material. Withers (1984) notes that "the scheme does appear to have established Gaelic more firmly in the educational system of those parts and has not alienated the language from its culture or its speakers" (p. 245). Murray & Morrison (1984) present a lively account of the Project, but no hard research evidence to determine its relative success in terms of a variety of educational outcomes.

Fourth, recent surveys have revealed increased parental interest in children being taught Gaelic. J. H. Grant (1983) investigated the feasibility of establishing Gaelic–English bilingual primary schools on the Scottish mainland. A substantial demand was revealed in Glasgow and Argyll in particular. This demand emanated from non-Gaelic speaking parents who nevertheless wanted their children to become more aware of their heritage and roots. Some parents also believed that learning both Gaelic and English would help language learning and education generally. "People talk of reclaiming 'a lost heritage', of how they would like their children to learn Gaelic even though as children they were seldom taught it and were rebuked if they spoke it" (Withers, 1984:246).

Gaelic is undoubtedly in a precarious position. In Southern Ireland, some 800,000 people speak Irish with a substantial but unquantified minority of the Northern Ireland population also speaking Irish. In Wales, the figure is close to 500,000 people speaking Welsh. In Scotland, only 80,000 speak Gaelic. Yet, as in Ireland and Wales, there is some fresh concern amongst both native speakers and monoglots for their Celtic language. The movement may be a minority one, but the interest goes beyond sympathy. Some commitment to bilingual education is beginning to appear in urban as well as heartland areas. This is encouraging, but possibly equivocal as far as a real restoration of the language is concerned.

Bilingual education in England

Bilingualism in England is a very different issue from current debates in Wales, Ireland and Scotland. In the three Celtic countries, bilingualism usually, but not exclusively, concerns protection and restoration of the indigenous minority language. In England, bilingualism refers to the great number of ethnic minorities who maintain their mother tongue in the home, temple, mosque, church or by voluntary education.

The minority languages of England include Arabic, Bengali, Cantonese, Gujerati, Greek, Hindi, Italian, Punjabi, Polish, Portuguese, Spanish, Turkish, Ukrainian and Urdu (Linguistic Minorities Project, 1984, 1985). The bilingualism which the presence of these languages invokes is found in school, work, religious affiliation, culture and mass media. The issues of bilingualism and bilingual education in England tend to have more in common with the USA than with the Celtic nations nearby.

Within Wales, Ireland and Scotland it is perhaps indifference rather than antagonism that characterizes the viewpoint of large numbers of inhabitants towards the heritage language. In England, while it is wrong to generalize and stereotype, there appears to be comparatively more antagonism, prejudice and distrust of bilingualism and bilingual education. This may stem in part from the nineteenth-century British imperialistic and colonialist viewpoint which regarded English as a superior language (Brook, 1980). Immigration into Britain in the period following World War II has instigated a growing debate about the place of these minority languages in British society in general, and within schools in particular. The debate, long and well rehearsed in the USA and parts of Europe, is being re-invented in England.

One element in the debate about bilingual education concerns the historical, economic and educational dominance of the English language. Martin-Jones (1984:426–7) summarizes the situation well:

"English is the majority language not only in terms of numbers of speakers and users, but, more importantly, in terms of legitimized power and control. The relationship between English and many minority languages in Britain, new and old, is embedded in a long history of colonization, with English as the language of rule. In Britain in the 1980s, English remains the dominant language of literacy in education, in the media, in the workplace, in government and in all aspects of British life. The ability to read and write Standard English is regarded as a crucial measure of educational performance, and as such it also serves as a means of discrimination in the labour market. Minority languages and literacies only have a legitimized place within minority institutions such as the home, the temple, church, mosque or the local community association. They also have a place within the marginalized sectors of the economy, such as the 'rag' trade or in small family businesses: the corner shop or the fast food business".

The attitude to minority languages in education in England has resultingly been assimilationist and transitionalist. The response to increasing linguistic diversity since the 1950s was to increase provision for the teaching of English as a second language (Viv Edwards, 1984). A Government pamphlet *English for Immigrants* (Ministry for Education, 1963) urged separate provision (withdrawal) of non-English speaking children within a school for intensive English language teaching. Concern was often expressed by parents and politicians that "normal" classes were being disrupted by the presence of a number of non-English-speaking pupils. Dispersal policies were developed with the notion that "the integration of the immigrants is more easily achieved, if the proportion of immigrant children in a school is not allowed to rise too high" (HMSO, 1965, para. 42).

In the last two decades, policy and philosophy, provision and practice have begun to project a slightly more pluralistic position. Recent reports and research as well as recent active measures and changes in classroom practice suggest a small movement towards a more multilingual and multicultural society. The evidence for this movement will now be considered. However, the rhetoric, the views of progressive educationalists and researchers tend to hide the probability that amongst the populace, rejection and antipathy to minority languages in England has changed little. The white majority viewpoint is likely still to be assimilationist and antagonistic to bilingual education. The pluralist movement is some light-years ahead of the public mind. This is not to argue that one viewpoint is right and the other wrong. As is examined in Chapter 4 when considering the USA, a variety of ideologies exist with different political, cultural and social assumptions.

There are three types of evidence suggesting that, in the last 20 years, new directions in bilingualism and bilingual education have emerged: reports, research and provision. Each of these will now be considered in turn.

Reports

The Bullock Report, *A Language for Life* (1975), was a milestone in an official viewpoint on minority languages. "No child should be expected to cast off the language and culture of the home as he crosses the school threshold and the curriculum should reflect those aspects of his life" (paragraph 20.5). "Every school with pupils whose original language is not English should adopt a positive attitude to their bilingualism and wherever possible help maintain and deepen their knowledge of their mother tongue" (paragraph 20.17). These two quotations illustrate a new and seemingly enlightened viewpoint of the intelligentsia.

In the same year, 1975, a Draft Directive from the Council of European Communities (EEC) requested Member States to teach within the school curriculum, the mother tongue and culture of the country of origin of EEC migrant workers. The Directive was passed in July 1977, allowing such education to be in accordance with national circumstances and legal systems. When the British Government relayed the Directive to local education authorities in July 1981, it became translated into exploring ways in which mother tongue teaching might be provided. Such provision could be during or outside school hours, but tuition was not to be considered as a legal right of an individual.

In terms of Reports, the most recent, more important and most considered is *Education for All* (1985), popularly termed the Swann Report. A Committee was established in March 1979 initially to report on West Indian children in school who were seen to be relatively less successful, and subsequently to report on the educational needs and attainments of children from ethnic minority groups. The Report carefully considers the type of multiracial society that should not be and should be fostered. Two notions are rejected and one is promoted. The traditional policy of assimilation is rejected. In varying degrees and in differing respects, minorities should maintain their distinctive nature. A policy of separatism is also rejected. A British society based on separate education, for example, is seen as a contradiction in terms. The essence of society is seen as a cohesive unity where shared experience and shared commitment to central values (e.g. justice and the right of dissent) is paramount. The Swann Report (1985) decided in favour of the aim of a pluralist multiracial society. Ethnic minorities within this philosophy should be allowed, and at times assisted, to maintain their own language and culture. If a pluralist society is not fostered at every level, the genuine risk of a fragmented society along ethnic lines is considered possible, threatening the stability and cohesion of British society. Schools where there are no ethnic minority pupils are equally encouraged to teach about the multicultural nature of British society. In one survey, schools almost without exception saw multicultural education as remote or irrelevant to their needs and responsibilities. The Report sees the necessity of changing the majority view that multicultural education is for "them" and not "us".

When the Swann Report (1985) considered a multilingual society as different from a multiracial society, there is evidence of possible inconsistency in the high value given to minority languages and the low value given to the place of such languages in the educational system. The Report calls for the equal acceptance of all minority languages. Mother tongues are perceived as a key factor in maintaining a community's identity and culture. Such linguistic diversity is also seen as an asset and resource for a school. From the pluralist viewpoint and the equality of languages viewpoint taken in the Report, a strong multilingual educational policy might have been expected. This does not appear to be the case. However, initially, there are elements of educational policy that do appear to follow logically from the stance taken. The Report is against separate language centres for minority groups to learn English. Such separatism would be assimilationist in that a child learns English in order to take his or her place in an unchanged mainstream school. Separate language provision is seen as discriminatory in outcome rather than intent. A similar case is made against withdrawal systems within a school. Instead, learning English as a second, but not foreign language is seen as a necessary and integrated provision within the mainstream school.

In the role given to minority languages within mainstream education there is a surprise. In essence, bilingual education is rejected. A distinction is made between three different possible aims with regard to minority languages. *Bilingual education* is perceived as using the mother tongue as a medium of instruction; *mother-tongue maintenance* is regarded as developing pupils' fluency in their own language; *mother-tongue teaching* is seen as the teaching of community languages as part of a modern language curriculum (e.g. in a similar way that French and German are taught in the secondary school). Bilingual education is rejected as the disadvantages are seen to be more numerous than the advantages. Mother tongue maintenance is not seen to be a school aim. Mainstream schools are not expected to take over the role of communities themselves in continuing their ethnic languages. The third aim, mother-tongue teaching, is seen as worth developing, with ethnic languages becoming a small part of the larger curriculum. Hence such languages may become a subject within the curriculum but not a medium in teaching the curriculum. Despite being home languages, they should be given the same status as foreign languages in the curriculum.

The recommendations of the Swann Report (1985) include the view that minority languages should be fostered, but not incorporated in any general way into the normal school curriculum. Fostering translates into allowing the community to use school premises, and a "bilingual resource" in the primary school classroom being available to support pupils with little or no fluency in English.

The Swann Report (1985) is a definite advance in "official" thinking about the nature of a multiracial and multicultural society in Britain. It contains a wealth of data and argument that adds very considerably to the minority language debate in England. With regard to bilingual education, it may appear relatively unenlightened. What is missing is a world-wide comparative perspective that evaluates traditions, initiatives, the evolution of policy and practice in countries such as Australia, Canada, the USA and Wales. If such a comparative stance had been taken on board, more positive attitudes to bilingual education amongst English educationalists might have emerged.

Yet at the same time, the Swann Report (1985) represents a middle way, a traditional English compromise. This is evident in the reactions to the Report which often attacked the recommendations from wholly opposite points of view. For some, the Report fails to concentrate on the perceived necessity of assimilating the variety of ethnic groups into an integrated, harmonious, unified and cohesive British society. For others, the Report fails to consider ethnic needs, the benefits of pluralism and multiculturalism and the advantages of bilingualism over monolingualism. A two-directional perspective on Swann (1985) is evident in the response of the National Council for Mother Tongue Teaching (1985) and a retort by Vanikar & Dalal (1986). The National Council for Mother Tongue Teaching criticizes the Swann Report for its over-emphasis on the English language and British identity, its dismissal of bilingual education and the implication that ethnic minority languages and cultures are divisive. Vanikar & Dalal's reply is that children in Britain need a shared identity, that bilingual education in England will "serve to accentuate the heterogeneous features of various sub-groups" (p. 424), will stop ethnic minority children from becoming multicultural as they will only taste English and their own ethnic culture, will hinder the development of English skills needed for academic and professional advancement, will give undue prominence to the languages of predominant groups among ethnic minorities and will lead away from a democratic society. As will be examined in Chapter 4 when considering the criticisms of USA bilingual education, the issues are complex and controversial, political and polemical. Swann (1985) tends, however, to provide a thoughtful, carefully balanced and well defended perspective, though of necessity, valued and contentious.

Research

Research specifically on various forms of bilingual education in England is sadly minimal. The type of research that has been successfully carried out in Canada and the USA, in particular on the role of two languages in education, has yet to flow in England. The major research areas have included surveys of the variety of languages and dialects in English schools, the possible underachievement of minority groups, particularly West Indian pupils, and curriculum development projects to further community languages and cultures. Thus research in London by Rosen & Burgess (1980) and by the Inner London Education Authority (ILEA) (1979, 1982) and the Linguistic Minorities Project (1985) in London and various areas of England provides important surveys of the hitherto undocumented extent of bilingualism in parts of England. Tansley & Craft (1984) surveyed mother tongue teaching and support for primary age pupils in England and Wales, documenting mother tongue policies within local education authorities and their support for community supplementary schools. Unfortunately this survey often combines the results for England and Wales, confusing policy which concerns the heritage language of Wales and the ethnic minority languages of England.

Tomlinson (1986), Figueroa (1984) and the Swann Report (1985) provide excellent analyses of the underachievement issue. Since the underachievement issue concerns ethnicity more than language, it is not considered in this section. However, three projects have been set up in England to further the mother tongue as a medium of instruction. The Bedford Mother Tongue Project (1976–1980) was sponsored by the European Community and produced teaching materials in Italian and Punjabi for pupils aged 5 to 8. Such materials concerned the language, history, geography, music, games and social studies of their ethnic origin (Simons, 1979; Tosi, 1984). The Schools Council Mother Tongue Project commenced in 1981 and aimed to develop materials for bilingual teachers of Greek and Bengali pupils in the 7 to 11 age range. The Project was also concerned with producing guidelines for teachers working in linguistically diverse classrooms in primary schools (Houlton & Willey, 1983). The third project took place in Bradford and took on an experimental design that provides the opportunity for a less subjective judgement on the value of a project. Termed the Bradford Mother Tongue and English Teaching Project, it provided a one-year experimental bilingual education programme for infants whose home language was Punjabi and who had little knowledge of English at the point of entry to school (MOTET, 1981). The research is unusual in education in that a group of some 66 pupils were randomly assigned to the experimental bilingual or "control" monolingual English group. After one year, the effects of bilingual education were assessed. The bilingual group were found to perform better in Punjabi, and overall, there was little difference in English. The conclusion was that there were no negative effects from bilingual education. On the contrary, there were the positive effects of mother tongue maintenance alongside equivalent English progress compared with the control group (Fitzpatrick, 1987).

It seems possible that research into bilingualism in schools in England may develop and flourish in the next decade. Given the excellence of recent British research into school effectiveness and the comparative technical excellence of much English research on education, an important tradition in bilingual education research may soon develop.

Provision

There is evidence of increased support and provision for minority languages both at a voluntary and institutional level. Such provision indicates that the previous emphasis on teaching English as a second language, while still the dominant viewpoint, is very slowly being supplemented by some interest in developing ethnic languages. The provision for ethnic languages mostly derives from community rather than official educational sources. Evening classes, Saturday schools and Sunday schools have been set up to meet political, religious and cultural goals (Linguistic Minorities Project, 1985). The instigators of such voluntary provision are sometimes religious bodies (Orthodox churches, synagogues, mosques and temples); in other places, groups of parents or local community organizations rent premises, such as schools, for mother tongue classes. Tansley & Craft's (1984) survey found that at least 28 different languages were being taught in over 500 community/supplementary schools. Asian languages such as Urdu, Punjabi, Bengali and Gujerati were often found in such community schools, but also European languages such as Greek, Italian, Spanish and Portuguese were being supported.

Most Local Educational Authorities throughout England have responded to the multilingual population that resides in many urban areas of the country. The LEAs differ considerably in their policies; many are in essence assimilationist, a few have pluralist sympathies. The lead has been taken by the Inner London Education Authority (ILEA) who formulated a multi-ethnic policy in 1977. The ILEA has sponsored voluntary schools, appointed an Inspector of Schools to oversee minority language education and devised bilingual resources for schools. Martin-Jones (1984) outlines the bilingual support given by other authorities such as Leicester, Peterborough, Nottinghamshire, Coventry, Birmingham, Walsall, Dudley, Manchester, Ealing, Brent, Haringey and Waltham Forest in providing bilingual teachers, inspectors, support services, materials, resources or special classes. Tansley & Craft's (1984) survey revealed some 126 primary schools in England where the mother tongue was supported as part of the school curriculum. The most frequently supported languages were Punjabi, Urdu, Gujerati, Bengali and Hindi. Eighteen LEAs paid for community teachers, 34 LEAs provided free accommodation for community schools, but in-service training of mother tongue teachers, an important issue if there is to be any progression in mother tongue teaching, was not greatly encouraged. Tansley & Craft (1984:383) conclude on both a pessimistic and then optimistic note:

> "there is a wide gap between the known number of bilingual children in local authority schools and support for their languages, varying

according to both the language concerned and the LEA involved ... there is perhaps an even wider gap between the knowledge LEAs have about the languages spoken by the community and those for which provision is sought".

This note of pessimism may suggest that a more informed and centralized policy needs to be established. The note of optimism paves the way for the evolution of a more co-ordinated policy.

"Educational opinion has markedly changed over recent years. From being referred to successively as 'immigrants', 'English as a Foreign language' learners and 'English as a Second Language' learners, pupils who speak a language other than English as a mother tongue are now being accorded recognition as 'bilingual'. Instead of being viewed as pupils with problems or deficiencies, bilingual children are now seen to have certain resources which they bring to the school and which can be of benefit to the whole class" (p. 383).

Bilingual education in Wales

Historical perspective

The history of the Welsh language in the twentieth century is a history of decline. At the beginning of the century there were some 930,000 Welsh speakers forming close to 50% of the population. By the 1981 Census, these figures had dropped to some 500,000 and 19.0% respectively. As Baker's (1985) analysis of the 1981 Census data revealed, the diminution in the size of heartland areas, the distribution of illiteracy in Welsh speakers and the distribution of age differences indicates a few silver linings set against the presence of a large foreboding cloud.

In the decline of the Welsh language in the twentieth century, education has been influential, alongside and interactive with immigration, emigration, mass media, transport, communications and employment. J.L. Williams (1974) provides the popularist view of English becoming the legal and administrative language, with the middle classes and then the working classes seeking English medium education for their children. To acquire English became a status symbol, a way of climbing the social and economic ladder of success. Education of monoglot Welsh speakers sometimes occurred through monolingual English teaching. While there exists a debate as to whether English was imposed upon reluctant Welsh speakers, or whether Welsh speakers were keen to acquire a majority language which had higher perceived status, potentially more economic value and the promise of greater affluence, it remains the case that education played its part in the decline of the language. Despite outstanding histories of education in Wales (e.g. G.E. Jones, 1982), there sadly exists no published authoritative, detailed and objective history of the Welsh language in education in Wales.

If education in Wales in the past has been, in part, a cause of language decay, it has, since World War II, begun to work for the maintenance of the language. Bilingual education in Wales has developed and flourished in the last three decades. This development is not uniform, undisputed or unprecedented. However, examples of its development will reveal the continued momentum of the bilingual school movement. The first independent but official bilingual primary school was established in Aberystwyth in 1939. By 1950 there were seven designated bilingual primary schools and today there are 63 such primary schools in predominantly English-speaking areas containing some eleven thousand children. Alongside these primary schools, there exist designated bilingual secondary schools. The first such school opened in 1956 in Clwyd (Ysgol Glan Clwyd); by 1970 a further three schools, and today there are 16 spread throughout anglicized parts of Wales. The degree of fluency in Welsh in primary schools has risen in the last decade. In 1977, some 12.8% of primary children were rated by their Headteachers as fluent in Welsh. In 1984, this figure had risen significantly to 15.3%. Baker (1985), Thomas (1986), T. P. Jones (1987), I. W. Williams (1987), Jenkins (1986) and Griffiths (1986) have documented further positive signs of increased bilingual education in Wales: in recent years an increase in the number of infants, but not junior, classes teaching Welsh, more secondary pupils being taught Welsh and taught other subjects through the medium of Welsh, and an increase in Welsh medium examinations being taken, both in terms of subjects available in Welsh and pupils sitting their examinations in Welsh.

There is, therefore, some evidence of attempts to reverse the replacement of Welsh by English. As in Ireland and Scotland, there are movements in education to establish bilingual schooling. Such movements have often been inspired by parents (e.g. Rhieni Dros Addysg Gymraeg: Parents for Welsh Medium Education), by activist movements (e.g. Urdd Gobaith Cymru: The Welsh League of Youth; Mudiad Ysgolion Meithrin: Welsh Medium Nursery Schools and Playgroups Association) and by community interests. The next section seeks to analyse whether research supports these developments.

Early research

Parallel to early investigations on bilingualism and IQ, research on the educational attainment of bilinguals and monoglot English speakers in Wales tended to find in favour of English monoglots. Thus Saer (1922), Smith (1923) and Barke & Parry-Williams (1938) found with tests of English vocabulary and composition that bilinguals were significantly behind monoglots in their progress. Such bilinguals were therefore seen to be at a disadvantage, not only from inadequate reading ability in English, but from other factors such as the ability to think in English with a sufficient degree of fluency and accuracy.

Similar to the early research on bilingualism and IQ, such studies had unredeemable experimental flaws in their design. Such differences could have been explained by other variables not held constant. For example, socio-economic class, IQ, classroom experience might each or all explain why one group labelled bilinguals scored lower than monoglots. Thus James (1947) found no difference between bilinguals and monoglots in general school subjects. This study was not perfect in experimental design, but illustrated that with different samples, different results could be obtained. Good control of factors which might otherwise explain differences is obviously necessary, and will be considered more fully in the next chapter.

Two early researchers did attempt to control extraneous variables. W. R. Jones (1933), using groups equal in non-verbal IQ and socio-economic status, found no difference in 10-year-old children on English attainment. Bilinguals performed equally as well as monoglots. Similarly, M. Williams (1953), using 9- to 11-year-old children, found no significant difference between English and bilingual groups in English reading and spelling when IQ was held constant.

The research of W. R. Jones

A series of researches by W. R. Jones in the 1950s analysed the relationship between bilingualism and educational attainment with greater experimental and statistical sophistication than had previously been achieved in Wales. His 1953 study found that the initial difference in reading ability, seemingly due to language background, could be explained by socio-economic status differences and teaching factors. This paved the way for the first large-scale investigation, using all (2,565) children in the old county of Caernarvonshire aged 10 and 11. Having tested reading attainment in English, Jones (1955) created four language groups: Welsh, Mixed Welsh (i.e. Welsh and English language background but Welsh predominating), Mixed English and English. By analysis of co-variance, differences between these groups in non-verbal IQ were held constant. Assuming that the mixed Welsh (and possibly the mixed English) were the more "balanced" bilinguals (q.v. Chapter 1), their standard of English reading was equal at 10 and 11 years of age to the English group. The Welsh group lagged behind the other groups in reading comprehension by about 10 months, suggesting that more "balanced" bilinguals, rather than dominant Welsh language children, had as good an attainment in reading as English monoglots, with the advantage of having skills in the minority language.

In an additional study, Jones et al. (1957) used a sample of 10- and 11-year-olds from a variety of locations in Wales. While testing English usage and reading as before, measures of mechanical and problem arithmetic were added as well as tests of reading and usage in Welsh. Even more so than in previous research, it is the mixed groups, regarded here as the more "balanced" bilinguals, who came out with the higher honours. On the tests of English reading comprehension and English usage, the two more bilingual groups (Welsh/English and English/Welsh) are not significantly different in attainment from the monoglot English group, non-verbal IQ being held constant. The less "balanced" bilinguals (dominant Welsh language) did perform at a lower level. If more "balanced" bilingualism did not affect English skills progress, it did affect Welsh attainment in a comparative but not necessarily in a criterion sense. Welsh dominants scored significantly higher than the Welsh/English group on the tests of Welsh reading and usage after differences in non-verbal IQ were taken into account.

While this research is dated and different results may be found in the very changed bilingual climate of the 1980s, it reveals a weakness of this kind of research, that Harris (1984) in Ireland (see p. 54) has avoided. Jones et al. (1957) found that on the two Welsh language tests, before adjusting for non-verbal IQ, the more "balanced" bilingual and dominant Welsh groups were not significantly different in performance. They were of similar achievement and progress. This raises the question, unanswerable from Jones' et al. (1957) research, as to whether both groups' performance was satisfactory in Welsh. Had both groups succeeded or not in reaching the level appropriate for their age group? Had they mastered the Welsh language skills suitable for 10- and 11-year-olds? Thus, Harris (1984) preferred criterion referenced tests to the type of norm referenced tests used by Jones et al. (1957). Norm referenced tests tend to be used to compare groups to show superiority and inferiority. Criterion referenced tests concern mastery of skills, relative to an order of progress within a curriculum area. Of course it could be argued that the norm referenced tests of Jones *et al.* (1957) show that the more "balanced" bilinguals may not have been fulfilling their potential. Since their non-verbal IQ was, on average, higher than the "dominant Welsh" group, were they capable of higher attainment in Welsh than the dominant Welsh group? The questions are important, intriguing and suggest that future research should seek by the same testing procedure to produce both pupil comparisons and skill referenced results.

Jones' (1957) results also focused on arithmetic. No difference between groups of differing language backgrounds was found on mechanical arithmetic. However, differences in problem arithmetic were found, with the more "balanced" bilinguals (Welsh/English) performing significantly better than monoglot English and "dominant Welsh" groups. This is intriguing as the test was in English. MacNamara (1966) found a different result, explained by Cummins (1977b) as due to Irish speakers being tested in English. While Jones *et al.* (1957) explains away the poorer score of the dominant Welsh group by the test being in English, the explanation does not cover the more "balanced" bilinguals performing better than the English monoglot group, even after differences in non-verbal IQ are controlled. Jones *et al.* (1957) mentions that the explanation of this may be in the unrepresentative nature of the Welsh/English group, although no specific causal reasons are provided for this explanation. An alternative explanation, that "balanced" bilinguals have some cognitive advantages, as was considered in Chapter 2, is worthy of consideration, but lacks precise confirmation from the data. Explanations might also be found in differences between the groups in urban–rural environment and socio-economic status.

There are researches of the same period that are on the surface not so positive as is the above interpretation of W. R. Jones' researches. Meirionnydd Education Authority undertook research similar to that of W. R. Jones (Evans, 1960) as did D. G. Lewis (1960) in Mid and South-West Wales. Both researches fail to examine the attainments of "balanced" bilingual pupils. Evans compares only two groups, Welsh and English, thus failing to extract a more "balanced" bilingual group. Lewis took schools rather than individual children as his unit of analysis, thus masking results sensitive to individual differences by concentrating on differences between internally heterogeneous institutions.

Therefore, the early research in Wales, only partially replicated, appears to suggest that the more "balanced" bilinguals were at least attaining in the majority language and in mathematics at a level commensurate with English monoglots. If it is accepted that the ownership of two languages rather than one language is a benefit and advantage, this early research suggests that "balanced" bilingualism is an additive and not a subtractive condition. If more careful interpretation of the research had been undertaken, with attention being focused on the effects of bilingualism rather than solely of the Welsh language, the bitter, polemical and inexcusable controversy between Jac L. Williams (1960a and b) and W. R. Jones (1960a and b) could have been avoided.

National surveys

A series of national surveys has been carried out in Wales by various researchers and organizations. The 1960 National Survey used a variety of mathematical, English and Welsh language skills tests to establish the attainments of children at 7, 10 and 14 years of age. Although language background was a variable allowing comparisons with attainment, no relationship between bilingualism and attainment can be validly discussed. As the Report itself notes, differences between Welsh, English and mixed language groups may be explained by parental occupation, parental encouragement, different cognitive ability rather than monolingualism and bilingualism (NFER/WJEC, 1969).

A survey of attitude and attainment in Wales, carried out by Derrick Sharp and co-workers (1973), included a variety of English and Welsh attainment tests. Relationships of these tests to gender, ability, socioeconomic background and attitude were considered, alongside language background. Although not controlling for variables which might explain the findings, Sharp et al. (1973) found that children from bilingual schools had the highest mean scores in Welsh attainment tests at 10, 12 and 14 years of age. Such children's performance in English attainment was at least comparable with children from anglicized backgrounds in primary or comprehensive schooling. A separate analysis was run for children in bilingual schools where Welsh was not the home language. On tests designed for first language speakers of Welsh, such second language children, by the age of 14–15 years, were as skilled in Welsh as first language pupils in the same schools, and better than first language Welsh pupils in comprehensive and secondary modern schools. Thus, in a criterion referenced sense, there is evidence that for second language Welsh pupils, bilingual education has no detrimental effects on English language progress and eventually secures skills in Welsh comparable to native speakers.

Wijnstra (1980a) re-analysed Sharp *et al.*'s (1973) data. Unfortunately he discarded data from children in the bilingual schools. However, his analysis confirmed results from a previous study of Frisian in schools (Wijnstra, 1980b). Once socio-economic factors are taken into consideration, children from Welsh language backgrounds progress in English as well as those from English language backgrounds. That is, bilingualism has no detrimental effect on progress in the majority language.

In fairness, neither Sharp *et al.* (1973) nor the 1960 National Survey set out to execute experimental research in the vein of early researches considered in the previous section. The aim was rather a fact-finding mission. Similarly, the recent APU surveys, commissioned by the Welsh Office and carried out by the National Foundation for Educational Research team based in Swansea, South Wales, are, by aim, fact-gathering assessment programmes rather than experimental research (Price, 1983). It is a paradox of recent international research, that the type of research which more validly tackles initial questions about bilingual education tends to be small-scale. Large-scale research has different, and equally important, issues in mind, yet often gathers most of the data, with the exception of a few crucial control variables, to allow generalizations about bilingual education that the small-scale research fails to provide. Another paradox is that national surveys tend to produce excellent tests and testing procedures and weak analyses. This is the case with a recent survey of speaking skills in Welsh (Price, Powell & Jones, 1981). The tests created for the research are of outstanding merit. When the statistical analysis is conducted, the results show that "success" in learning to speak Welsh is statistically significantly related to gender, teaching method, years of learning Welsh, number of days in a week Welsh is taught, hours of Welsh taught in a week, being taught by a fluent Welsh speaker, use of Welsh in the life of school, type of school and size of the age group. Interesting and important as each finding may be, the more important issue for bilingual policy, provision and practice is ignored. Which of these independent variables has the most or least effect on learning to speak Welsh? What is the order of importance of the independent variables in predicting success in learning to speak Welsh? The analysis, executed in England, is not the most helpful to Wales as it concentrates on individual statistical differences and not on the relative effects of these differences. In statistical terms, the analysis of variance technique used is far less helpful than correlational types of techniques. Statistical significance is exalted at the expense of the relative degree of relevance of the variables.

Schools Council Bilingual Project

A project was set up in 1968 to develop a programme of bilingual education for primary schools in anglicized areas of Wales. The Project was influenced by the Gittins Report (1967) on primary education in Wales, which recommended the establishment of bilingual schools for pupils from predominantly English language areas. Welsh was to be a medium of instruction in part of the school curriculum for both infants and juniors. Sixty schools participated in the Project which was based on the teaching methodology advocated by C.J. Dodson (1983, 1985a & b), an educationalist who has greatly aided Welsh language curriculum developments in both primary and secondary schools. The teaching methodology of the Project did not use Welsh in the manner of Canadian immersion education (see Chapter 4) or designated bilingual schools (Ysgolion Cymraeg). In these situations, the second language is accorded more time in the school day. In this sense the Project is closer to partial immersion bilingual education, although as Cummins & Genesee (1985) have considered, Dodson's approach to second language is unique and contains important differences from Canadian approaches, especially in "being one of the first communicatively-orientated theories to have been implemented on a large scale and to have been systematically evaluated" (p. 46). The Project integrates medium-orientated and message-orientated communication, combines structure in language learning and oral communication, showing that

> "there is a middle ground between teaching strategies which emphasize acquisition of linguistic structures divorced from students' communicative needs on the one hand, and those that emphasize message orientated communication which is divorced from considerations of linguistic structure, on the other" (Cummins & Genesee, 1985:46).

How successful was the Project? There are pieces of important non-experimental evidence which point to the success of this partial immersion experience. The Project spread after its official life of nine years. Having started with 60 schools, by 12 years after its inception, 1,047 infant and junior classes in 187 schools were using the Project's language learning approach. Data collected by Price et al. (1981) on the speaking skills of learners of Welsh found Project schools significantly ahead of other learner schemes. Children in the Bilingual Project obtained a significantly higher mean score on each of the three oral tasks, although such a result may be explained by increased time spent on Welsh in Project schools than by the scheme itself. The qualitative evaluation report on the Project by

Dodson himself (1978, 1985c) is cautiously positive. Dodson considered that infant achievement, linguistic and non-linguistic, was superior, sometimes outstandingly so, compared with previous traditional approaches to learning Welsh. At the junior school level, Dodson (1978, 1985c) regarded the Project as less successful due to four major factors: teachers devoting inadequate time to Welsh lessons, fewer materials and resources available for teaching Welsh, teachers lacking the training to teach successfully by the Project methods, and the desk-bound, teacher-directed, more academic written approach of junior compared with infant classes being less compatible with project methodology. Dodson (1978) concluded that the Project had "a greatly beneficial impact on a large number of children throughout Wales" (p. 53).

The experimental and psychometric evaluation of the Bilingual Project was executed by Eurwen Price (1978, 1985). Her evaluation is noteworthy not only for the experimental approach, but also for the cautious interpretations which do not confuse statistical with educational significance nor whose interpretations go further than the results permit. The evaluation sought to answer two questions which are commonly voiced about bilingual education programmes:

1. How will the programme of bilingual education affect pupils' general development and attainment?
2. What standard of bilingualism are the pupils likely to reach after following the bilingual programme?

Eight infant project schools were chosen as representing the variety of project schools. Eight infant control classes were also selected, being matched with the project (experimental) classes on IQ, socio-economic class and urban–rural background. This was repeated for junior classes, except that socio-economic background was not perfectly equated or controlled. Hence, the junior results were reported for separate socio-economic groups.

In attempting to answer the first question, infant children were tested on non-verbal ability, reading and English progress, and junior children were additionally tested on mathematics and verbal ability. For both infant and junior classes, there were no real differences between the project and control groups. Thus the first question may be answered with clarity. Bilingual education had no detrimental effects on progress in majority language skills, in reading and mathematics, nor on measured IQ.

The second question was tackled by the construction of tests of Welsh language skills. The two infant tests comprised measures of oral language and listening comprehension; the junior tests consisted of measures of reading comprehension and an oral test. The tests were obviously less appropriate for control schools. While the amount of time spent using Welsh, attitude of teachers and language background affected the degree of attainment, understanding Welsh and speaking Welsh were generally well established by 7 years of age, with further progress and consolidation over the next two years.

The overall picture is positive. Not only did children in the bilingual education programme not fall behind on English and maths attainment, they also benefited, compared with monolingual programmes, by gaining some communicative competency in a second language. Far from suffering, the pupils appeared to gain. They lost nothing, but gained bilingualism. Like almost all evaluations of bilingual programmes throughout the world, data are lacking about the long-term effects of such bilingual education. Do such children lose their second language ability or does their bilingualism flourish into adulthood? Does early bilingualism have positive educational consequences in a cumulative and long-lasting manner? Such questions form a research agenda for the next decades.

Conclusions

Previous surveys of Welsh research have tended to be negative, or at best neutral, about bilingual education. There are two explanations for this. First, early research failed to control for alternative explanatory variables. The poorer performance of bilinguals compared with monoglots, ascribed in the past to language background, could have been absent or negligible if IQ, social class, urban–rural differences, for example, had been controlled. Second, the focus was placed on the Welsh language and not on bilingualism. The issue was perceived to be whether children from Welsh language backgrounds suffered in their educational attainment. This led to much breast-beating and controversy in the 1960s. A re-examination of the research has suggested a fresh interpretation. When children who are "balanced" bilinguals are investigated, bilingual education has no detrimental effects; rather there are the positive advantages of progressing in two languages rather than one. This conclusion is also reached by Geoffrey Thornton (1986) in an independent appraisal of the findings of the Assessment of Performance Unit. Reviewing the language performance of school pupils in England and Wales, the finding was that in Wales "there were no significant differences in either reading or writing at either age in any year, and the mean scores for second-language speakers of English (all but a handful of whom were native speakers of Welsh) were sometimes fractionally higher than those for monolingual English speakers" (Thornton, 1986:61). A positive note is also struck by the Schools Council Bilingual Project. Children learning Welsh in a partial immersion situation gain facility in a second language and lose nothing in attainment in English and maths.

While research on bilingual education in Wales is by no means extensive, its implications are in the direction of support for such education. Cummins & Genesee (1985:47) sum up the insufficiency of research, the importance of such research and the implications of research. They suggest that there has been

"relatively little research conducted on the educational effectiveness of different forms of Welsh language instruction. The Canadian experience suggests that collection and dissemination of this type of information may be a precondition for the continued expansion of bilingual education for anglophone children in Wales. In this regard, it would seem important that parents and educators be made aware of the general educational advantages of full bilingualism and the fact that very strong emphasis on Welsh throughout school will not detract from children's English skills".

Conclusions on Celtic and English bilingual education

This chapter has sought to examine research, reports and recent movements in bilingual education in Britain and Ireland, and three conclusions appear warranted.

First, there is a lack of research to examine whether bilingual education developments since the War have been positive or not. Such developments would seem to require research as part of the *raison d'être* of the development. Members of the public and politicians need informing; administrators need evidence; teachers and parents need answers to their questions. Research can replace innuendo, guesswork, hunches, prejudice, false claims, polemic and propaganda. Bilingual education has not become a mainstream research area in the UK, nor does the topic appear on the agenda of the major research bodies. Research is badly needed in England and the Celtic countries to educate about bilingual education.

Second, from the little research that exists, it seems reasonable to conclude that bilingual education is not detrimental. There is a lack of evidence in Ireland and Wales particularly of negative effects. The very tentative conclusion in the 1980s must be that bilingual schooling is unlikely to affect progress in the majority language of English. Indeed, the possession of a Celtic language where the home background is English, or the maintenance and enhancement of a minority home language in all four countries may seem a beneficial extra given by bilingual education. Does immersion in bilingual education produce more skilled and sympathetic future citizens than those who swim through mainstream education?

Third, in all four countries, there is evidence of grass-roots movements to promote and produce bilingual education. Pre-school playgroups in all three Celtic countries, the expansion of adult classes learning a Celtic language, the fight by parents to obtain bilingual provision in Ireland, Scotland, Wales and England and the growth of voluntary minority language classes in England, all suggest that pressure for, and the development of, bilingual education is coming more from the bottom than the top. Pressure groups, community groups and language activists have probably affected the development of recent bilingual classes, units and schools to a greater extent than administrators, politicians and professional educators. The growth in bilingual education in the four countries has tended to be a trickle rather than a flood. Yet the way the tide is moving in all four countries is the same: irrigating bilingual education.

4   Bilingual Education: The Judgement of North American Research

Introduction

Research from Canada and the USA on bilingual education is both plentiful and penetrating. Britain, Ireland, the other European countries, Australasia, Israel, Mexico, the mid and far East all tend to look at the North American experience and evaluations. The aim of this chapter is therefore not only to review and illustrate the research findings on North American bilingual education, but also to examine and investigate the limit of the generalizations that can be made from such research by noting the extent of its relevance to non-American situations and the ideology and assumptions of the research. What is the message? Can the message be reasonably broadcast across the Atlantic and Pacific? Does the medium of research on which the message is based affect the message?

United States of America

Historical perspective

In terms of multilingualism, the USA has historically been a willing receptacle of peoples of many languages: Spanish, French, German, Italian, Dutch, Portuguese, Chinese, Polish, Greek, Japanese, Welsh, and various indigenous Indian languages to name but a few. The receptacle of immigration was transformed into a melting-pot to achieve assimilation and acculturation. The dream became a unitary America, with shared common social, political and economic ideals. Roosevelt in 1917 urged all immigrants to adopt the English language.

"It would be not merely a misfortune but a crime to perpetuate differences of language in this country ... We should provide for

79

every immigrant by day schools for the young, and night schools for the adult, the chance to learn English; and if after say five years he has not learned English, he should be sent back to the land from whence he came" (quoted in González, 1979).

Between the World Wars, diversity was discouraged so that harmony would hasten a healthy and homogeneous nation. A common language would provide, it was thought, common attitudes, aims and values. A common language and culture would cement society. A God-blest-English-speaking America was preferable to the threat of Babel.

An alternative viewpoint to the dominant melting-pot, assimilationist policy developed in the Lyndon Johnson era of the 1960s. Increased concern about disadvantaged groups, symbolized in the Civil Rights movement, caused interest in linguistic minorities. Following a United States Senate Subcommittee on Bilingual Education, a landmark was achieved in 1968 with the passing of a Bilingual Education Act (Title VII of the Elementary and Secondary Education Act). The Act recognized the feasibility of non-English instruction and was designed to "build the capacity" of bilingual education by an initial funding of 7.5 million dollars in 1969. By 1981, the Title VII program had supported over 200 bilingual education programmes and had received 157 million dollars. The Act was, however, more concerned with *transitional* bilingual education than maintenance or enrichment bilingual education. Perceived as a disadvantaged sector of society, minority language groups were seen as requiring remedial and compensatory attention. A temporary use of the home minority language would help successful transition into majority language education. The use of home language in school was seen as a means of securing the eventual successful use of English. Use of the home language was not regarded as a worthy goal in itself. The clientele of the bilingual programmes were children of minority language status. Monolingual English speakers were rarely involved. This is further evidence of bilingual education not aimed at achieving a truly bilingual or multilingual or multicultural society.

Another United States landmark in bilingual education was a lawsuit. A court case, brought by Chinese pupils against the San Francisco School District in 1970, concerned whether or not non-English-speaking students received equal educational opportunity when instructed in a language they could not understand. The failure to provide bilingual education was alleged to violate both the equal protection clause of the 14th Amendment and Title VI of the Civil Right Act of 1964. The case, known as Lau v. Nichols, was rejected by the federal district court and a court of appeals, but was accepted by the Supreme Court in 1974. The verdict outlawed English submersion programmes and resulted in nationwide "Lau remedies". Such remedies reflected a broadening of the goals of bilingual education to include the possible maintenance of minority language and culture. As Teitelbaum & Hiller (1979) have documented, Lau remedies created some expansion and further establishment in the use of minority languages in schools, although they rarely resulted in true enrichment programmes.

The Reagan administration has tended to reverse the development of minority language education in the United States that occurred in the 1960s and 1970s. President Reagan himself has openly expressed unsympathetic attitudes towards bilingual education (Hakuta, 1986). The Secretary of Education has withdrawn proposals for revising the Lau guidelines and cancelled regulations intended to help school districts comply with the Lau decision. Since 1980, bilingual education funding has been cut by 33 million dollars (Cohen, 1984).

The recent change in approach to bilingual education has been justified by an important major review by Baker & de Kanter (1983) of relevant research. As Cohen (1984:225) noted: "The Federal Government justified its approach to bilingual education through a major study commissioned by the Education Department, which concluded that research evidence offered little justification for bilingual programmes on the basis of educational gains". The change in attitude is not unpopular. There is much public support for the demise of bilingual education, such education being seen to foster separatism, divisions in society and minority group political and economic self-interest.

Various reviews of bilingual education in the United States had been undertaken before that of Baker & de Kanter (1983). Troike (1978), Dulay & Burt (1978, 1979) and Zappert & Cruz (1977) had each concluded that bilingual education effectively promoted majority and minority language skills with minority language students, and was preferable to monolingual English programmes. Baker & de Kanter's (1983) review is more recent, much more comprehensive and has had much attention because it was both promoted by the United States Education Department and was used to promote policy change. Therefore, the approach, findings and conclusions of Baker & de Kanter will now be reviewed.

Baker & de Kanter's (1983) review of the effectiveness of bilingual education

In a chapter entitled "The Effectiveness of Bilingual Education", Baker & de Kanter (1983) pose four instructional alternatives with regard to United States language minority children:

1. Submersion. Language minority children are placed in an ordinary classroom amongst English speakers to either sink or swim. The home language is not used in the classroom. This type of programme was found unlawful by the Supreme Court ruling on the Lau v. Nichols case.

2. English as a Second Language (ESL). Language minority children are placed in a submersion experience, except that they are withdrawn for a small part of the day for compensatory English instruction.

3. Transitional Bilingual Education (TBE). Language minority students are taught in their home language until their English is good enough for them to participate in a mainstream classroom. While minority language literacy may be included as a school subject, the aim of Transitional Bilingual Education is for the use of the home language to decrease in direct proportion to increasing use of English in the classroom. The reasoning is that, unless children's skill in English is quickly established, they are likely to fall behind their majority language peers in various curriculum areas.

4. Structured Immersion. Language minority pupils are taught by teachers fluent in that minority language. Pupils are allowed to talk to each other and the teacher in their first language, but the teacher will generally reply in English. "The curriculum is structured so that prior knowledge of L2 is not assumed as subjects are taught. Content is introduced in a way that can be understood by the students. The students in effect learn L2 and content simultaneously" (Baker & de Kanter, 1983:34).

Despite posing four alternatives, Baker & de Kanter focused their study on Transitional Bilingual Education. Thus the two central issues became:

(i) *Does Transitional Bilingual Education lead to better performance in English?*

(ii) *Does Transitional Bilingual Education lead to better performance in non-language subject areas?*

The positive rather than null hypothesis is strange given the scientific approach of the evaluation. The way the questions are posed hints at the desirable answer. Also, the narrow range of "effects" or "outcomes" is apparent. English and non-language subject areas are regarded as the desirable outcome of schooling. Neither self-esteem nor employment nor the preservation of minority languages and cultures are considered as other valuable alternative outcomes. That is, there are many other possible effects of schooling than proficiency in English and subject areas. Moral, social, personality and employment effects are a few other outcomes of schooling that pupils or parents or various interest groups in society may value.

Baker & de Kanter (1983) gathered together over 300 studies from North America and the rest of the bilingual world. Of these they rejected all but 39 researches. To be included in this meta study, researches had to conform to the following six criteria.

1. Relevance. Only studies which used outcome measures concerning English and non-language subject area performance were used. Studies which used other outcome measures were excluded. This is difficult to defend given the variety of possible educational outputs in a pluralist society (C. Baker, 1985; Dunkin & Biddle, 1974).

2. Matching. As has been considered in previous chapters, comparisons between two or more groups can only validly occur if initial differences between the groups have been controlled. To find, for example, that immersion pupils make better progress with English than do transitional bilingual education pupils may be due to differences in age, socio-economic class or language background, rather than the type of educational programme. Baker & de Kanter (1983) provide other alternative explanatory variables, which show the difficulty, even impossibility, of making absolute judgements about a bilingual education programme. These factors include ethnicity, pupil motivation and self-concept, parental support and encouragement, IQ and cognitive abilities, place of birth (i.e. immigrant or native-born), degree of home language dominance, teacher–pupil ratio, teacher skill and motivation, type of classroom and school environment, volunteering for bilingual education or its enforcement and home–school relationships. The vastness of variables that can affect outcomes of bilingual education is returned to in the final chapter when the input–output–process–context model is considered.

3. Statistics. A difference between two average scores is insufficient to argue that one programme is better than another. Such differences may have occurred by chance, so that with further equal samples, a different result may be found. Tests of statistical significance provide evidence of the degree of confidence that a set of results has not occurred by chance alone.

4. Norm referenced comparisons. Some studies were rejected because they compared the rate of progress of an experimental group with national averages for a particular subject area. Such a comparison is unfair in that it assumes equal rates of progress between monolingual English speakers and bilinguals, and also that taking the test in English is fair to bilinguals (instructions in the weaker language may for example, negatively influence bilinguals' test score).

5. *Gain scores*. A study was rejected if it only showed that the experimental group pupils had progressed over a term or a year. Nearly all children show gains during a year as a result of any form of schooling and as a result of out-of-school learning. Relative or comparative gains are required as evidence for the effectiveness of bilingual education. For example, comparing a transitional bilingual programme with a submersion programme provides data on the differential effects of each approach.

6. *Grade equivalent scores*. Research was rejected where outcomes centred on American grade equivalent scores. Since there are problems of comparability and compatibility, such scores are not accurate and precise measures of outcome.

The 39 studies found satisfactory on the above criteria were either experiments where pupils had been randomly assigned to the experimental and control groups (thereby matching the groups) or where existing groups' initial differences were controlled for as far as possible. Occasionally control over alternative explanatory variables is achieved by matching pupils in pairs. More often control of initial differences is by the statistical technique of analysis of co-variance. Neither of these methods is perfect.

What are the conclusions that Baker & de Kanter (1983) draw from their 39 steps through the research literature? The 39 studies are found to have no consistent thread. In short, the results have no pattern and disagree with each other. For example, of the "true" experiments, some found in favour of transitional bilingual education, some in favour of English submersion, some found no difference between transitional bilingual education and submersion, and another found immersion superior to transitional bilingual education. Similarly, non-experimental research relying heavily on statistical sophistication found a variety of outcomes; no difference between transitional bilingual education (TBE) and ESL or between TBE and submersion; positive effects for TBE and negative effects for TBE.

If attention is given to large sample studies, mixed conclusions are still necessary. Danoff *et al.* (1977, 1978) found submersion better than TBE with a sample of almost 9,000 pupils. McConnell (1980) found TBE better than submersion with over 1,000 pupils, while Matthews (1979) and Stebbins *et al.* (1977), again with 1,000 plus samples, both found TBE no different from submersion.

The conclusion: "The literature makes a compelling case that special programs in schools can improve the achievement of language-minority children. There is no evidence, however, that any specific program should be either legislated or preferred by the federal government" (p. 49).

"Although special programs of one sort or another have been shown to be effective, this conclusion says nothing about the effects of any particular instruction approach. The Federal Government should not place exclusive reliance on TBE ... The literature on the effectiveness of TBE, however, does not justify such heavy reliance on this one method of instruction ... In general, findings of no significant differences predominate, and negative effects for TBE are almost as frequent as are positive effects" (p. 50).

If transitional bilingual education, despite being United States government policy, is no better or worse than submersion, immersion or teaching English as a foreign language, it might have been expected that Baker & de Kanter (1983) could conclude in praise of immersion education. Unlike the other three programmes, immersion provides support for the home language and culture. That is, immersion has as its educational aim the fostering of bilingualism and biculturalism. Since immersion education is the only additive scheme, some support might have been forthcoming.

From the 39 researches considered, there is supportive evidence for immersion education. Immersion is better than TBE in three different studies, and no different from TBE in one study. That is, in no study does immersion come out as inferior to another type of schooling. Admittedly, of the three studies finding immersion superior to TBE, two are Canadian and only one is from the United States. Nevertheless, Baker & de Kanter (1983) tend to ignore the potential of immersion education. Thus bilingual immersion education is not tried and found guilty. The evidence is apparently ignored in favour of a narrow line of enquiry.

This narrow line of inquiry leads to a conclusion that seems at variance with the evidence:

"The common sense observation that children should be taught in a language they understand does not necessarily lead to the conclusion they should be taught in their home language. They can be taught successfully in a second language if the teaching is done right. The key to successful teaching in the second language seems to be to ensure that the second language and subject matter are taught simultaneously so that subject content never gets ahead of language. Given the American setting, where the language-minority child must ultimately function in an English speaking society, carefully conducted second-language instruction in all subjects may well be preferable to bilingual methods" (p. 51).

It is this last sentence that reveals all. Perhaps because it was an official, Government sponsored study, the dominant Government assumption and ideology have seemingly affected the conclusions. Functioning in an English language rather than in a bilingual society is the assumption. Assimilation is the aim. This is one reason for disputing the Baker & de Kanter (1983) study despite its very influential nature in terms of United States policy.

There is a second reason for disputing the analysis. The conduct of their meta survey is open to criticisms. These may be listed as:

1. A consideration of only a narrow range of outcome measures (e.g. self-esteem and absenteeism are ignored). As Willig (1981/82) notes this is a fault of the research rather than of Baker & de Kanter.

2. Focusing on transitional bilingual education led not only to ignoring the full issues but possibly implicitly devaluing them as well (e.g. preservation of a child's home language and culture). As a footnote to Table 2C-1 (p. 69) conveys, "Studies that do not address our questions are not listed".

3. Adopting a rigid and selective criteria for inclusion and exclusion of research studies. The choice excluded some well known studies (e.g. the Rock Point Navajo research) and included studies with relatively small samples and of consequent questionable generalizability. Thus 28 of their 39 favoured studies have a sample smaller than 300 pupils. All educational research has limitations, such limitations existing on a dimension (or more precisely on multiple dimensions). A good review will look for patterns in the results, not just at the one "good" end of the dimension, but through its middle ranges as well. Sometimes patterns occur across studies despite those studies having varying limitations.

4. In most studies, the assumptions of the analysis of co-variance technique are not met. Similarly, matching of children in experimental and control groups only equates on a small number of variables (e.g. sex, IQ, socio-economic class). Given the variety of human differences, matching is an aspiration rather than an achievement. Thus the American Psychological Association (1982), writing on the 1981 final draft of the report,

noted that "Inconsistencies are apparent in the application of the methodological standards utilized. The evaluation question addressed by the study was limited, and an arbitrary and narrow definition of 'acceptable data' was utilized" (p. 9).

5. The review methodology is of a "voting" type (Glass, McGaw & Smith, 1981). A tally is kept of the number of studies in favour of a type of programme and the number against. The winner is the type of programme with the highest number of ticks rather than crosses. A more sophisticated statistical approach, meta analysis, has been developed, allowing for methodological flaws in a systematic way and taking a variety of intervening variables into account (Glass *et al.*, 1981). However, as Kelly (1986) has shown, meta analysis, sometimes called quantitative research reviewing, is not totally objective. "Personal decisions enter into many points of a meta analysis, from selecting studies to read, to deciding how to code the data" (Kelly, 1986:39). This, together with further issues and limitations is explored by Willig (1981/82).

Willig's (1985) and Cummins' (1983a) review of United States bilingual education

Of the reviews of United States bilingual education research evaluations that exist, Zappert & Cruz (1977), Troike (1978) and Dulay & Burt (1978, 1979) each took the voting approach. The most important recent review (Willig, 1985) adopts the statistical meta analysis approach of Glass *et al.* (1981). Only 23 studies were used for the meta analysis, such studies being selected from Baker & de Kanter's (1981) review. All 23 studies concern United States bilingual education evaluations and deliberately exclude Canadian immersion evaluations. Willig's (1985) meta analysis is important not only in that it is more sophisticated, and more, though imperfectly, objective than that of Baker & de Kanter (1981, 1983). It also contains a thorough and erudite discussion of the methodological weaknesses of United States bilingual education research.

"A major result of the current synthesis has been the revelation that bilingual education has been badly served by a predominance of research that is inadequate in design and that makes inappropriate comparisons of children in bilingual programs to children who are dissimilar in many crucial respects" (Willig, 1985:312).

Willig convincingly shows that "it is virtually impossible to truly equate groups of children from dual language environments on all of the factors that constitute an adequate research design by attempting to match students or to employ statistical adjustments" (p. 312). Her answer to such methodological inadequacies is the random assignment of pupils to experimental and control groups. This is usually illegal and a doubtful ethical procedure.

When statistical controls for methodological inadequacies are made in the meta analysis, Willig (1985) found bilingual education to be generally superior to submersion education. Small to moderate advantages were found for bilingual education pupils in reading, language skills, maths and overall achievement, when the tests were in English. Similar advantages were found for those curriculum areas plus writing, listening, social studies and self-concept, when non-English tests were used. Ann Willig's (1985) conclusion about United States bilingual education is more positive and seemingly more fair than that of Baker & de Kanter (1981, 1983). It is also in accord with a review by Cummins (1983a) and Genesee (1985).

Cummins (1983a), in a literature review of heritage language education, chose evaluations which "illustrate the theoretical principles that appear to be operating in bilingual programs for minority students" (p. 23). Such theoretical principles will be examined in the final chapter. Suffice to suggest at this point that a sophisticated theoretical explanation for the diversity of findings is preferable to a "vote". Cummins (1983a) has argued a strong case for some pattern in world-wide results (see Chapter 7). However, his explanation for "the relative paucity of positive [USA] evaluations in comparison with the total number of bilingual programs" (p. 22) is because of their recency, implementation difficulties and methodological inadequacies. These three reasons are insufficient grounds for concentrating on positive evaluations. Cummins (1983a) considers the results of the Colorado State-wide evaluation, the Rock Point Navajo study, the Nestor School Bilingual Program, the Californian Bilingual Kindergarten programs, the Head Start Bilingual Bicultural Pre-School Programs and the Carpenteria Intensive Pre-School program. Each illustrates that the language minority pupil's progress in some form of bilingual schooling is as good as, and sometimes better than, that of pupils in monolingual schools. That is, the programmes which succeed illustrate, but do not prove, that the acquisition of English language skills is not impeded by some form of bilingual education which includes a pupil's first language.

Cummins' (1983a) conclusions on the United States research are well argued, and, on existing evidence, appear to summarize well the positive side of United States experience. Cummins has four conclusions. First, the available evidence dispels the myth that instruction in the home language will impede the acquisition of English. "Less time spent in English-medium instruction exerts little negative effects on the development of English academic skills" (p. 29). Second, bilingual schooling has been partly instrumental in the academic progress of minority pupils who would typically fail in school. That is, some recognition by the school system of a pupil's minority language and culture can facilitate progress where lack of recognition may be connected with failure. Cummins then makes a key point: improvement of a pupil's performance is not an automatic consequence of using the minority language in school, whether it be with the aim of language maintenance, enrichment or transition. In other words, using a child's first language in school does not by itself cause progress. Other factors such as attitude, motivation, teaching approach, cultural transmission in the school may interact and combine to create an optimal setting. This leads directly to Cummins' third conclusion. Parental interest and involvement is an important factor, as is community participation, for the success of bilingual education. Bilingual education prospers by conviction and not by conformity. Fourth and finally, bilingual education does not exist in a vacuum. There are cost implications and perceived threats to a uniform mainstream education on the negative side, increased concern and professional development amongst teachers on the positive side. A change in a part can affect the whole. Bilingual education invokes different policies, provision and practices that may have a small ripple effect through mainstream thinking.

Criticisms and conclusions

Willig (1985) and Cummins (1983a) are in accord that immersion bilingual education has positive advantages over other forms of bilingual education. Yet many USA politicians and much of the English-speaking United States populace support transitional bilingual education rather than maintenance or enrichment bilingual education. To conclude that academics are correct and the populace wrong is untenable. The difference may at first sight be between research and public prejudice, between rationality and popular passions. Underneath there appear to be varying assumptions, different political and social beliefs, different ideologies of society. The underlying difference may be about ethnic groups maintaining their own identity and ethnic groups being assimilated into one integrated American society; about diversity and unity, minority language survival and majority language supremacy, cultural pluralism and cultural communality.

It is therefore important at this stage to represent the major criticisms of bilingual education, especially in terms of their relevance to the USA:

1. As Hernández-Chávez (1984) has noted, there is an important distinction between immersion bilingual education for majority language and for minority language pupils. The former is an additive enrichment situation. Immersion bilingual education for minority language children is ambiguous. It could be interpreted as immersion in English, which may create a subtractive, displacement situation. It could also mean in Baker & de Kanter's (1983) term "structured immersion", the use of a child's home language (and culture) with the second language gradually introduced.

2. Immersion education, as occurs successfully in Canada (see below), cannot be directly exported to the USA or any other country. Between countries are important social, political, cultural, economic and educational differences. "The Canadian enrichment model is not appropriate for language minority children in the United States because the requisite sociopolitical, sociolinguistic, and educational conditions for the successful conduct of an enrichment program are completely different" (Hernández-Chávez, 1984:168).

3. Factors such as parental co-operation, positive pupil motivation, the socio-economic background of pupils, the status of a minority language in society and pupil self-esteem may be important in the success or failure of any form of immersion or bilingual education. A great variety of factors determine the extent to which any form of bilingual education is successful.

4. Cultural pluralism is often seen as a positive outcome of bilingual education. However, as Edwards (1981) has shown, pluralism can itself increase inequality and separation within society when it is owned by those already assimilated (i.e. élitist pluralism) or is used as a condition to maintain the minority status of ethnic language groups. Van den Berghe (1967) and Higham (1975) have noted that pluralism is often not regarded as conducive to democratic order. Higham (1975) suggests that a consequence of a badly-conceived proliferation of pluralistic values may be the increased fragmentation of society, more discord, less harmony, less integration. This suspicion about pluralism is often a suspicion about a variety of forms of bilingual education.

5. Fishman (1977) and Edwards (1981) have suggested that much research and writing on bilingual education is committed, prescriptive in nature, with interests, idealism and ideology mixed with investigation and intelligent discussion. "Bilingual education is not merely a disinterested exercise in the application of theory and research to real-life situations. It is also an exercise in social policy and ideology" (Edwards, 1981:27). Most writers

on bilingual education support ethnic diversity, minority language rights and cultural pluralism, and are opposed to transitional bilingual education and assimilation. Bilingual education is not a purely pedagogic question with pedagogic answers. Support or criticism of bilingual education involves questions of a social, political and cultural nature.

6. Support for bilingual education is mostly from academics. We have negligible evidence as to the degree of parental, public or pupil support for the various forms of bilingual education. We have almost no evidence from ethnic groups themselves as to their educational priorities (Edwards, 1981).

7. The idea of assimilation and the melting-pot is usually negative in connotation. Edwards (1981) argues that assimilation into mainstream society can be attractive, sought after rather than coerced. It may not be seen by an individual as the "treacherous repudiation of heritage and tradition" (p. 38), but as a new adventure and a natural development of living in the United States.

The experience and judgement of research on bilingual education in the USA shows the dangers of assuming that there can be a perfectly objective, rational investigation and conclusion. To expect research to provide a best bet or an incontrovertible and indisputable lead on bilingual education is to be too optimistic. The record shows that meta studies of the count, statistical or theoretically derived variety fail to agree. While Baker & de Kanter (1983) tend to understate the immersion results, Willig (1985), Cummins (1983a) and previous reviewers tend to underestimate the social, political and cultural ideologies that underpin the ambiguity of immersion bilingual education. While evaluations of USA immersion education show the language benefits and other academic benefits of such education, the aims of immersion education are themselves valued, contentious and not necessarily in accordance with USA public consensus wishes. Issues about bilingual education ultimately cannot be divorced from political, cultural and societal issues. Research and evaluations can and should inform that debate. They cannot conclude the debate.

Canada

Historical perspective

The first colonization of Canada occurred in 1534, when the Frenchman Jacques Cartier discovered this part of the New World. In 1763, the British defeated the French near Quebec and began their colonization.

Thus Canada has two mainstream European traditions and cultures, two majority languages that are spoken world-wide. The 1867 British North America Act, an act similar to the American Declaration of Independence, did not given equal status to the French and English language. Bilingualism was official only in Quebec. One hundred years later, in 1969, the Official Languages Act gave equal status across Canada to the two languages. Canada has also adopted an official policy of multiculturalism recognizing majority and minority cultures amongst its population.

Legislation did not create a bilingual country. Of the ten provinces, only New Brunswick recognizes French and English as its official languages, with Quebec recognizing only French and the other eight provinces recognizing only English as their official language. The policy of the provinces reflects the language balance of their populations.

Approximately a quarter of the Canadian population speak French as a first language. Despite this high proportion, despite French being an official and a major world language, the English language dominates. As Genesee (1984) has noted, in commerce and business, English is predominant. At social and business occasions French speakers will switch to English to a greater extent than English speakers will concede and switch to French. Social psychological research has revealed by the use of well controlled experiments that, around the adolescent period, French Canadians develop more positive attitudes to English speakers than their own language group (Day, 1982). Of the two majority languages, one is more in the majority than the other in both a numerical and psychological sense. The discontent in Quebec since the early 1960s is further evidence that French is not perceived as being accorded sufficient status, even in a province where some 80% speak French as their first language.

It is against this historical background that Canadian bilingual education has recently evolved. The Canadian bilingual education movement started in the mid 1960s, and in the last 20 years has become famous world-wide for its experiments in immersion education. Such experiments were revolutionary, imaginative, evaluated with precision and sophistication, and tend to dominate discussion of the effects of bilingual education.

The St Lambert experiment

Although extensive evaluation studies had previously been published (e.g. in South Africa by Malherbe, 1946) and bilingual education has a history going back to early civilization (Lewis, 1977), the St Lambert experiment marks the start of a twentieth-century movement of carefully controlled and well analysed immersion education.

In the small suburban community of St Lambert outside Montreal, English speakers became disgruntled by their incompetence in French. The fault was attributed to the inadequate methods of second language teaching in schools. Such schools had traditionally taught French as a second language for one short 20–30 minute period a day. The teacher was not necessarily fluent in French and taught vocabulary and grammar by drill and practice. After 12 years of such school lessons, many pupils could not communicate in French with French Canadians.

Like many recent Welsh, Irish, Scottish and English developments, the move for bilingual education came not from government agencies or educational establishments, but from interested and committed parents. Remarkable and different from most bilingual education movements was the fact that parents consulted University experts. Whereas political lobbying often comes at the start of most parental pressure group movements, the advice of Wallace Lambert and Wilder Penfield of McGill University was sought. Their advice was given, as was their support. Together the parents and University academics persuaded the local school district administrators to set up an experimental kindergarten class in St Lambert in September 1965. A set quota of 26 children had enlisted within five minutes of opening the books (Lambert & Tucker, 1972).

The aims were: for pupils to be competent to speak and write in French while promoting and maintaining normal levels of achievement in all subjects including the English language, comparable with children in monoglot English education; for pupils to appreciate the culture and traditions of French Canadians as well as that of English Canadians.

The method of approach was "early total immersion". All curriculum areas were initially taught in French for one hour a day and by the end of elementary schooling, 60% of the curriculum was taught in English and 40% in French. Children were allowed to speak to each other and to the teacher in their first language until ready to switch to their second language. When using French of their own volition, children were encouraged and reinforced by the teacher, and the use of French was for meaningful and interesting communication and not just for repetitious practice. Conscious learning of vocabulary and grammar was absent. Instead the second language was acquired in a way similar to that in which the first language is unconsciously acquired. By learning maths or music, enjoying sport or art in school, language acquisition is said to occur naturally and at an individual's own rate of progress.

Respect for the home language was maintained by not forcing children to speak French. Respect was also achieved by the presence of English speakers amongst administrative and ancillary workers in the school, thus ensuring a positive and significant presence for English. "The children are exposed to many positive English-Canadian models in the home, in the community and in the media. Consequently, the support for the French language and culture is never achieved at the expense of the children's home language and culture" (Genesee, 1984:46).

Lambert & Tucker (1972) investigated the success or failure of the experiment by a psychometric–statistical rather than a case study approach. This set the standard and trend for further important evaluations of the spread of Canadian immersion education. A control group of pupils were located and matched on IQ and socio-economic class with the immersion children. Both groups were given tests of achievement in French and English, maths and IQ, as well as tests of attitude. To attempt to avoid a novelty effect, tests were given to subsequent immersion classes in the St Lambert experiment.

The results suggested the success of the experiment. Tucker & d'Anglejan (1972:19) summarized the results as follows:

"the experimental pupils appear to be able to read, write, speak, understand, and use English as well as. youngsters instructed in English in the conventional manner. In addition and at no cost they can also read, write, speak and understand French in a way that English pupils who follow a traditional program of French as a second language never do".

Attitudes and achievement were not hindered by the immersion experience. Tucker & d'Anglejan (1972) added one caution. Children used English at home and in their social milieu. Thus French was a school experience that did not necessarily become activated in the wider community context. This may make full bilinguality difficult to achieve.

The St Lambert immersion experiment is important in several respects. *First*, it shows the grass-roots power, foresight and educational inventiveness of parents. It is unusual if not unique for an innovation in schooling of such importance to be launched by parents. *Second*, new trends, innovations and vogues come and go. Language laboratories, educational television and programmed learning were each hailed as innovations that would change the face of education. Each was tried and found little better or worse than existing methods. Computer-based learning is beginning to experience the same tide of enthusiasm and then agnosticism. Immersion came and stayed. It has spread to most of the major cities of

Canada as well as influencing bilingual practice across the world. *Third*, as Stern (1984) noted, most innovations are advocated and installed. As an afterthought, evaluation is tacked on. With the immersion experiment, evaluation was there at the start, and had an important effect in publicizing and extending the programme. Parents, who stood to lose by an evaluation using strict forms of procedure and analysis, in fact gained. *Fourth*, the evaluation found success. This was far from predictable. Studies of computer-based learning, the audio-visual language method, language laboratories and progressive education have often led to the debunking of their claims of superiority. With immersion education, the finding was not only that attainment in English and other curriculum and cognitive areas did not suffer, but the children learnt a good deal of French, and certainly more French than solely having French language lessons. The St Lambert experiment suggested that more could be gained and little or nothing lost by changing the style of schooling.

Immersion education since the St Lambert experiment has spread across Canada. Not only has it developed geographically, but also linguistically and numerically. By 1986 there were over 120,000 pupils in immersion classes, with immersion not solely in French but in German, Hebrew, Chinese, Arabic and Ukrainian. In Montreal there is trilingual immersion involving English, French and Hebrew. The Ontario Institute for Studies in Education predicts that up to 20% of anglophone Canadian children will be in French immersion programmes by the early 1990s (Beaty, 1985).

Stern (1984) speaks of the quiet language revolution in Canada which has been fostered in a crucial respect by immersion education. "If immersion had not occurred, I am convinced, the other factors by themselves would not have produced the startling effects" (p. 507). Given the perceived success of immersion programmes it is necessary to define the aims, methods and evidence for the success of such programmes.

There are a number of excellent reviews of the immersion movement which tend to convey a very similar picture (Swain & Lapkin, 1982; California State Department of Education, 1984; Cummins, 1983a; Genesee, 1983, 1984). The reviews provide unusual uniformity in interpretation, such that relatively more stable and valid conclusions can be made than with the United States experience. Nevertheless, the limitations of this research will be considered at the end of the chapter.

Aims and methods of immersion education

Since the St Lambert experiment, the aims and methods of immersion education have changed little. The essential features are as follows:

(a) immersion education is optional not compulsory.

(b) the second language is the medium for the teaching of all or most school subjects.

(c) children are allowed to use their home language for up to 1½ years for classroom communication. There is no compulsion to speak the second language in the dining-room or the playground. The child's home language is appreciated and not disparaged.

(d) the teacher is bilingual, but initially appears to the pupil to be able to speak the second language (French) but only understand and not speak their first language (English).

(e) pupils in immersion education experience the same curriculum content as those in non-immersion education.

(f) classroom communication in the second language must be meaningful, authentic and relevant, never contrived, repetitive or tightly controlled. The content of the curriculum becomes the focus rather than correct communication. Thus second language learning is seemingly incidental, mirroring the manner a first language is acquired.

(g) emphasis is placed on comprehension competency before production competency. Listening with understanding comes before speaking with understanding.

(h) pupils commence the immersion experience with the same lack of skill in the second language. Classrooms start with relatively homogeneous pupils in terms of their monolingualism.

Further details of classroom methods in immersion education may be found in Lapkin & Cummins (1984).

Types of immersion education

Immersion education is an umbrella term. Within the concept of immersion experience are a variety of Canadian programmes varying in terms of the following:

(a) *age* at which a child commences the experience. This may be at the kindergarten or infant stage (*early* immersion); at 9 to 10 years of age (delayed or *middle* immersion), or at secondary level (*late* immersion).

(b) amount of *time* spent in immersion in a day. *Total* immersion normally commences with 100% immersion in the second

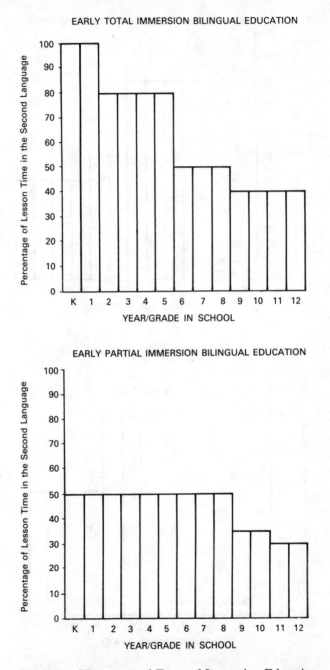

FIGURE 1.   Histograms of Types of Immersion Education

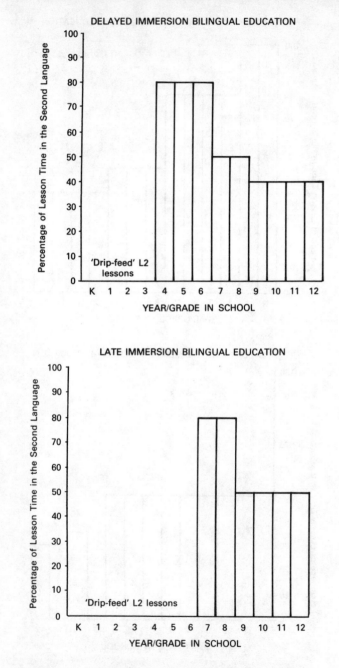

FIGURE 1 (*continued*)

language, after two or three years reducing to 80% for the next three or four years, finishing junior schooling with approximately 50% immersion. *Partial* immersion provides close to 50% immersion in the second language throughout infant and junior schooling. The histograms in Figure 1 illustrate the various possibilities.

(c) language of immersion. Apart from immersion in French as a second language, there are also double immersion programmes where both Hebrew and French are taught (Cummins, 1983a).

Results from the evaluations of immersion schooling

The results from a large number of evaluations have centred on French immersion, and the trends and patterns found may be summarized as follows.

Second language (French) learning

It is easy to predict, and clearly the case, that immersion pupils greatly and quickly surpass pupils being given French lessons for approximately 30 minutes a day. The more important question is whether immersion students reach native-like fluency in French. Pupils in early total immersion programmes approach such fluency at around 15 years of age, with pupils from early partial immersion programmes only a year or so behind. Late immersion students, while making better progress in French than students given 30-minute French lessons a day, tend not to progress as well as early total or partial immersion pupils. However, when early immersion pupils whose French curriculum was decreased to 40% after four years of immersion were compared to a late immersion group given 80% exposure to French for two years in secondary schooling, there were few differences (Swain & Lapkin, 1982). This suggests that early immersion needs adequate reinforcement throughout schooling. While the result may on the surface suggest the feasibility of late immersion, such programmes tend not to result in near native-like French proficiency.

To the credit of the evaluation studies, measures of French achievement go further than mere achievement tests. Such varied measures also reveal the limitations and paradoxes of immersion programmes. Early immersion students, while generally able to follow French TV programmes and magazines, report little self-initiated experience of various French media. Whilst having the potential, immersion students were not frequent in practising their French outside school. A further paradox is found in that immersion students' speech tends to be acceptable to native French speakers yet they are not active in seeking out or initiating conversations with French speakers. Genesee (1978) found that immersion students did not use French outside school any more than those given 30-minute a day French lessons. Why is it that immersion students are competent to react but are cautious to act in French? Potential does not mean production (Pawley, 1985; Singh, 1986). Avoidance motivation does not seem the cause. Such immersion pupils tend to regard themselves as skilled in French (Lambert & Tucker, 1972). Is it, as Stern (1984) suggests, that immersion has remained mainly a classroom language learning phenomenon? Research in Wales has suggested the crucial nature of culture in the promotion and maintenance of a second language (Baker, 1985). To support a language without supporting its attendant culture is to fund an expensive life-support machine attached to someone culturally dead or dying. To support the culture attached to a language is to give a life-saving injection to that language.

As Stern (1984:514–15) noted, the classroom immersion experience needs extending to contacts with native French Canadian children and the kind of values, beliefs and culture of such "French" children.

"An immersion program ideally should not be just an English program offered in French; it should of course be equivalent and have the same educational qualities, but it should also widen the immersion students' cultural horizon and sensitize them to francophone cultures and values and thus open the students' minds to the Canadian and world francophone. In other words, an immersion program is an invitation not only to become bilingual but also bicultural. But curricula that reflect these principles have not yet been widely developed. There has not yet been a serious discussion on the type of curriculum that immersion classes should promote".

First language (English) learning

The previous section shows that the immersion experience provides a distinct advantage for second language learning. But is this second language success at the cost of the first language? Like a weighing balance, does one increase as the other decreases? Most parents who enter their children in immersion education want success in French but not at the cost of English.

The trend that emerges for early total immersion is positive and encouraging. For the first four years of early total immersion, such pupils tend not to progress in English as monolingual English pupils do in mainstream classes. Reading, spelling and punctuation, for example, are not so developed. Since such children are usually not given English language instruction for two or three years after starting school, these results are to be expected. The initial pattern does not last. After approximately six years of schooling, early total immersion children have caught up with their monolingual peers in English skills. By the end of elementary schooling, the early total immersion experience has not generally affected first language speaking and writing development. Parents of these children believe the same as the attainment tests reveal. Indeed, when differences between immersion and mainstream children have been located by research, it is normally in favour of immersion pupils (Swain & Lapkin, 1982). This finding links with Chapter 2 which discussed the possible cognitive advantages consequential from bilingualism. If bilingualism permits increased linguistic awareness, more flexibility in thought, more internal inspection of language, such cognitive advantages may explain the possible faster English progress of early immersion pupils.

Partial early immersion pupils also tend to lag behind for three or four years in their English skills. Their performance is little different from that of total early immersion pupils, which is surprising since early partial immersion has much more English language content. By the end of elementary schooling, partial early immersion children catch up with mainstream peers. Unlike total early immersion pupils, partial immersion children do not surpass English comparison groups. Similarly, late immersion has no detrimental effect on English language skills (Genesee, 1983).

The evidence suggests that immersion children learn French at no cost to their English. Indeed, not only is there the gain of a second language, there is also good evidence to suggest that immersion results in possible extra benefits in terms of English proficiency. Rather than acting like a weighing balance, early total immersion, in particular, seems like cooking. The ingredients, when mixed and cooked, react together in additive ways. The product becomes more than the sum of its parts.

Other curriculum areas

If immersion provides some degree of fluency in French and no detrimental effect on English, do immersion pupils suffer in other curriculum areas? Is the accent on language acquisition at the cost of progress in subjects such as mathematics, science, history and geography? Does immersion cause negative effects on pupils' motivation, interest, attitude or study skills?

In *early total immersion*, all the curriculum is initially taught in French. Later in the elementary school some subjects are taught in English. Swain & Lapkin (1982) note that the choice of language of instruction depends on a variety of factors: teacher expertise, administrative constraints, likely pupil achievement and the usefulness of a curriculum area to develop rich, creative French language proficiency.

When children are taught maths in French, and even when the test is in English, the balance of evidence suggests no difference in mathematics attainment between *early total immersion pupils* and English-educated peers. Similarly science, history and geography achievement is generally neither positively nor negatively affected by the early total immersion experience.

Although not a curriculum subject, but a possible effect of education, research has examined changes in IQ, creativity scores and other cognitive skills. Although not extensive and well replicated, there is more than a hint in available studies that *early total immersion* has a more positive effect on general cognitive development than comparable English-only education. Such early total immersion pupils tend to show greater increases in IQ, have higher verbal and non-verbal creativity scores, perform better on measures of divergent thinking, cognitive flexibility and work-study skills compared with monolingual control pupils (Swain & Lapkin, 1982). These results reflect the cautious conclusion of cognitive advantages for "balanced" bilinguals found in Chapter 2.

The overall findings for *early partial immersion* are not so positive. In acquiring mathematical and science skills through French, early partial immersion children tend to lag behind comparable mainstream children, at least initially. The relatively inferior performance may be due to their French skills being insufficiently developed to deal with the subject matter of mathematics and science. However, general intellectual functioning does not appear to be detrimentally affected by early partial immersion (Swain & Lapkin, 1982).

The overall results for *late immersion* tend not to form a clear pattern, with the existence of some positive and some negative results. One key factor appears to be the extent to which late immersion pupils have received French instruction before the immersion experience. When previous French instruction has been consistently provided since the start of schooling, little or no negative effects tend to be found. If the prior experience of French is more limited, detrimental effects may occur. One major explanation seems to be the same as for the early partial immersion findings. Second language skills need to be sufficiently developed to cope with fairly complex curriculum material.

Attitudes and adjustment

Immersion education attempts to avoid children's self-esteem and attitude to school becoming negative by allowing them to use their home language freely for 1 to 1½ years. Nevertheless, it is still possible that immersion has effects on a child's attitude to education and feelings of self-worth.

The relatively small number of studies in this area tend to suggest that *early total immersion* has positive rather than negative psychological effects. Pupils in early total immersion tend to adjust fairly quickly to this experimental type of schooling and are positive about being in immersion education. Parents also tend to express retrospective satisfaction with both learning and individual psychological outcomes of the immersion experience.

Early immersion students also tend to have made some kind of bridge with French Canadian society in terms of attitude. Genesee (1977, reported in Swain & Lapkin (1982)), using multidimensional scaling, found that early immersion pupils perceived less social distance between themselves and French Canadians than did comparable English pupils, while still maintaining their basic "English" identity. Attitudes to French Canadians also tend to be most positive with the early total immersion pupils. However, this tends to be an initial rather than a lasting effect, with attitudes still remaining favourable. Lack of sustained contact with French Canadians may explain the levelling out of attitudes to French Canadians over time, with immersion students having no really different attitudes to their English speaking peers in the later stages of schooling.

In comparison with late immersion pupils, the early immersion pupils tend to adjust more readily to the school experience and are more positive in attitude towards their education. Whether this is an effect of immersion education itself or stems from parental views and beliefs is not clear from the research.

The effectiveness of different forms of immersion schooling

With a variety of styles of approach, early total, early partial, delayed and late immersion, the question naturally arises as to whether one is superior or inferior to another. Genesee's (1983) review of the relative effectiveness of the different approaches suggests:

1. None of the alternatives has a negative result on pupils' English language development. All programmes appear to result in first

language development comparable with mainstream schooling.

2. All the alternatives provide greater proficiency in French than achieved by "core" or "drip feed" programmes where French is taught as a second language for approximately 30 minutes a day. Immersion programmes, including early total immersion, do not result in native-like bilingualism. As Stern (1984) has observed, "reading and listening comprehension reaches near-native standards. They also acquire a certain fluency in talking which is generally lacking in traditional language learners. But their grammatical accuracy remains somewhat inadequate and they seem to lack the social and stylistic sense of appropriateness of language use which the native speaker possesses intuitively" (p. 514).

3. Early total immersion pupils tend to achieve higher French proficiency than early partial immersion pupils, with this latter group achieving higher levels than the middle/delayed pupils. Early immersion pupils tend to achieve higher French proficiency than late immersion pupils.

4. Genesee (1983) provides three qualifications to the predictable result of earlier exposure and more exposure to French resulting in higher French attainment. First, intensity of exposure may be more important than length of exposure. Second, teaching techniques can change the pattern of results. "Individualized, activity-based teaching techniques may be more effective than traditional group-oriented approaches" (p. 20). Third, other variables being constant, older pupils learn a second language more efficiently than young learners.

5. Early total immersion pupils and late immersion pupils with a continuous experience of "core" French lessons since the start of elementary schooling achieve as well as mainstream children in science and maths even though these subjects are taught in their second language. Early partial immersion and late immersion pupils without extended prior French lessons tend to lag behind their peers when taught other curriculum subjects through their second language. This lag tends to be temporary and rectifiable. Too little evidence exists on middle or delayed immersion to make valid conclusions.

Trilingual schooling

A bold extension of immersion education is double immersion. Double immersion experiments involve the use of two second languages, French and Hebrew, as mediums of instruction in elementary schooling in Montreal. The French medium lessons included mathematics, science and social studies; the Hebrew lessons included history, religious studies and cultural studies. English was not introduced until 8 and 9 years of age in one experiment (early double immersion). In another experiment, the three languages were all used in varying proportions throughout elementary schooling (delayed double immersion).

The evaluation report of the experiments shows a complex variety of results (Genesee, Tucker & Lambert, 1978a & b). The analysis suggests that, with some qualifications, by the end of elementary schooling:

(a) English language proficiency did not suffer. English skills were comparable to those of single immersion and mainstream pupils.

(b) with French language proficiency, double immersion pupils were achieving higher than "core" mainstream pupils. Early double immersion resulted in higher French attainment than late double immersion, with the former pupils having achievement comparable to early single total immersion pupils.

(c) Hebrew proficiency tended to be greater for early double immersion than late double immersion children.

(d) much early use of a child's first language in the curriculum interferes with second language learning.

(e) general academic achievement was not impaired.

The children in the trilingual experiment tended to be highly motivated and able children. This does not mean that such a trilingual programme is irrelevant to other children, merely that the evidence for generalization to different populations has yet to be produced.

Canadian enrichment programmes

Apart from the teaching of French by immersion, similar evaluated experiments in Canada concern the use of Ukrainian in Alberta and Manitoba. Most of the pupils in the evaluation came from homes where Ukrainian was spoken but the children lacked fluency in that minority language. About one in ten children had no Ukrainian linguistic skill or ancestry. This is not so different from some schools in Ireland, Scotland and Wales where there is a mixture of language skills. The classroom time allotted to each language was approximately equal. For example, mathematics and science were taught in English, music, art and social studies were taught in Ukrainian.

Cummins (1983a:8) summarizes the results:

"students acquire satisfactory levels of Ukrainian skills and appreciation of Ukrainian culture at no cost to achievement in English and other academic subjects. Student affective outcomes, as viewed by parents, teachers, and principals, also appear to be positive".

Thus minority language experiments, while not being so numerous and well replicated as majority language immersion experiments, do seem to have similar results.

The limitations of the Canadian immersion research

The evaluations of immersion education are numerous, well replicated and mostly technically good. So far, the results have been considered uncritically, almost as if there are law-like patterns. This section considers two topics: three potential criticisms that appear to. be at least partly answerable, and three limitations that further research may address.

There are three criticisms that have sometimes been voiced about the limitations and assumptions of immersion education in Canada which appear to be answerable, either fully or partly.

1. Many experiments use only a narrow range of educational and psychometric tests which may lack breadth in terms of curriculum outputs, and fail to address the issues that parents, industry and other interested parties may raise. There is evidence in the immersion experiments of a wide range of tests used within a curriculum area (e.g. French language or English language representing a variety of skills). A number of different curriculum areas and not just languages have been evaluated, and importantly, the views of pupils, parents, teachers and administrators have often been sought. Therefore, some breadth of curriculum output has been considered. Added to this, there are psychological investigations of the attitudinal and affective outcomes of immersion. The result is a multicoloured canvas in comparison with many educational experiments which have a very restricted sketch and use of colours.

2. The results of experiments can sometimes be explained by a novelty or a "reactive" effect. A new teaching scheme may lead to improved results because of the enthusiasm that usually accompanies new developments. The immersion experience has continued since the early St Lambert experiment, so that any initial novelty effect should have become extinct. Similarly, the act of being in an experiment can lead the guinea

pigs into behaving differently (Hawthorne effect). Since the experiments have developed into customary and accepted forms of alternative education, the experimental effect would not seem to explain the immersion results. However, over time, situations change, commitments vary, values and needs of parents and society alter and develop. There is a sense in which experimental results say something about what has been, not what will always be. They do not guarantee that as circumstances change, results will be stable across time.

3. Does the immersion experience only work with children of high ability and from the middle classes? The majority of immersion programmes in Canada are populated by above average ability children from middle- to upper-middle-class families. However, the evidence, which admittedly is not great and is in need of replication and extension, suggests that children of lower socio-economic backgrounds and children of below average ability may both be successful in immersion schooling. Research has found that working-class immersion children performed as well as mainstream control children on tests of English and other curriculum areas, and their French proficiency develops to a high level (Genesee, 1983). Genesee (1985), reporting on the Cincinnati Immersion Programme in the USA, finds positive results for children of lower socio-economic background and of average and below average levels of ability. However, Canadian research tends to concern working-class children in classes with many middle-class peers. Whether the same positive findings would occur in more deprived working-class communities and more homogeneous working-class schools has yet to be revealed, although Genesee's (1985) findings in the USA are tentatively positive.

Results for average IQ and below average IQ pupils show no different trends from those from above average IQ groups, so long as equivalent control groups form the basis of the comparison. These results hold for English and general academic achievement (Genesee, 1983). The evidence for children with learning difficulties has provided controversy and debate (Cummins, 1984a; Trites, 1981). Trites (1981) is critical of the immersion experiments, partly because of insufficient data about experimental mortality (the type and number of children dropping out of the immersion classes) and the effect of this on the overall results, and partly because aggregate results hide the passage of individuals, some of whom may have been unsuccessful. Trites' (1981) interpretation of his own research suggests that children with learning difficulties cannot make satisfactory progress in early immersion schooling. However, extensive criticisms of Trites' (1981) research have been made (Cummins, 1984a; Genesee, 1983). Bruck's (1978) research found that children with learning difficulties did not suffer from the immersion experience. Rather, they gained some second language proficiency. Trites (1981) has criticized Bruck's (1978) research for lack of controls, experimental mortality and the non-representative nature of the learning difficulty group. While Cummins (1984a) finds in an extensive discussion of Trites' (1981) and Bruck's (1978) research support for Bruck's conclusions, it may be more fair to await the evidence of more large-scale, multi-variable, better replicated research before a definitive answer can be provided about the value of immersion for children with learning difficulties. Such research will need to follow the lead of Bruck (1985a) who found that, although cognitive academic variables are necessary conditions for children to transfer out of immersion education, such variables are not sufficient conditions. Children who opt out of immersion education tend to have relatively negative attitudes to schooling in general, poor motivation and conduct or behavioural problems. Attitudinal and motivational factors are of primary importance in pupils' success in bilingual education, especially with children experiencing learning difficulties. Bruck (1985b) further found such children who opted out of immersion education neither improved their attainment more than comparable children remaining in immersion, nor did their negative attitudes and poor motivation improve after transfer. This innovatory research of Bruck (1985a & b), while requiring replication, provides early hints that immersion does not disadvantage children with learning difficulties.

There are three further criticisms voiced about immersion education that are more difficult to answer, and suggest avenues of further exploration.

1. The outputs of the research mostly concern that which is measurable. This is an essential part of most evaluations. However, it may not reveal the whole canvas. Evaluations have tended to follow the one methodological tradition, the experiment. In particular, case studies, or the illuminative evaluation tradition, have rarely been used. MacDonald *et al.*'s (1982) evaluation of bilingual schooling in Boston, USA, follows this alternative, intensive and holistic approach. Sometimes case study reveals the complexity of interactions between and amongst teachers, pupils, curriculum materials and the school environment. An experiment is like judging a dramatic production on an applause-meter reading. The data is quantifiable, replicable, reliable and comparable across productions. A case study is comparable to drama critics' notes. The evaluations will differ from critic to critic, but may sometimes be more vigorous, insightful, rich in detail and interpretative. The evaluation of immersion education has produced a well developed skeleton. Qualitative evaluations could add some flesh to ·that experimental skeleton.

2. The evaluations concern immediate outputs. Pupils' performance at the end of the year is regarded as very important. It is a limitation not just of this research, but of most educational evaluations, that more long-term effects are not examined. Do immersion pupils stay bilingual throughout life? Do immersion pupils become bicultural in the years after schooling? Do immersion pupils find employment more easily? Do immersion pupils have advantages in vocational success? Do immersion pupils marry bilinguals? Are their offspring brought up bilingually? More follow-up research is needed to answer these important long-term questions.

3. While every endeavour is made to match immersion students with a mainstream control group, absolute equivalence is impossible. To match pupils statistically or by pairing for social class, IQ and age, will still leave differences between immersion and control groups that are not randomly distributed. Immersion pupils may have parents who are motivated for one reason or another to gain, through education, bilingual children. Such parents may therefore be the more enthusiastic, committed and interested parents. As Swain & Lapkin (1982) note themselves, "the experimental group may have one or more characteristics (such as high motivation) which are absent in the comparison students" (p. 30). A further example is late immersion students who tend to be above average at French before they start the immersion experience. Thus their motivation is different from the control group. The conclusion is that the results may not be due solely to immersion education. The special characteristics of the pupils may be a small part explanation as well. In a similar way, immersion teachers as, opposed to the immersion practice may well affect results. Are immersion teachers more committed than the average teacher? Such is the evidence from designated bilingual school teachers in Wales (Roberts, 1985). Are immersion teachers more skilful and experienced? Further research needs to indicate how "teacher proof" is the immersion experience. What effects does school ethos have on the results? To say that immersion education is superior is very non-specific. What are the essential features and non-essential factors in the success equation? What factors are more and less important in the recipe?

Conclusions

The North American experience is not a unitary one. The tradition of the United States is bilingual education for transition and assimilation. Speakers of minority languages have historically been expected to adjust to monoglot English education through some form of bilingual education. The many become one. A recent movement in Canada has been immersion bilingual education. Given the recognition of French and English as the official languages of Canada, immersion education seeks to create bilinguals from monoglot English pupils. One becomes two.

Thus, countries geographically joined together are separated by two different philosophies of language and culture. One seeks commonality, the other plurality. The United States has the goal of common aims, ideals and values. Canada has the goal of bilingualism and biculturalism. The vision of a unified nation wrought out of diversity is an American dream. The vision of Canada is to celebrate its multiple language heritage by encouraging bilingualism and multiculturalism.

The themes of this chapter reflect the difference in ideologies between the two countries. The recent major review of bilingual education in the United States focused on the relative effectiveness of different bilingual education programmes in aiding the transition from minority home language to English. The United States official concern is with bilingual education for assimilation. The review of Baker & de Kanter (1983) suggested that various types of bilingual education could lead to satisfactory transition, this including immersion education. The review of the dominant trend in Canadian research on bilingual education focused on the effectiveness of immersion education in creating bilingual pupils. The review suggests that immersion education is capable of producing bilingual children at no cost to their first language or general achievement throughout the curriculum. Immersion education seems to realize the Canadian dream of linguistic diversity.

It is tempting to see in Canadian and United States research a link between the dream and the data. Has the ideology of sponsor and researcher affected the findings and conclusions? Certainly, criticisms of the Baker & de Kanter review have suggested that, by asking a very narrow range of questions and possibly by too narrow a selection of "good" research, the conclusions reached tell a partial "truth" and not the whole "truth". Critics of the positivist approach to educational research would see in the methodology of the Canadian research the ideology of social engineering and change. The observation of this chapter is that the data have in part created and fuelled the dream. The research has been a major influence in advancing the possibility of a bilingual Canada. The research is rigorous and well replicated, with strong patterns emerging from the variety of research. There are no absolute truths in educational research findings, no unalterable laws of educational behaviour. A change in parts can affect the whole in unexpected ways. Nevertheless, immersion education, and particularly early total immersion, has been well tested, tried in a variety of courts, and found not guilty of any detrimental effects. Rather, immersion has benefits in terms of bilingualism. Children learn a second language without cost.

If immersion education is transported across the Atlantic and Pacific, there are conditions which may make for success or failure. *First*, immersion needs to be optional, not enforced. The convictions of parents, teachers and peers affects the motivation and achievement of pupils. Immersion education appears to depend on conviction and not on conformity. *Second*, children need to be homogeneous in language skills at the start. Varying degrees of ability in the second language may detract from a well structured and sequenced curriculum. *Third*, respect is shown for the child's home language and culture, allowing the child to use that language whenever and wherever he or she needs. Immersion allows children to speak to their teacher in their first language until skilled enough to communicate naturally in the second language. *Fourth*, teachers need to be committed to immersion education, to be able to understand the child's first language, and to have not merely tolerance of a child's home language, however low in prestige it may be, but a progressive, liberal and pluralistic view of a multilingual and multicultural society. This includes majority language situations where the minority language is the home language as well as situations where the indigenous minority language is endangered. *Fifth*, the method of language teaching needs to be well thought out and to defy traditional practices of formal teaching of rules, grammar and construction. The theories of Krashen (1981), immersion education (Lapkin & Cummins, 1984) and Dodson (1985a) are each recent considerations of progressive practices. *Sixth* and finally, research needs to go hand in hand with immersion innovation. Research informs the inquisitive parent and agnostic administrator. The Canadian experience is that research aims at evaluating in retrospect but in turn creates a prospect for immersion education.

To transport immersion education across continents entails close consideration as to immersion in what and for what reason. The danger is to conceive of the Canadian experience as appropriate for the immersion of minority language children in a majority language (e.g. English in the USA, Britain or Quebec) where that language may replace the home language. Immersion can in this case imply assimilation. The danger is also to conceive of the Canadian experience in purely pedagogic terms. Immersion education has underlying political, social and cultural assumptions which need consideration before implementation in other contexts, other countries. In the last analysis the immersion experience is not just in a second language.

5 Attitudes and Bilingualism

Introduction

In the life history of a language, attitude may be crucial. In language growth or decay, restoration or destruction, attitude may be central. The status and importance of a language in society and within an individual derives in a major way from adopted or learnt attitudes. The success of language policy is partly predicated on attitudes surrounding that language. As E. G. Lewis (1981:262) succinctly observed:

> "Any policy for language, especially in the system of education, has to take account of the attitude of those likely to be affected. In the long run, no policy will succeed which does not do one of three things: conform to the expressed attitudes of those involved; persuade those who express negative attitudes about the rightness of the policy; or seek to remove the causes of disagreement".

An attitude predisposes yet is capable of change. It is individual yet has origins in, and effects on, collective behaviour. An attitude is a hypothetical psychological construct yet impinges in an important way on the reality of language life. This chapter, after explaining briefly the concept and measurement of attitudes, uses research from Wales, Ireland and Scotland to illustrate the importance of attitudes in any discussion of bilingualism.

Attitude theory

Input and output

One idea of an attitude to a language is something an individual has which defines or promotes certain behaviours. A person who owns a positive attitude to Welsh may wish to learn the language fluently or engage in indigenous Welsh cultural forms (e.g. eisteddfodau). In this

112

sense, attitude causes certain behaviours. But while attitude is certainly a causal or *input* variable, it also needs to be thought of as an *output* or outcome variable. For example, the end product of Welsh lessons in school may not only be greater facility in the language, but also a positive attitude to the language. Watching Welsh language programmes on television may not only result in enculturation but also a positive attitude to Welsh cultural forms. In this sense attitude is an end product.

Attitude conceived as an outcome of education is important because it may provide a complimentary or even an alternative and more long-lasting effect than examination achievement. A majority of the public may regard examination success as the most important outcome of schooling. Yet knowledge specific to pass examinations may be short-lived, easily forgotten. A positive attitude towards a subject may be a more enduring outcome than knowledge gained to pass an examination. Rules of grammar, syntax, spelling and pronunciation may be quickly lost. Attitude to a taught second language may last.

Cognitive, affective and action components

In theory, attitudes are said to have three parts (Triandis, 1971). In practice it is much more difficult to separate out and identify these parts, which interact and merge. These three parts are the cognitive, affective and active. Attitudes may have a *cognitive* component. An attitude to a minority language may be thought about and be capable of being transmitted by words or other symbols. Secondly, attitudes may have an *affective* component. Feelings and emotions may be attached to attitudes. A person may think that coloured people are equal to whites yet feel in a way that is dissonant to rational thought. A love of one's native language may be felt deeply in ways that words or symbols could never adequately convey. For example, Welsh people may speak of a "hiraeth" which inadequately translates into English as a deep-seated longing. Thirdly, attitudes relate to readiness for *action*. A positive attitude may predispose certain behaviours. While there may well be consonance between cognitive, affective and action parts of attitudes, there may be dissonance. A person may have positive thoughts about a language, yet behave in a negative way. The context of actions sometimes sets constraints on latent attitudes.

The absence of a strong relationship between attitudes and actual behaviour is a well documented research finding (Triandis, 1971). The classic example is LaPiere's (1934) research. He travelled through the USA with a Chinese couple. Service was refused to the Chinese only once in 250 visits to hotels, motels and restaurants. Yet only 8% of hotels, motels and restaurants said, in response to a letter, that they would serve a Chinese couple. Actual behaviour compared with attitudes expressed in a verbal form were markedly different. The implication is that attitudes in reality are:

(a) different from, and not always congruent with actual behaviour. Gardner, Lalonde & MacPherson (1986) found, for example, in a study which included the relationship between attitudes and second language attrition, that language usage was independent of attitudes.

(b) affected very significantly by the context. As the props change on the stage where attitudes are enacted, so behaviour connected with attitudes may alter with changed scenery.

(c) just one determinant of behaviour. Personality, abilities, rewards, situation, drives and needs, for example, are also helpful, additive, hypothetical or real explanatory factors.

(d) different for reality and hypothetical reality. An attitude to Chinese people in general is not the same as an attitude to two individuals present in person. An attitude towards a mother-in-law may be modified when in her presence.

(e) different for "I" and "they". People's attitudes to screening for cancer differs widely according to the target of the screening. In response to the question "Should people (you) have a regular screening for cancer?" almost 100% of individuals are in favour of "people" in general being screened. When the question is "you" the percentage drops to approximately half.

Nature of attitudes

Attitudes are usually regarded as hypothetical constructs. An *attitude* to the Welsh language cannot be directly observed. Attitudes are inferred, conceptual inventions hopefully aiding the description and explanation of behaviour. Attitudes are learned predispositions, not inherited or genetically endowed, and are likely to be relatively stable over time. Our attitudes tend to persist. However, attitudes are modified by experience, such that attitude change is an important notion in bilingualism. If people's attitudes are open to change, then attitude to a minority language, to learning a second language, to participating in a second culture may be both positively or negatively affected. Factors promoting attitude change will be considered later in the chapter.

The dichotomy of attitudes being positive or negative (e.g. for or against the existence of the Welsh language) needs extending into the idea of a dimension. Attitudes will vary in degree of favourability and unfavourability, with all shades of favourability existing between the extremes. In the middle comes neutrality, with no opinions or feelings one way or the other.

Separate from the positive and negative nature of attitudes is their complexity. This again will vary from person to person. One pupil may hold a simple negative attitude, hating all foreign language lessons. Another pupil may have a relatively more complex attitude, with positive and negative feelings and thoughts about such lessons that are dependent on the type of lesson, sex and age of teacher and size of the class. One adult might believe that bilingualism is good for all, another have a complex belief with a large number of constraints (e.g. age, ability, status of language, economic realities) variously combined.

Attitude measurement

A variety of alternative methods exist for measuring an individual's attitude: Thurstone & Chave (1929), Likert (1932), Guttman's Scalogram analysis, the Semantic Differential Technique, the Repertory Grid Technique, Factor Analysis and Sociometry being varied examples. Document analysis, content analysis, interviews, case studies, autobiographies and the matched guise technique are also well established alternatives. The specific attitude under investigation may include attitudes to language groups (e.g. Welsh speakers), a language itself, its features, uses, cultural associations, learning a language, bilingual education as product or process, language preference, policy and practice (Giles, Hewstone & Ball, 1983).

Perhaps the most popular method of attitude measurement is to produce an attitude scale composed of statements such as:
"Welsh people speak too much English" or
"Welsh should not be forced on non-Welsh pupils".
Responses may be Agree/Disagree or be measured more exactly with a five point scale:

Strongly	*Agree*	*Neither Agree*	*Disagree*	*Strongly*
Agree		*nor Disagree*		*Disagree*

Summation of scores on various statements may finally produce one score per respondent, or, if factor analysis is used, several scores on sub-scales.

Most techniques are uni-dimensional in structure, resulting in one score on a general scale. Factor analysis allows multi-dimensionality, with the idea that attitude to Welsh, for example, may better be broken down into components (e.g. attitude to the language; attitude to Welsh-speaking people; attitude to the functional or instrumental use of Welsh).

The Semantic Differential Technique is less popular but may sometimes tap the affective component as well as the cognitive component of attitudes. A good example is to be found in Sharp *et al.* (1973). Meanings attached to a stimulus (the Welsh language) can be profiled for an individual person or, when calculated as an average, for a group. For example:

The Welsh Language

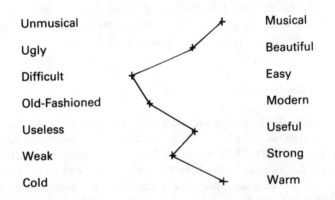

Unmusical	Musical
Ugly	Beautiful
Difficult	Easy
Old-Fashioned	Modern
Useless	Useful
Weak	Strong
Cold	Warm

The above hypothetical profile of a group suggests the Welsh language is seen as particularly Musical, Difficult, Old-Fashioned and Warm. Certain pairs of bi-polar adjectives may non-exclusively represent cognitive aspects of attitude (e.g. Useless–Useful); other pairs may tap feelings regarding meanings (Cold–Warm). Profiles of different groups may be compared, as well as individuals contrasted.

The measurement of an individual's attitudes is unlikely to reveal their attitudes perfectly. There are a number of reasons why attitude measurement is rarely, if ever, totally valid, and three of the more important of these are listed below.

1. People may respond to an attitude test in a way that makes them appear more prestigious, more good than is real. Consciously and unconsciously people tend to give socially desirable answers. We may wish to appear unprejudiced towards minority peoples or languages, when the reality is something different.

2. People may be affected in their response to an attitude test by the researcher and the perceived purpose of the research. The ethnic identity, gender, status, age, language in its verbal and non-verbal forms, and social class of the researcher may each affect how an individual responds. The perceived aim and objective of the research (e.g. pro-minority language or anti-immigration) may similarly affect replies, as may the context or environment of the testing.
3. A good attitude test will encompass the full range of issues and ideas involved in a topic. The initial item pool must of necessity cover the fullest range of possible attitudes in terms of topic, complexity and favourability and unfavourability, just as the item analysis on the item pool (to find the most reliable statements and exclude unreliable items) must be executed on a representative and not atypical sample of people.

As with almost all psychological measurement, attitude scores for individual people are imperfect representations of their attitudes. Nevertheless, there are examples of well conducted attitude test construction which demonstrate that attitude measurement, although imperfect, is feasible, relatively valid, reliable and provides important findings. The research of D. Sharp *et al.* (1973) in Wales and CILAR (1975) in Ireland, both considered later in the chapter, are two worthy examples.

Having briefly considered the concept and measurement of attitude, it should now be possible to better understand bilingualism-attitude research. The remainder of this chapter centres upon such research, focusing on two overall particular issues in "Celtic" countries:

1. the role of attitudes in language maintenance and restoration
2. the role of attitudes in language learning and bilingual education.

It is not the intention to examine all research from each country under geographical headings. Rather, what follows chooses research paths followed in "Celtic" countries to draw out important themes.

Attitude to Welsh: Decline with age

The diverse researches that have examined attitude to Welsh appear to have a common thread. There is the constant theme of a positive attitude to Welsh decreasing as age increases. This symbolizes the plight of the Welsh language this century. A decline in Welsh speakers in the population, in proportional and absolute terms, is matched by, and probably related to, children becoming less favourable towards Welsh as they become older. The work of four researchers who have considered this age decline theme will now be examined.

W. R. Jones (1949, 1950)

W. R. Jones (1949, 1950) first researched attitude to the Welsh language in the wake of World War II. Using a 22-item Thurstone scale with children from the Rhondda Valley (Cwm Rhondda) and Cardiff, Jones plotted the change in attitude with age. The Cwm Rhondda and Cardiff children from secondary modern schools (i.e. of average and below average ability) showed the similar downward trend with age illustrated in Table 3.

TABLE 3.   *Change with Age in Attitude to the Welsh Language*

Age	Average Scores Cwm Rhondda (Jones, 1949)	Cardiff (Jones, 1950)
1st Year (11/12 years)	6.74	6.74
2nd Year (12/13 years)	6.23	6.64
3rd Year (13/14 years)	5.97	6.41
4th Year (14/15 years)	—	5.52

Note: The higher the score, the more positive the attitude. A score of 6 represents a neutral attitude.

The decline in a favourable attitude to the Welsh language with increasing age is constant, with a particularly noticeable drop in the Cardiff sample from the third to the fourth year. As leaving school approached, the adolescents veered towards a negative attitude, having started secondary schooling on the positive side. Age, of course, was not the only variable connected with decline. Being a girl and having a Welsh-speaking mother were connected with less decline. Attitude and attainment were also connected, as expected. A less favourable attitude to Welsh was connected to relatively lower attainment in Welsh. Whether attitude is the cause or effect of attainment is not clear. Possibly both reciprocally are the cause and effect of each other. Jones (1950) concluded that "attainment in Welsh is increasingly influenced by the pupil's attitude in the later stages of the course" (p. 132).

D. Sharp et al. (1973)

The work of W. R. Jones was essentially small-scale. The impossibility of generalizing from two schools makes these studies mostly of historical interest. In contrast to Jones' studies is the large-scale research of Sharp et al. (1973) which used stratified random sampling to obtain a representative response from children of ages 10/11, 12/13 and 14/15. Measurement started at about 10 years of age because under that age attitude can be measured, but with less reliability and validity.

The great majority of children at age 10/11 years were mildly positive towards Welsh. By the fourth year in the secondary school, the average trend was downwards. However, as Table 4 shows, the average score of those in designated bilingual schools stayed on the positive side. In comparison, the average score of those *not* attending a bilingual school veered towards neutrality by age 14/15.

TABLE 4.   *Age and Average Attitude to Welsh (Scores *)*

Welsh-speaking population density of neighbourhood	10/11 Years	11/12 Years	14/15 Years
68–81% Welsh	3.97	4.10	4.98
48–55% Welsh	4.22	4.70	5.14
3–26% Welsh	5.39	5.67	5.80
Children attending designated bilingual schools	3.21	3.55	3.72

* Score 0–5 = Positive Attitude
   Score 5–6 = Neutral Attitude
   Score 6–11 = Negative Attitude
(Extracted from Sharp et al., 1973)

Sharp et al. (1973) found that attitude to Welsh was connected with gender (girls more favourable in attitude than boys), length of residence in Wales (a less favourable attitude tends to be held by immigrants), attainment in school (a more favourable attitude to Welsh is linked with higher attainment with some age and L1/L2 qualifications); ability (younger children of higher ability tend to be more favourable), and the Welsh-speaking density of neighbourhood (the higher the density of Welsh speakers, the more favourable the attitude). These are all relatively stable and enduring variables. In contrast, the type of schooling is comparatively more open to "social engineering". Thus, if maintaining a positive attitude to Welsh is desirable, does the concept of extending bilingual schooling in Wales require consideration?

Caution must be taken in using Sharp et al.'s results to support bilingual education. Pupils attending bilingual schools started with the most positive attitude (mean attitude score = 3.21). This represents a favourable attitude higher than that of pupils from Welsh-speaking heartland areas. Therefore it may not be bilingual schools alone that keep their average pupil's attitude positive rather than neutral. Nor may it be bilingual schools alone which, in themselves, reduce the amount of decline (0.51 decline in bilingual school pupils compared with children from more Welsh backgrounds, whose decline was 1.01 for pupils from 68–81% language background and 0.92 for pupils from 48–55% language background).

Does the causal factor lie in parental values, beliefs and motivations, the extended family and the influence of local friends as well as, or rather than, the effect of bilingual education? The interconnections between factors are complex. Bilingual schools often exist because of parental pressure, with such pressure (and the institution of bilingual schools) stemming from a variety of attitudes and motives. No simple causal chain can be postulated. Rather, there is a network of inter-related and reciprocating causes and effects.

However, a hint of the nature of declining attitude to Welsh with age lies in Sharp et al.'s (1973) examination of the relationship of attitude to English with attitude to Welsh. The relationship tends towards being a reverse reflection, the higher the one, the lower the other. Sharp et al. suggest the presence of a see-saw effect. Over time, attitude to English becomes more favourable. Table 5 demonstrates that this is constant, irrespective of type of language background and bilingual schooling.

The temptation is to consider the increasing favourability to English with increasing age as an explanation of declining attitude to Welsh. Indeed the rank–order correlations presented by Sharp et al. (1973) range between −0.79 and −1.0, giving a very high predication of one attitude by the other. Sharp et al.'s suggestions are that the relationship is logically interconnected. The relationship is symbolized in the statement "English will take you further than Welsh". Part of both attitude to English and attitude to Welsh is language loyalty. Loyalty to Welsh may breed a comparatively less favourable attitude to English. Loyalty to Welsh did not prevent attitude recognition of the value and position of the English language. However, the evidence of Sharp et al. (1973) suggests that with increasing age, loyalty to Welsh decreases and loyalty to English increases. To extend the analogy, the see-saw swings toward English with age. But the question is about why the balance shifts. Is it the status of English, its utilitarian, instrumental value that affects the balance? There is evidence in Sharp *et al.*'s attitude tests that English was seen in an increasingly pragmatic, utilitarian manner. Are television, schooling, youth culture, employment and Welsh culture explanations of the movement?

TABLE 5. *Age and Average Attitude to English (Scores*)*

Welsh-speaking population density of neighbourhood	10/11 Years	11/12 Years	14/15 Years
68–81% Welsh	5.87	5.25	4.81
48–55% Welsh	5.66	5.16	4.92
3–26% Welsh	5.06	4.82	4.58
Children attending designated bilingual schools	6.75	6.43	5.76

* The lower the average score, the more favourable the attitude.
(Extracted from Sharp *et al.*, 1973)

Sharp *et al.*'s (1973) study stands out for the national sampling which provides sound generalization of results. In retrospect, it suffers from (a) the absence of multivariate analyses (e.g. to examine interactive effects between age, sex, ability, attainment, length of residence and socio-economic class on attitude); (b) the cross-sectional design which can note age differences between different groups, but cannot examine longitudinally the same pupils to seek explanations of how and why they change. Large-scale longitudinal studies require considerable funding, and funding bodies are rarely prepared, in recent years, to finance such large-scale research; (c) the absence of a theory or model of how attitude change is created (the research is closer to a survey than an experiment or an evaluation). However, the research was a pioneer study and innovative in its time.

There is also the weakness which runs through almost all inter-national attitude research. Attitude to bilingualism and biculturalism is ignored. The content of attitude to Welsh and attitude to English scales, in itself, may, through restricted choice of items or by reactive effects when pupils complete the tests, artificially create a picture of two separate attitudes. Operationally, it may be preferable to add statements about bilingualism. The use, value and nature of being bilingual could be represented by attitude statements such as "Speaking both English and Welsh is an advantage". A factor analysis of items from all three sections would then identify the existence of the multi-component structure of attitudes to languages. Grosjean (1985) argues that "many surveys are still done solely in terms of the two separate languages" (p. 470), showing that "what we know about bilingualism today is tainted — in part at least — by a monolingual fractional view of bilingualism" (p. 470).

E. Glyn Lewis (1975, 1981)

E. Glyn Lewis (1975, 1981) extended the age range findings of Jones (1949, 1950) and Sharp *et al.* (1973) literally and metaphorically. First, he found (1975) that age effects continued after school. Declining attitude to Welsh was shown by a comparison of school pupils (from Sharp *et al.*'s (1973) study) with a sample of 100 adults aged 20 to 30. During adolescence and the twenties, attitude to Welsh becomes less favourable and attitude to English more favourable. Second, Lewis (1975) makes a conceptual distinction between various components on his attitude to Welsh tests. These may be summarized as:

(a) *General Approval*, e.g. "I like speaking Welsh"
(b) *Commitment to Practice*, e.g. "I want to maintain Welsh to enable Wales to develop"
(c) *National Ethnic Tradition*, e.g. "We owe it to our forefathers to preserve Welsh"
(d) *Economic and Social Communication Importance*, e.g. "Welsh offers advantages in seeking good job opportunities"
(e) *Family and Local Considerations*, e.g. "Welsh is important in family life"
(f) *Personal, Ideological Considerations*, e.g. "Welsh provides a range of aesthetic experiences in literature".

The conceptual analysis is interesting in that it reduces a potentially insensitive global measure of attitude to Welsh to more realistic sub-dimensions. However, a preferable categorization is by factor analysis or cluster analysis or multi-dimensional scaling, which seeks to locate the sub-dimensions in the data rather than from the guesses of the researcher. Guesswork is risky because the researcher cannot know how the *respondents* subdivide the various components at a manifest or latent level.

Third, Lewis (1975) mentions the Achilles heel of attitude research: the discrepancy between what people say and what they do. Verbal behaviour, upon which many attitude tests rely, may be different from actual behaviour. Lewis shows that positive attitudes may be linked in a seemingly less than logical fashion with negative reported practices. People with a positive attitude may discourage their offspring experiencing Welsh language schools, television, radio and reading. However, the behaviour was reported behaviour and not observed behaviour.

E. Price-Jones (1982)

From the late 1940s to the 1980s, the well replicated finding is that attitude to Welsh declines with age. This is also the pattern with attitude to Irish (CILAR, 1975). Partly because different authors use different attitude scales, it is not possible to say whether, in the three decades, attitude has declined historically. Trends over time are not validly discernible.

From the late 1940s to the 1980s, Welsh attitude research was cross-sectional. Pupils of different ages were compared at one point in time. A preferable design may be to study the same children over a period of time. Such a longitudinal design is more helpful, though still problematic, in attributing cause and effect. The research previously considered found links and relationships with attitude to Welsh declining with age: language background, type of school attended, gender and attitude to English in particular. Each link could be part of an explanation for age trends. Attending a bilingual school may be one explanatory variable of less attitude decline with age. A cross-sectional design does not allow the inference of cause–effect on statistical grounds, although some authors will argue for causality on the basis of the results fitting a theory.

Research previously considered also tends not to consider either the relative or cumulative effect of variables such as language background, type of school attended, gender and attitude to English. Which has most and least influence on attitude age decline? What combinations are particularly influential, negatively or positively?

The small-scale research of Emrys Price-Jones (1982), further analysed in Baker (1985), is both longitudinal and examines combined effects of a variety of variables. Having found the usual decline of attitude to Welsh with age, further analysis (multiple regression and path analysis) showed that seven cultural activities appeared most related to that decline. Three of these were activities that had changed over the three years of the research. Between the ages of 10 and 13, a decline in attendance at Welsh Church or Chapel, a decline in reading Welsh language newspapers, comics, books and magazines and an increase in watching English TV were all related to age decline in attitude to Welsh. Four cultural activities, representing more customary, stable behaviour from age 10 to 13 were also linked to age decline in attitude: relatively less attendance at Welsh language religious services, less reading of Welsh printed matter, less use of Welsh records and cassettes and relatively greater watching of English language TV programmes. Welsh language TV did not appear to have any direct effect on attitude change, nor did language background.

The conclusion from the path analyses was that attendance at Welsh Church or Chapel was the variable most associated with attitude change. Those who attended Welsh services were relatively more likely to retain a favourable attitude to the Welsh language. Those who attended less frequently, never, or whose attendance decreased between 10 and 13 years, were relatively more likely to decline in attitude. A discussion of the results suggested that the active, participatory culture embodied in Welsh Church and Chapel life could be more influential than the passive, receptive culture of the mass media. Being involved in the Welsh-speaking community (e.g. participating in eisteddfodau) rather than restrictively experiencing the one-way communication of the media could be important in fostering and maintaining a favourable Welsh attitude.

Conclusion

Research on attitude to Welsh has moved on from the finding that a favourable attitude to Welsh declines with age, to seeking a variety of connections with such age decline (e.g. language background, type of schooling, attitude to English), and thence to seeking to locate more or less influential connections. Much more research is required on the causes of age decline. However, one strong effect may be the type of active, participatory culture in which pupils engage. Halting the age decline, therefore, may need cultural planning to ensure language survival.

Attitude to Gaelic and Irish: Public support and personal scepticism

Introduction

In Scotland, the 1981 Census reported the existence of 79,307 Gaelic speakers aged over 2. In the Western Isles the density of Gaelic bilinguals is high (79.5%) numbering some 23,447 people, with the concentration of Gaelic speakers in towns being low in density but significant in raw numbers (e.g. Glasgow with 9,076 bilinguals). Overall, Gaelic bilingualism in Scotland is found in only 1.6% of the population, and only about half of these bilinguals are literate in Gaelic.

In Ireland, the density and size of the Gaelic bilingual population has been shown to be problematic (Greene, 1981). The 1971 Census returned 28.3% of the Republic of Ireland population as speaking Irish. This figure was doubted partly because of the manner in which the Census questions were framed. A major research investigating the attitudes of Irish people to the Irish language at the same time as the 1971 Census found that, in reality, the percentage was close to 9.3% (Committee on Irish Language Attitudes Research, 1975, hereafter termed CILAR). The Census returned three million people as speaking Irish, the CILAR research less than 300,000. The Census figure appeared to represent attitude and not actual behaviour, support rather than speech. In both countries, attitude to the minority language is important in indicating survival prospects. Research from Scotland and Ireland has examined this survival issue.

Scotland

A major attitude survey regarding the place of Gaelic in Scotland was undertaken by MacKinnon in 1981. Commissioned by An Comann Gaidhealach, Inverness, the survey sought to assess opinion on the official recognition of Gaelic and its place in public life, education and the mass media. Four quota samples from the Western Isles, Skye and Lochalsh, other Highland regions and the Lowlands were taken, totalling 1,117 people aged 15 and over. Each person was interviewed in English, asked eighteen questions, and could respond in terms of agreement, disagreement or no feelings/no response.

On most of the major issues, MacKinnon (1981) found that between 40% and 50% of the total sample were positive towards Gaelic and the remainder neutral or negative, as shown in Table 6.

TABLE 6.

		% Agree	% Disagree
(i)	Gaelic language as important for Scotland as a whole	41.2	41.5
(ii)	More public money available to encourage Gaelic	45.9	38.0
(iii)	Gaelic allowed in dealing with public authorities	41.2	31.5
(iv)	Gaelic speakers appointed to public posts in Gaelic areas	43.0	13.3
(v)	Gaelic encouraged throughout Scotland as a whole	49.0	27.3
(vi)	More radio and TV programmes for Gaelic learners	47.3	19.4
(vii)	Gaelic used with English on public signs, notices and adverts	42.2	19.6

Set against the figure of 1.6% of the population in Scotland speaking Gaelic, the 40% to 50% support on each of these questions must be encouraging for the minority language. Two further results were even more positive. First, on being asked, "Do you think that Gaelic should be officially recognized in Scotland?", 54.2% agreed compared with 27.0% disagreeing. A marginal majority say they favour the kind of official status partly given to Welsh in the Welsh Language Act of 1967 and to Gaelic and Welsh in the 1982 Nationality Act. Second, the most optimistic result came in response to "Should children in any part of Scotland be able to learn Gaelic at school if they or their parents want it?" Seventy per cent of people agreed; only 1.5% disagreed. There exists a minor ambiguity in the question (the use of "or" creates two questions, one about parents, the other about pupils, with the option of pupils and parents in joint consent logically ignored). However, a two-thirds majority is clearly in support of Gaelic in education as a bilingual alternative to mainstream monoglot English education.

These results have an underlying theme. Each attitude concerns relative impersonality. Gaelic is portrayed in general terms, Gaelic for the general population rather than for "me". Compare question (i) in the interview schedule in Table 6 with an alternative not presented. Question (i) asked "Do you think that the Gaelic language is important for the Scottish people as a whole?" An alternative or complementary question could have been "Do you think it is important for you to learn/speak Gaelic?" The first question is generalized; the second is personalized. From a Scottish Health survey, a generalized "Should teachers have regular chest X-rays?" produced a 95% agreement. A personalized "Should you have regular chest X-rays?" produced only 55% agreement. Therefore, the danger is to assume that there is personal commitment to Gaelic. In reality, the results may be closer to the "good for other people so long as it doesn't affect me" attitude to minority language. Permitted rather than committed.

Two results lend support to this argument. First, on being asked "Would you yourself welcome more opportunities for adult education in Gaelic?", only 24.4% answered "yes", 42.1% responding "no". This contrasts significantly with the 40% to 50% positive responses to the generalized questions. Second, MacKinnon (1981) asked an open question at the end of the interview. "If Gaelic became more noticeable in everyday life in what way would this affect you?" Although, as interviewers of politicians are aware, hypothetical questions produce fanciful answers, a content analysis of answers is revealing.

Category of Response	%
Antipathetic	14.8
Indifferent	37.2
Supportive	23.4
Would learn Gaelic	10.8
No response	13.8

(Analysis weighted by geographical area)

The same kind of pattern is found as with the adult education question, although not so strongly. Fifty-two per cent are negative, 34% are more positive.

MacKinnon's (1981) results initially look encouraging for attitude to Gaelic in Scotland. This is especially so given the Census figure of 1.6%

of people in Scotland actually speaking the language. The generalized form of the questions and possible impersonalization of response adds a caution to this initial conclusion. There is also a second caution. The phrasing of the questions is, unfortunately, not without error. Almost all the items are potentially leading questions. That is, there is a hint in the phrasing of the questions as to a possible preferred answer. "Do you think that the Gaelic language is important for the Scottish people as a whole?" is expressed only in the positive. A clue is given in the word "important". It may suggest the "desired" answer. A more correct phrasing would be, "Do you think that the Gaelic language is *important or unimportant* for the Scottish people as a whole?" Adding "unimportant" as well as "important" obtains a balance. Nine of the 13 "attitude" (as distinct from factual) questions have this inbuilt bias. Along with this, there are two other response biases in the questionnaire. First, the respondent may pick up what were "desirable" answers in terms of the intention of the exercise, type of questions, interviewer and order of questions. Respondents are prone to give socially desired answers, placing themselves in a favoured light or pleasing the interviewer. Second, the acquiescent response bias results in people marginally but significantly preferring to "agree" than "disagree". A bias towards "agreeing" would favour favourability in attitude to Gaelic.

The leading questions, the socially desirable and acquiescent response biases each separately and cumulatively point to the possibility of the favourability to Gaelic being a little overstated in the results. Each bias tends to increase slightly the chances of more positive, encouraging findings. If the difference between expressed attitude and actual behaviour is added, then further caution must be expressed.

Nevertheless, the survey is important, innovative and informative. It was undertaken at a national level and provides valuable evidence to combat guesses, prejudices, innuendos, fabrications and ignorance. MacKinnon (1981:66) asserts that:

"In the debate between individuals, organizations and public bodies it is important that there should be some body of factual data obtained in an objective and scientific manner to which such debate might refer. Too often it has been the case that the tenor of both non-official and governmental voices on issues affecting Gaelic has been in terms of assertions, assumptions and anecdotal impressions".

MacKinnon's (1981, 1984a) contribution to the Gaelic debate is significant. However, the survey evidence must be treated with caution.

Given a cautious inspection of the results, the concluding possibility appears to favour the attitude to Gaelic being more favourable than the 1.6% of the population speaking Gaelic might predict. Attitude to Gaelic seems to be more positive than use of Gaelic. The problem may be the transformation of attitude into action.

Ireland

Introduction

From Southern Ireland comes a very large-scale and detailed attitude survey. After a 5-year monumental study, the Committee on Irish Language Attitudes Research (CILAR) published a voluminous 478-page report (1975). This investigation of attitude to the Irish language is probably unique in terms of its breadth and depth of research. Joshua Fishman (1975) described it as "the best country study of a language that I've read ... the most thorough and the most voluminous" (quoted in J. Edwards, 1984b). With some forty staff, great technical care in sampling and attitude scaling and an enormously detailed analysis, the research symbolizes the emphasis that those concerned with minority languages place on attitudes.

The terms of reference were to report on (1) current attitudes towards the Irish language and towards efforts to restore it as a general means of communication; (2) the extent to which the public would support policy development aimed at restoring Irish.

Sampling

A stratified random sample of the adult population formed the major research group. Approximately 13 adults in every 10,000 of the population were randomly selected for interview. One in five of those chosen were either incapable of responding, could not be traced or refused to be interviewed. The results from this sample are based on 2,443 people. In addition, special groups were studied in more depth. Important among these groups was a stratified random sample of people living in the Gaeltacht. (The Gaeltacht are areas defined by the Irish Government in 1956 as officially Irish-speaking.) Gaeltacht areas contain approximately 3% of the Irish population, but contain relatively high population densities of Irish-speaking people. Other groups studied were secondary school pupils, teachers and the Civil Service personnel in Dublin. The consideration of pupils and teachers as special groups symbolizes the customary belief that education is a strong agency for minority language transmission.

The inclusion of the Civil Servants was based on Civil Service entry (until 1974) being dependent on Irish language proficiency tests. However, as the CILAR report (1975) found, "Even in the designated Irish-usage sections the majority of Civil Servants, generally speaking, rarely if ever *spoke* Irish in those sections during work hours, either currently or in the past" (p. 196).

Factor analyses

Seventy individual attitude items were included on the interview schedule. Examples of such statements are:

(Q3)   "All children should be required to learn Irish as a subject".
(Q37) "Using the Irish language more would make Ireland more independent of England".
(Q57) "People who know Irish well have a better chance to get good jobs and promotion".

Responses were requested on a five point scale:

Strongly Agree	Mildly Agree	No Opinion	Mildly Disagree	Strongly Disagree

Since individual questions may be inconsistently answered by a person and not be very reliable in accurately measuring attitudes, factor analysis was used. This reduces the initial pool of attitude items to categories or groups of more reliable items. Responses from the national sample yielded six factors. That is, the statistical analysis of 2,443 responses suggested that people's attitude to Irish falls into six latent, underlying dimensions.

Factor One was termed "Irish as a Symbol of Ethnic or National Identity". The highest loading item on this dimension was the statement "Ireland would not really be Ireland without its Irish-speaking people". Two-thirds of the population agreed with this statement; one third disagreed. Included also on this factor were items relating to public support for Irish to guarantee its transmission (e.g. "The Government should spend more money on improving methods of teaching Irish").

Factor Two was labelled "Attitude to Irish in the Schools". Items included in this factor included "Children doing subjects through Irish don't do as well at school as those doing them through English" and "Most children resent having to learn Irish". Sixty per cent agreed with the first statement; 66% agreed with the second statement. Factors one and two seem paradoxical. On Factor one, 68% of people agreed with the general statement "All children should be required to learn Irish as a subject in school". On Factor two, responses to specific practices in the use of Irish in school reveal apparently opposite attitudes to Factor one.

Factor Three concerned personal commitment to the use of Irish (e.g. "I will sometimes speak Irish if spoken to in Irish").

Factor Four was called "Beliefs about the Viability of Irish". Items loading highly on this factor included "If nothing is done to prevent it, Irish will disappear in a generation or two" and "Most people just don't care one way or the other about Irish". Seventy-one per cent agreed with the first statement; 80% agreed with the second statement. As with Factor two, Factor four needs contrasting with the positive general attitude of Factor one. The majority of the population are negative about the eventual fate of the Irish language. Serious doubts are expressed by about half to three-quarters (depending on individual statements) of the sample. These doubts concern Gaeltacht areas dying out, the language and culture attached to Irish as being too old-fashioned, and the negative effects of being in the European Economic Community. Irish is perceived as being the badge of backwardness, not as the placard of prestige. For many, should the Gaeltacht areas die, the language will die also, indicating that many feel the fate of Irish depends on its survival in a separate, designated speech community. This reflects the arguments about a designated heartland area for the Welsh language (Y Fro Gymraeg) considered by Baker (1985).

Factors Five and Six in themselves represent the paradox of support and pessimism, general concern and personal non-commitment. *Factor Five* was labelled "Attitude towards the Gaeltacht", and revealed public support for the Gaeltacht. The majority opinion was that the Government should provide more employment, more training, more self-determination and not close small schools in the Gaeltacht. *Factor Six*, in contrast, reflects an opposite attitude. The majority opinion was apathy towards an irrelevant language. Seventy-nine per cent agreed with the statement "Irish is less useful than any continental language". The same percentage agreed that most people do not care about the fate of the language.

The underlying paradox of the results is well portrayed by CILAR (1975:24):

"The average individual, for instance, in the national population feels rather strongly that the Irish language is necessary to our ethnic and cultural integrity, and supports the efforts to ensure the transmission of the language. At the same time, under present policies and progress, he is not really convinced that we can ensure its transmission. He has rather negative views about the way Irish has been taught in school and has a rather low or 'lukewarm' commitment to its use, although in the latter case the average person has not sufficient ability in the language to converse freely in it. On the other hand he strongly supports nearly all Government efforts to help the Gaeltacht, but at the same time feels that the language is not very suitable for business life".

Irish tends to be given attitudinal support as a symbol of culture, heritage and identity. Yet Irish people are pessimistic about the way it is taught in school, and are against compulsion or preferential treatment associated with the language. They want support for the Gaeltacht as an isolated community but see Irish as an old-fashioned and decaying language in the wider European community. The population is not committed at a personal level of restoration of the language but favours its retention in school. It is desirable that children know Irish even though they are unlikely to use it in public and private adult life. Does this mean that Irish people in general regard schools as important in language maintenance, but do not perceive schools as willing or able to be the only or major source of language restoration?

Surveys date quickly. Ten years after the CILAR Report, Institiúid Teangeolaíochta Éireann, with a smaller questionnaire and smaller sample (N = 791), ran a parallel survey (Ó Riagáin & Ó Gliasáin, 1984). In that decade, the shift has been towards more favourable attitudes. This may be partly explained by the removal of compulsory Irish for examination purposes. On questions relating to Irish as an ethnic symbol and on public support for Irish, attitudes which were previously favourable have become even more favourable. For example, reactions to "Without Irish, Ireland would certainly lose its identity as a separate culture" rose from 56% to 66% agreement. Similarly, there is increased public support for the teaching of Irish in schools, with a possible reversal from 1973 to 1983 in the perceived effects of Irish immersion education. In 1973, 60% agreed with the statement "Children doing subjects through Irish don't do as well at school as those doing them through English". By 1983, this had reduced to 44% agreement.

Despite continued, even increased, favourability to Irish language education and Irish as a symbol of ethnic identity and of cultural value, the paradox remains and is even extended over the decade 1973–1983. As with Gaelic, Irish is permitted rather than committed. The negative side of the paradox is: a 3% increase in the numbers who think that Government revival attempts will fail, no change in the size of the majority who have doubts about the future viability of Irish, and a clear majority who prefer Irish taught as a subject only and do not want bilingual education for children. "Beliefs in the viability and utility of Irish continue to be generally pessimistic" (Ó Riagáin & Ó Gliasáin, 1984:32). Between 1973 and 1983, the paradox in Irish attitudes has not only continued, but appears to have been extended. Support is growing in attitude but not in active commitment and participation.

Conclusion

The attitude survey research from Scotland and Ireland appears to show the same pattern. There exist positive public attitudes but private scepticism. There exists interest in the survival of a minority language, but not in involvement. As a symbol of ethnic history, heritage and national culture, the languages are valued. As a tool of widespread personal communication, as a medium of mass education, the languages are less valued. Positive attitudes to a minority language are safe where left dormant as cognitive representations. When attitudes are related to personal action, the surveys suggest that there is apathy, pessimism, even antagonism. When the personal balance sheet includes employment, educational success and interpersonal communication, the credit of positive attitudes towards language as a cultural and ethnic symbol is diminished by the costs of perceived prior needs and motives. Goodwill stops when the personal pay-off is not great.

J. R. Edwards (1984c) gives the choice of summary. We can either say that people are linguistically pragmatic. Or we can take the wit of Ussher (1949) — "the Irish of course like their Irish, but they like it *dead*".

Attitude change

Introduction

The research from Wales, Scotland and Ireland reveals that surveys of attitudes towards minority languages symbolize the plight of minority languages. In each of the three countries, the indigenous language has declined significantly in the last century. Attitudes, in harmony with that trend, decline with age and reveal a distance between public and personal, symbolic and pragmatic attitudes.

Yet, at the same time, each country has produced research which provides some glimmer of optimism. In Wales, attitudes are favourable when there is immersion in the indigenous culture. In Scotland, 70% of respondents thought that Gaelic should be taught at school anywhere in Scotland if parents desired it. Almost the same percentage in Ireland thought that Irish should be compulsory in schools. In Ireland, there was majority support for language zoning in the Gaeltacht. This raises the question about whether or not attitude change is possible in a minority language context. What are the possibilities of attitudes becoming more favourable to private usage, interpersonal communication, bilingual education or whatever mechanism or support function exists to further a minority language?

In this section, the intention is not to examine specifically how age decline, bilingual education or language zoning may be treated to foster minority languages. These are considered in Baker (1985) and elsewhere in this book. Rather, the intention is to extract from the great variety of psychological theories of how attitude change occurs, ideas that may be considered viable and important in minority language survival and maintenance.

Attitude functions

Katz (1960) provides four functions for an individual's attitudes. The four functions have important implications for attitude change.

1. The utilitarian or instrumental function. Attitudes may change when there is some reward. Acquisition of a minority language, using and maintaining a language or acquiring a positive attitude to that language may depend on gaining reward and avoiding punishment.

For example, the CILAR (1975) research showed that approximately half the national sample believed that "there is too much punishment associated with Irish in schools" (factor two). In Wales, the "Welsh Not" was a very severe method of attitude change. Any child, during much of the nineteenth century, heard using Welsh in school was required to wear a wooden halter around his or her neck. When another child was heard speaking Welsh, the halter was transferred to that child. At the end of the school day, whoever was wearing the halter was beaten. Rewards in school for speaking a minority language may be more subtle: praise and encouragement from the teacher, more attention, more eye-contact, more interaction with the teacher. A language learnt in school needs encouragement and reinforcement outside. In Wales, Yr Urdd, the Welsh League of Youth, exists to foster a wide range of popular and traditional cultural activities through the medium of Welsh. Having left school, adults need rewards to use a minority language, employment prospects which utilize or allow minority language usage. For minority language speech events to become more frequent, some tangible, social or individual reward system needs ideally to exist. Minority language television, discos, pop music, novels, papers, concerts, for example, all provide the stage upon which the prestige and status of a language is viewed and acted out. Such status and prestige supply and control the rewards and reinforcement for speaking a minority language. Where everyday events of perceived high status are almost entirely in the majority language, there is little hope of attitude change. Attitude change can be made more probable when rewards can be gained and punishment avoided for speaking a minority language. Such punishment may be latent and barely obvious: the raising of a friend's eyelids in speaking Irish in public; being given less attention in shops when speaking Gaelic in Scotland; speaking Welsh when the disco music is North American and English. Providing appropriate rewards for minority language activity depends on identifying what is perceived by the pupil or the employee as a reward. Praise for speaking a second language may work well with young children, but have the opposite effects to that intended if delivered by a teacher to a delinquent older pupil.

2. *The ego defensive function.* Basic inner security is essential for psychological health. People who hold attitudes which lead to insecurity, embarrassment and anxiety are likely to change their attitudes to achieve greater security and less anxiety. Speaking a minority language in a majority environment may lead to such anxiety. Being a peripheral member of a group, not sharing the common threads of identity of a group, lacking some of the status attributes of a reference group may lead to attitude and behavioural change. Majority group members may defend their egos by denigrating a minority language. Fearing minority language groups being given privileges or greater worth, majority groups may hold negative attitudes towards such minorities to enhance their own self-worth and distinctiveness. Attitude change strategies therefore need to ensure ego defence mechanisms are either enhanced (e.g. by adding to self-esteem) or are not threatened nor attacked. Threats need to be removed, or catharsis needs to occur, or an individual needs to develop more self-insight (Katz, 1960).

3. Value-expressive function. Katz (1960) suggested that attitudes are expressed and activated when they are congruent with personal values and the self-concept. Those who value Welsh cultural forms or who regard themselves as being very Welsh, whose core self-identity is Welsh rather than English, may express attitudes logically emanating from such values. For minority language attitudes to become more favourable, it is evident that deep-rooted personality characteristics need to be considered (Herman, 1968). The psychological notion of self-concept, the picture we hold of ourself, may be a powerful governor of attitude change. When, for example, self-concept in adolescence moves towards conformity with peer group identity, the peer group may become an important determinant of change towards, or away from, minority language and cultural identification. If social comparison occurs with majority cultural forms (e.g. the Anglo-American pop culture), then self-concept and attitudes may change accordingly. If the social comparison process occurs with indigenous cultural forms, minority language and culture may be more open to positive attitude change.

Attitudes do not exist in a vacuum. They are part of an individual's whole psychological functioning (Bain & Yu, 1984). An individual with certain personality characteristics may be more or less open to attitude change.

4. Knowledge function. As expressed when considering attitude theory earlier in the chapter, an attitude is said to have a cognitive or knowledge component. Attitudes facilitate understanding of people and events. Katz (1960) contended that attitudes are more susceptible to change when the knowledge function is known and understood. For example, adolescents for whom knowledge of Anglo and American pop music is necessary in order to gain peer status or to conform to group norms, will be likely to have, or change to, attitudes congruent with pop culture and their peer group.

Knowledge of minority or majority culture, social organization, politics and education, for example, can affect attitude. In this sense knowledge precedes attitude, and helps explain attitude. Knowledge that participating in a Welsh male voice choir, a Scottish dance party, or in Irish folk music is invigorating, rewarding and enjoyable helps form or change an attitude.

Classical conditioning

Attitudes towards stimuli may become more favourable if they are associated with pleasant events. This is the essence of Pavlovian or classical conditioning. A simple experiment will illustrate. In Staats & Staats' (1985) study, positive words such as *beauty*, *sweet* and *gift*, were presented simultaneously with one group of male names (e.g. Jack, Tom, Bill). When more negative words such as *bitter*, *ugly* and *sad* were presented with a different set of male names, the first condition resulted in a positive attitude towards the male names, the second condition in a decrease in positive attitude. Ryan's (1979) research suggested that when children of bilingual parents observe the contexts that accompany use of their second language, such children form negative and positive attitudes towards that language. If the child perceives the contexts as having pleasant enjoyable properties, favourable attitudes may develop towards that second language. For instance, parents taking their children to an enjoyable Welsh-speaking chapel are conditioning attitudes to Welsh by association of speaking Welsh with a pleasurable context. One reason among many why a positive attitude to Welsh declines with age may be due to children perceiving that certain Welsh-speaking contexts are not pleasurable, or that English-speaking contexts are more pleasurable. Discos, football, pop music and videos provided potentially pleasurable contexts for adolescents which are often English rather than Welsh in language. Such contexts may condition attitudes to second or minority languages.

Reinforcement and operant conditioning

Attitudes may be made more favourable by the suitable arrangement of reward. This is the essence of operant conditioning. Insko (1965) found that students who were reinforced with "good" when they agreed or disagreed with certain statements of attitude, changed their attitudes over a one-week period in the expected direction. Thus maintaining favourable attitudes to minority languages or changing attitudes in a favourable direction may require constant reinforcement. Such reinforcement cannot be arranged in the precisely pre-determined manner of operant conditioning experiments with both human and non-human subjects. Nevertheless, institutional and individual reinforcement may be required for favourable language attitudes to be fostered. Children soon learn the positive and negative rewards, outcomes and reinforcements attached to speaking a minority language. Such reinforcements may be non-verbal (e.g. raised eyebrows, smiles) or verbal (e.g. praise, criticism), overt (e.g. congratulated for speaking a second language) or covert (less eye contact from other members in a peer group), individually presented (e.g. reinforcement from a teacher) or expressed publicly (e.g. attributions about Welsh speakers conveyed in the mass media).

Favourable attitudes may be fostered by the experience of success. Perceived success may be critical in establishing positive attitudes. Success of a learner to communicate in an accepted way in a minority language, failure in eisteddfodau competitions, positive or negative experiences in attempted attachment to minority language groups may each affect attitudes.

The reinforcement of attitudes need not be social and external. Self-reinforcement is an important idea especially, but not exclusively, in analysing resistance to change. Children's self-control over their aggression is an example of how early parental reinforcement of self-control eventually becomes self-reinforcing. Most children achieve self-control without the need for external reinforcement. In the same way, attitudes can change from external reinforcement to self-reinforcement. Encouragement for a favourable attitude to Irish or Gaelic given early on may eventually become self-reinforcing, partly because such an attitude relates to ego identity, self-esteem and self-respect. Self-reinforcement is also an important concept in that it reveals that external reinforcement may have little or no effect on changing attitudes. Encouragement of a favourable attitude to Welsh may be not enough given self-reinforcement for holding a neutral or unfavourable attitude.

Human modelling

Imitation of someone else may be a powerful source of attitude change. Human models need to be highly regarded, respected, admired and credible in what they say and do. Imitating the attitudes of the model becomes positively reinforcing. The imitator attempts to take on some of the attributes of the favoured model, thus positively affecting feelings of status and worth. Models can range from parents, siblings, peers, teachers, to cultural and media figures.

Attitude may change as a result of the content of a model's speech, conversation or message. Unfortunately, research has failed to give consistent results, mainly due to the variety of variables involved and their interactive nature (Kahle, 1984; Cacioppo & Petty, 1982). Who is speaking may be more crucial. Triandis (1971) suggested that physical attractiveness, clothes, speech, expertise, age, race and nationality are some of the variables affecting how persuasive is the communicator. Models have to be perceived as having the appropriate status for their verbal communications to effect attitude change. Where the ingroup is a majority language group and the outgroup a minority language group, finding a model to maintain favourable minority language attitude may be difficult.

Consistency

A variety of social–psychological theories (e.g. Heider, 1958: McGuire, 1981; Festinger, 1957) suggest that attitudes change when an individual has to strive to achieve consistency and an internal logic in attitude systems. For example, it would be difficult for a person to hold a positive attitude to the Welsh language and a negative attitude about bilingual education in Wales. Festinger's (1957) Cognitive Dissonance Theory assumes that our attitudes must be in harmony, but when discordant or cacophonous attitudes arrive, attempts will be made to harmonize and seek concert.

An original research in support of cognitive dissonance theory is rather striking. Festinger & Carlsmith (1959) promised either one dollar or twenty dollars to subjects who would deceive another subject by describing a very boring task as enjoyable, fun, interesting, intriguing and exciting. Cognitive dissonance theory predicts that attitude change will be greater when people are induced to behave inconsistently with their attitudes with the minimum of inducement. That is, being given twenty dollars (in the mid 1950s) may be seeming justification for lying. A one dollar reward is much less justification, hence there may be more dissonance. To reduce dissonance the subject may decide that the experimental task *was* fun. The results supported dissonance theory, in that after the experiment, subjects offered one dollar reported that they actually enjoyed the experiment more than did the twenty dollar group. Operant conditioning theory predicts the opposite. The higher the reward, the more the attitude change. In this situation, striving for consistency seemed to be more important than cash.

An important piece of research by Bourhis & Giles (1977) shows how cognitive dissonance may work in speech style and identity in Wales. Bourhis & Giles (1977) formed two groups of people from South Wales: those who valued their Welsh identity and those who did not. When engaged in conversation with an English person, the Welsh people who valued their national identity emphasized their less prestigious Welsh accents when the English person derogated Wales. In contrast, Welsh people who did not value their Welsh identity responded to the English person's derogation by attenuating their Welsh accents. In each case, the two groups appeared to obtain cognitive consistency by changing their speech style. The first group did this by becoming more Welsh, thus maintaining harmony with their value of being Welsh; the second group by becoming less Welsh, identifying more with the English speaker and thus harmonizing with their lesser valuation of being Welsh.

Attitude change may be induced when discrepant components exist in an attitude. Attitude to a minority language may be positively engendered by the neighbourhood, negatively affected by Anglo pop culture or English-language mass media. An individual, in striving for inner consistency, may have to reject one in favour of another. Welsh chapel is spurned; English pop music and discos replace religion. A school where there are cliques of pupils with different language attitudes (e.g. anti-Welsh and anti-English), may require a bilingual and bicultural pupil to develop a partisan attitude. Alternatively, reminding people of their indigenous cultural and language heritage may induce the inconsistency in attitudes which in turn spawns change favourable to an indigenous language.

Conclusion

Attitude changes both as a function of individual needs and motives and as a function of social situations. The need for success, reward and cognitive consistency interacts with the effect of pleasurable contexts and environments and valued models. Attitudes can change through activity which is self-directed and purposefully planned, as well as through the need for security and status within a group and through societal demands. Attitude change is essentially a cognitive activity, yet is formulated through social activity.

Final conclusions

The chapter has attempted to spotlight the nature of attitudes and of attitude change, particularly with regard to minority languages in a bilingual setting. Two particular components reveal the present and the possible. At present, attitudes to Welsh, Gaelic and Irish evidence pessimism. In Wales, a decline in favourability to Welsh occurs with age. In

Scotland and Ireland, there appears a wide gap in favourability to Gaelic and Irish between general public support and personal commitment. The present situation for Wales, Scotland and Ireland seems clouded with pessmism, although a few silver linings may be present. Much theory and research in social psychology has indicated the plausibility and possibility of attitude change. While the educational and social engineering of favourable attitudes cannot be achieved as easily as in psychological experiments, the basis in attitude change theories does exist to consider ways in which age trends may be halted or reversed. Attitude change theory suggests possible paths to translate concern for minority languages into commitment, permission for existence into participation, attitudes into action. Unless greater consideration is given to bilingualism and attitude change, for the Celts at least, the evidence from attitude surveys is pessimistic. To adapt Ussher's half truth, the Celts of course like their heritage language, but they like it dead. In attitude change lies one hope for language life and resurrection.

6 Bilingualism and Motivation

Introduction

There are various ways in which people explain what drives and shapes human activity. For the ancient Greeks, the will and the power of gods was thought to promote and explain behaviour. Primitive tribes may explain and understand the presence of disease, harvest or rain by the enactment of rituals. Unless these rituals are religiously and punctiliously performed, disaster may occur and evil spirits may not be overcome. Christians believe that the Holy Spirit leads and guides behaviour. A chance meeting where help is given may be thought to have been promoted by divine guidance. Some psychologists on the other hand tend to assume that behaviour is promoted by an inner force (Peters, 1958). The description of a person's inner drives, needs and motives is one way in psychology that helps explain "why" a certain piece of behaviour occurs (M.D. Vernon, 1969). Needs and motives are purely hypothetical constructs inferred from the energy, direction and persistence of behaviour. Certain actions are repeated time after time, people strive after certain goals repeatedly. To explain such recurrent actions, an energy is postulated, and termed a drive, need or motive. These terms also help account for the variations in the behaviour of a person at different times and individual differences between people in the goals they pursue (Argyle, 1964).

The motivation to want to become, or to continue to be, bilingual is an important idea in bilingual theory. It helps explain *why* a person may wish to learn a second or further language. What is the carrot that encourages such learning? Or what is the stick that drives language learning? What are the motives and needs that lead a person to stay bilingual or reject one language in favour of another?

While there exists some overlap between the psychological concepts of attitude and motivation, they have been kept apart by two relatively independent traditions in psychological theory. Before considering the motivations for becoming, staying or rejecting being bilingual, a brief consideration of aspects of the theory of motivation that underlies most of such bilingual research will provide the necessary foundation to consider bilingualism and motivation.

The definition of terms

Three relevant terms tend to be used interchangeably in ordinary speech: drives, needs and motives. Psychologists tend to make more defined and specialized usage of these terms. *Drives* normally refer to innate, automatic physiological forces, especially in animals. People and animals have a hunger drive and a sex drive. A baby at birth has drives but no motives. At first the infant expresses a hunger drive by crying and sucking. Later, when an infant has learnt that food is pleasant, a hunger motive may co-exist with the hunger drive (McKeachie & Doyle, 1966).

Not all behaviours stem from physiological forces (Kagan, 1971). Wanting to become bilingual, working for the maintenance or restoration of minority culture, clearly is not a physiological drive. It is not innate, unconditioned or automatic. When the force or energy exists to behave in a directed or recurrent manner, and when there is no evidence of a drive, then a *motive* is postulated. A motive, like an attitude (see Chapter 5), is a hypothetical construct used to describe the stored potential or predisposition to behave in persistent fashion. Thus McClelland (1958) defines a motive as a relatively stable and enduring strength.

If the origin of a motive is not physiological, the origin would seem to be in cognitive processes. Kagan (1972), in this fashion, defines a motive as a "cognitive representation of a future goal that is desired" (p. 53). Unconscious motives would not seem to be excluded. Unconscious motives could still be regarded as having a cognitive basis, but without a person having awareness of the nature, even existence, of that cognition. When the goal is successfully to learn a minority language or to become bicultural, the motive may be known, thoughtful and introspectively understood by the person. Alternatively, the motive may be more hidden, implicit, and latent. In this case, a person is not particularly aware of the motive or motives that determine the learning of a second language.

Another theoretical distinction that needs to be made is between motives and motivation. A motive is a stored potential that may at certain times become activated or may lay dormant. *Motivation*, on the other hand, is the activation of that motive. When a motive that has lain dormant is triggered off and represents itself in goal-directed action, the temporary arousal of that motive is called motivation (Kagan, 1971). "Motive" refers to a relatively stable, static disposition; "motivation" to the ongoing dynamic energy gained from activation of a motive.

An example will illustrate this important distinction between motive and motivation. A person may have acquired a stored predisposition to identify with a minority language group of people. This may be seen as a relatively enduring characteristic of an individual and as a dimension along which people vary in terms of their goal to identify or not identify with a minority language group. When that motive is triggered off, the ongoing energy that realizes itself in actual behaviour is termed motivation. When an individual has the activated urge to attend, for example, adult language classes or engage in some expression of minority culture, some defined motivation may describe the event.

What changes a motive into motivation? Kagan (1971) suggests six different causes:

1. The *strength* of the latent motive. People vary in their desire or urge to learn a second language. The Motivation Intensity Scales (see below) along with other tests of motivation are usually constructed to measure varying strengths of motives.

2. The likelihood that a *situation* will activate a motive. Context is very important in triggering off a motive, and tends to be understated and relatively un-emphasized in the literature. Working daily in a bilingual environment is clearly a favourable context for a motive to act bilingually to become activated into motivation. The type of school a pupil attends, the language balance of the neighbourhood, the use of two languages in the nuclear and extended family, the relative dominance of majority languages in the mass media, the peer or reference group to which a person is affiliated, the work environment, social and leisure activities each may constrain or promote the activation of motives related to bilingual activity. Contexts may also work in a negative, constraining fashion, stopping a motive becoming activated. A motive to learn a second language may be kept latent by the peer group scorning such a motive, for example.

3. The degree to which strong *feelings* accompany the motive. Just as attitudes may have an affective component, so with motives. When pleasure and enjoyment or satisfaction and gratification are likely to result from the activation of a motive, motivation is more probable. Enjoying an adult language class, gaining pleasure from interacting with close neighbours or work colleagues in their preferred language and being happy in immersion education are each examples of affect accompanying

and promoting motivation. In a contrary fashion, strong negative feelings may accompany a motive. This is separately considered below (6).

4. The availability of *actions* that can gratify the motive. A motive cannot become motivation unless the behavioural repertoire exists to support the realization of the motive. The motive to learn a second language needs the person to join a group, or diligently work with tapes and books at home. The motive to be accepted by a minority group requires the social skills and interpersonal actions to support that motive.

5. The *expectancy of success*fully obtaining the goal. Learning a minority language or engaging in a fresh cultural form (e.g. participating in eisteddfod competitions) is aided when the person believes that a positive outcome is probable. When people believe their aptitude for languages or ability is rather restricted, the motive to learn a second language may be kept dormant.

6. The *freedom from anxiety* and conflict that can prevent action. A motive and motivation can be blocked by fear of failure. Whether such fear is unrealistic or not, one strong personal reason for not becoming bilingual or bicultural lies in fear of failure; fear of not being accepted by the minority language group, fear of failing to be able to hold a sensible conversation in a second language, fear of being taunted and spurned by the majority group, or anxiety of change and the unknown. This idea leads to a descriptive distinction between approach and avoidance motivation. Two people may have the same strength of motive to become bilingual. However, each may show different reactions when the motive is aroused. One person may have the actions, exist in an encouraging context and expect success. The motive in this case becomes approach motivation. Another person may lack the behavioural repertoire, be placed in a non-encouraging context, and expect failure. The motive in this second case translates into avoidance motivation.

Three final comments need to be made. First, psychologists have tended to use the term "*need*" as an umbrella word, to include both drive and motive. Thus Maslow (1954) talks of physiological needs (drives) and cognitive-based needs (motives). Second, behaviour is rarely prompted by a single motive. In reality, actions often stem from a variety of interacting motives. For example, attending a bilingual school may be from multiple motives: for academic achievement, friendship, security, status and self-enhancement. The simplicity of stating motives often belies the complexity of real motivation. Third, there are many other psychological explanations of the origins of behaviour: psychoanalytical, behaviourist and physiological for example. These are not discussed here, as the relevant mainstream tradition in bilingual research has centred on motivational theory.

The measurement of motivation

In everyday situations, people ascribe motives to actions. Teachers describe pupils as "highly motivated" or "unmotivated". Doctors may describe their clients as having the will to get better. Such descriptions may imply measurement. Motives exist on dimensions, with the strength of the motive being the most obvious, but not the only, variable to measure.

There are a variety of ways in which motives may be measured:

1. In-depth interviews.   An in-depth interview may be used to assess the dominant conscious motives of people, and sometimes, by inference, their unconscious motives. A person may be interviewed as to why they chose to learn Welsh, or why they do not send their children to a bilingual school.

2. Observation.   Observation of the behaviour of young children may reveal needs and motives. Such observation may provide evidence in vigorous prose or, if systematically recorded, provides data which are quantitative and capable of statistical analysis (Croll, 1986). A child may be observed using two languages in a play group, such that inner motives may be revealed.

3. Repertory Grids.   Repertory Grids attempt to analyse a person in their own terms (Kelly, 1955; Bannister & Fransella, 1971). The Repertory Grid method provides details about an individual's constructs, which are not equivalent to motives, but are close enough to merit consideration. Also, since the remainder of the chapter deals with nomothetic approaches (comparing people on the same dimensions), this idiographic approach (analysing an individual as an unique entity) will be developed in terms of an example relevant to bilingualism.

Supposing a researcher was interested in an individual's constructs (and, by inference, motives) regarding bilingualism and biculturalism in Wales. The following elements may be presented to a person, each written on a small card:

(a) Eisteddfodau (Welsh cultural festivals)
(b) Designated Bilingual Schools
(c) Welsh Language
(d) English Language
(e) Sianel Pedwar (S4C) (the partly Welsh TV channel)
(f) Plaid Cymru (Welsh Nationalist Party)
(g) Welsh Office
(h) Gareth Edwards (Welsh rugby hero)
(i) Mrs. Thatcher (British Prime Minister)
(j) Yr Urdd (Welsh League of Youth)
(k) Ysgolion Meithrin (Welsh Pre-School Play Groups)
(l) B.B.C. (British Broadcasting Corporation)
(m) Daily Newspaper (named by person; all of which are in English)
(n) Papurau Bro (Community newspapers in Welsh)
(o) Manchester United (English football team)
(p) *Top of the Pops* (English TV pop music show)
(q) Parliament at Westminster, London
(r) Gwynedd people (who are mostly bilingual)
(s) Gwent people (who are mostly monolingual English)
(t) Welsh male voice choirs

A person is invited to select two cards which are, in an *important* way, regarded as similar by that person. That person is then questioned in order to elicit *why* the two elements are seen as similar. This reply forms the first construct. For example, a person may see Ysgolion Meithrin and Designated Bilingual Schools as similar, saying that each fosters the Welsh language in young children from English backgrounds. The testing moves on, with the person picking out a third card which is, in an *important* way, different from the other two. For example, the B.B.C. fosters English language development in children. The three cards are then returned to the pile, and the same process is repeated until the person begins to repeat the constructs previously given.

Each construct may be regarded as existing on a dimension or continuum, e.g.:

fosters the Welsh language in children .... fosters the English language in children

promotes Welsh culture .... indifferent to Welsh culture

supports Welsh nation .... uninterested in Wales

radical and aggressive .... peaceful and in favour of status quo

interesting .... boring

a waste of time and money ... worth keeping going at all costs

serious and worthwhile .... entertaining

pleasant .... unpleasant

killing the Welsh language .... keeping the Welsh language afloat

Having elicited constructs, the normal procedure is for the person to rate the elements on each of the constructs. This may be achieved by ticks and crosses (binary scale), a 5-point or 7-point rating scale or by ranking the elements in order of one end of each construct in turn. Thus a subset of elements and constructs may produce the following hypothetical and simplified grid.

	Eisteddfodau	Daily newspaper	Top of the Pops	Welsh male voice choirs	
promotes Welsh culture	√	x	x	√	indifferent to Welsh culture
supports Welsh nation	√	x	x	√	uninterested in Wales
killing the Welsh language	x	√	√	x	keeping language afloat
waste of time & money	x	x	√	x	worth keeping going
interesting	?	√	x	√	boring

Ticks refer to the left hand construct; crosses to the right hand construct; ? implies not sure, undecided or irrelevant

Personal constructs are not the same as motives, but the Repertory Grid technique does provide an interesting and flexible tool to analyse an individual in their own terms through their own language and perceptions. Motives need to be inferred from analyses of the resulting grid, hence the method is indirect.

4. Questionnaires and self-completion tests. By simple questions or statements, a number of people at one time may be tested. Such self-completion measures are similar to attitude scales. An example is Gardner & Lambert's (1972) Motivational Intensity Scale which attempts to measure strength of motivation with regard to a second language (French). Examples of items are:

(a) If French was not taught in this school, I would probably
  (i) not bother learning French at all
  (ii) try to obtain French lessons somewhere else
  (iii) pick up French in everyday situations
  (iv) none of these

(b) Compared to others in my French class, I think I:
  (i) do more studying than most of them
  (ii) do less studying than most of them
  (iii) study about as much as most of them

5. Projective techniques. Projective tests usually try to hide the intent of the test from the respondent. This is usually justified on the grounds that questionnaires, self-completion tests, repertory grids and responses in interviews are open to response tendencies which decrease the validity of the measure. For instance, the social desirability effect is a major source of invalidity. Social desirability concerns the conscious or unconscious tendency of people to give answers which make them appear "better" or more favourable than is real. There is a tendency to give oneself a "halo" or to give oneself the characteristics that gain most approval in a peer group or in society in general. Projective tests attempt to overcome this social desirability problem.

Projective tests usually start with an ambiguous stimulus: a picture, an inkblot, an ambiguous sentence or story. In response, the testee is expected to tell, write or complete the sentence or story. Believing that the response is to test imagination and creativity, a person may reveal in his or her story inner drives and motives, unconscious urges and wishes. The person projects into the story inner thoughts and feelings, dreaming out loud. It is hoped that people will forget their inhibitions and defence mechanisms and give an X-ray picture of their motivations. This idea originates with the Freudian idea of "projection", and has been most used in the Thematic Apperception Test and the measurement of need for achievement (Kline, 1983).

In bilingual research, a picture may be presented showing, for example, the outside of a bilingual school with an individual (of indeterminate gender) looking towards the school. Ideally the person in the picture should be such that the respondent can identify with that person (e.g. should be of the same age group). In writing a creative and free-flowing story, a person may reveal his or her inner motives regarding bilingual education, positive or negative, simple or complex, strong or weak. Such motives may be consciously or unconsciously hidden from the researcher when answering a questionnaire.

Problems and limitations of motive measurement

Motivational measurement needs firstly to be reliable over time; secondly, internally consistent within a test, that is, self-consistent; and thirdly, valid. Of the three, the most important is validity. Validity occurs in terms of degree, and requires a test to really measure what it claims to measure. Validity may be tested by the ability of a scale to predict future bilingual behaviour. The Motivational Intensity Scale should predict who does well or less well in learning French as a second language, as well as who tries hard or not to learn French. Social desirability is one factor producing decreased validity; unreliability is another. Projective tests, for example, suffer from being somewhat internally inconsistent and relatively unreliable over time (P.E. Vernon, 1963).

As Kline (1983) has shown, the measurement of motives is far more primitive than the measurement of personality traits (e.g. extraversion and neuroticism). The best known of the tests of motivation is the EPPS (Edwards Personal Preference Schedule, 1959), which derives from Murray's (1938) theory of needs. The test lacks evidence that it usefully captures human motives; factor analytic evidence suggests that it does not. Also, the validity of the scales is in doubt (Baker, 1976; Kline, 1983), as is Murray's theory of needs. However, the tests of motivation which have been most used in bilingual research are much less primitive than the norm. Gardner & Smythe (1981) and Gardner (1985b) have produced evidence to show that measures of integrative and instrumental motivation (see below) have reasonable reliability as well as construct and factorial validity.

An overview of bilingualism and motivation

Most of the research on bilingualism and motivation has centred on two concepts: integrative and instrumental motivation. These will be considered in the next section. However, it is clear that the motives surrounding becoming and staying bilingual or allowing bilingualism to decay will be more and wider than integrative and instrumental motivation. Therefore this section briefly considers some of the hypothetical motives from motivational theory that would seem to be relevant to bilingualism.

Descriptive theories of motivation tend to have low status amongst psychologists (Kline, 1983). Thus Maslow's (1954) theory of motivation with its hierarchical structure of survival needs, security needs, social and status needs, autonomy and self-actualization needs, has intuitive appeal but little empirical foundation.

Maslow's (1954) hierarchical theory does, however, appear to make one important point with regard to bilingualism. Motivation to learn a second language, to maintain one's bilingual abilities, or motivation to reject a language previously spoken will differ on an individual basis due to the level reached in the hierarchy. Learning a second language in order to gain security and status within a peer group (e.g. in an immigrant situation) is unlikely to be preceded by learning a second language for self-actualization. This latter motive can only operate when prior needs have been mostly or fully satisfied. Teachers cannot expect children to be motivated to learn a second language for personal enjoyment and fulfilment if the child has prior needs; security and love, for example. The same point can be made at a societal level. A nation or ethnic minority concerned with physical survival is less likely to be interested in bilingualism for cultural enhancement. Fostering bilingualism may require prior identification of the level of needs at which an individual or group is presently located.

A separate general structural theory of motivation which has implications for bilingualism comes from McClelland (1961) and Atkinson (1958, 1964). In particular, their research, which has used and adapted projective techniques, has located the need for achievement and the affiliative motive as two central human motives.

The *affiliation motive* is the need for warm, close, friendly relationships. Learning a language may sometimes be partly or mainly caused by the need to have and maintain close friendships. The need to belong and to identify with close friends may be an important source of learning a second language when in adulthood. Wishing to preserve a minority language may also be based on affiliation needs, even at an unconscious level. When friendships operate through minority groups, such groups will be reinforced in their existence. When friendships evolve outside the minority group, language erosion may be more probable. Findling (1969) investigated the affiliation motive of Puerto-Ricans living in Spanish-speaking ghettos of New York. The sample comprised bilingual Puerto-Ricans who spoke Spanish with their family and friends, but spoke English at work. Findling (1969) proposed that this group's affiliative needs would be fulfilled in their home surroundings, but being an "outgroup" in white American surroundings they would feel deprived of affiliation with English speakers. In comparing Spanish and English responses to a Word Association Test, he found that affiliation motive scores were greater in English than Spanish.

The *need for achievement* has been linked with success at an individual level and at a societal level. Success in economic or interpersonal terms, reaching a standard of excellence, is related to need for achievement. So bilingualism may be related to this trait. Learning a language may be driven by success and achievement needs. Those who metaphorically and sometimes literally fight for minority language rights may be partly powered by an inner need for achieving. Need for affiliation and need for achievement have a separate research tradition to integrative and instrumental motivation, yet have a degree of overlap and relatedness. It is to these latter motivations that the chapter now turns.

Integrative and instrumental motivation

Definitions

Two motives have dominated discussion of motivation in language learning and bilingualism: integrative and instrumental motivation. The pioneering and dominating work of Gardner & Lambert (1972) introduced the terms to answer a simple question: "How is it that some people can learn a foreign language quickly and expertly while others given the same opportunities to learn, are utter failures?" (Gardner & Lambert, 1972, p. 1).

Placing emphasis on integrative and instrumental motives depends partly on their being an influence distinct from ability. While ability and aptitude both play a determining role in second language learning, various researches have found that motivation is an independent factor in such learning (Gardner & Lambert, 1959, 1972; Clement, Gardner & Smythe, 1977, 1980). Having the ability and aptitude without the motivation results in lesser achievement than having both aptitude and motivation.

If motivation is a crucial dimension in second language learning which causes individuals to succeed or fail, it is likely that such motivation is not the same for all. A variety of motives exists. Gardner & Lambert (1972) argued that diverse motives will tend to fall into two headings, instrumental and integrative. Instrumental motivation reflects utilitarian motives, being keen to succeed and get promotion in employment, for example. An instrumental orientation is characterized by "a desire to gain social recognition or economic advantages through knowledge of a foreign language" (Gardner & Lambert, 1972:14). The motivation is mostly self-oriented in a non-social, individualistic sense. It is conceptually close to need achievement and the idea of "extrinsic motivation", but has been conceived and analysed separately in research. Integrative motivation reflects personalized, interpersonal motives, for example, wanting to be liked and accepted by a group of people. Integrative motivation is conceptually similar to the affiliation motive, and has been defined as "a desire to be like representative members of the 'other language community" (Gardner & Lambert, 1972:14).

The integrative motivation is a concern to develop personal relationships with a group speaking another language, and this was originally thought by Gardner & Lambert (1972) to result in more effective motivation than instrumental motivation, because desired attachment to people may be more long-lasting. The motivation to become bilingual may need to be sustained as mastering a second language can be slow. An integrative motive in its original conception was thought to be a more sustaining motive than an instrumental one, due to the relative endurance of personal relationships and group attachments.

Measurement

Orientation

Gardner & Lambert (1972), in their original investigation, chose a simple questionnaire method of measuring the integrative and instrumental motivation dimensions. Pupils responded on a 7-point scale ("not my feeling at all" to "definitely my feeling") to the following statements concerning the reasons for learning French as a second language:

Integrative orientation

(i) It will help me to understand better the French people and their way of life.

(ii) It will enable me to gain good friends more easily among French-speaking people.

  (iii) It should enable me to begin to think and behave as French people do.
  (iv) It will allow me to meet and converse with more and varied people.

Instrumental orientation

  (i) I think it will some day be useful in getting a good job.
  (ii) One needs a good knowledge of at least one foreign language to merit social recognition.
  (iii) I feel that no one is really educated unless he is fluent in the French language.
  (iv) I need it in order to finish High School.

Motivational intensity

Gardner & Lambert (1972) used a second test of motivation. If integrative and instrumental motivation represents goal-directed behaviour, the measure of motivational intensity measures amount of effort and zeal. The Intensity scale contains six items, where a respondent chooses one from four possible responses. Two examples will illustrate:

(i) If French was not taught in this school, I would probably
  (a) not bother learning French at all
  (b) try to obtain lesson in French somewhere else
  (c) pick up French in everyday situations (i.e. read French books and newspapers, try to speak it when possible, and go to French movies)
  (d) none of these (explain)

(ii) Considering how I go about studying for French, I can honestly say that I:
  (a) do just enough work to get along
  (b) will pass on the basis of sheer luck or intelligence because I do very little work
  (c) really try to learn French
  (d) none of these (explain)

Evidence for the reliability and validity of this scale is provided by Gardner (1985b) and Gardner & Smythe (1981).

Research evidence

Early studies

Before the 1970s, the customary explanation for a pupil learning a second language was through ownership of ability and aptitude. If a child had the necessary intelligence and had a particular skill in picking up a second language, then bilingualism was a possibility. A significant change in the traditional explanation came as a result of research on motivation and language learning.

Most research starts in reality with an expectation, a positive rather than a neutral or null hypothesis. The research on Integrativeness and Instrumentality was no exception. Lambert (1977:23) tells the story.

"We saw many possible forms the student's orientation could take, two of which we looked at in some detail: an 'instrumental' outlook, reflecting the practical value and advantages of learning a new language, and an 'integrative' outlook, reflecting a sincere and personal interest in the people and culture represented by the other group. It was our hunch that an integrative orientation would sustain better the long-term motivation needed for the very demanding task of second-language learning."

The hunch was first tested by Gardner & Lambert (1959) who found that motivation was an important variable in second language learning. While the possibility existed that those with higher ability or greater aptitude for learning languages were the same pupils as the more highly motivated, a factor analysis of the data showed this not to be the case. Included in the variables entered into the factor analysis were achievement ratings by teachers, Carroll's Foreign Language Aptitude Battery, an Orientation Index which did not distinguish between integrative and instrumental reasons, and the Motivational Intensity Scale. Four groups of variables were located by the factor analysis. Factor one was labelled a linguistic *aptitude* factor, and factor two as a *motivation* factor particularly concerned with a desire to be valued by a language community. Both factors were significantly related to achievement. That is, aptitude and motivation were regarded as working relatively independently in producing achievement.

Furthermore, Gardner & Lambert (1959) concluded that "the integratively oriented students are generally more successful in acquiring French than those who are instrumentally oriented" (p. 271). Gordon (1980) also found that people who were integratively motivated tended to have stronger motives in second language learning than those instrumentally motivated. However, there are certain reservations to be made. *First*, learning a second language and the act of becoming bilingual may invoke increased integrative motivation (Strong, 1984). Integrative motivation may both be the cause and effect of becoming or staying bilingual. As will be seen in the final chapter, the evidence suggests that the most customary chronological order is integrative motivation affecting learning. *Second*, people who score highly on the integrative dimension may not necessarily be motivated to learn a second language or maintain their bilingualism. Integrative motivation may be directed at friendships, sociability or gregariousness without being focused on language learning or maintenance. *Third*, some research has shown that motives other than an integrative one promote the learning of a second language. Lukmani (1972) found that female school pupils in Bombay gave instrumental rather than integrative reasons for learning English. Gardner (1985a) notes two weaknesses in this conclusion: the measurement by Lukmani (1972) concerned orientation, which is not precisely the same as motivation; and a lack of statistical significance in the comparison of orientations. *Fourth*, the classification of reasons for learning a language into instrumental and integrative categories need not be straightforward (Oller, Hudson & Liu, 1977). For example, there is a difference between Burstall *et al.* (1974) and Lukmani (1972) who both include travelling abroad as an item in their measurement scales. The former authors regarded such travel as integrative, the latter author as instrumental. Factor analysis (e.g. Gardner & Smythe, 1975) does help a considerable amount in the clarification and classification of individual items on a scale. However, different groups of people from different contexts, different countries, may validly interpret the same item in different ways. Travelling abroad, for example, could be an integrative motive for one person or ethnic group, an instrumental motive for another person or group. *Fifth*, these two motivations have been studied by research which concentrates on learning a second language. Little research exists on the way these motives explain the continuation of bilingual skills or the erosion of a language or bilingualism.

The potential exists for these two motives to become helpful explanatory variables in language decay where minority languages are declining or in peril. The lack of an integrative motive with respect to relationships with, and amongst, the minority group may be a valuable concept at both the individual and societal levels of explanation. Similarly, lack of an instrumental motive for economic, political, social, educational or vocational reasons may be a source of personal and group reasons for minority language decay. However, the power of these motives in both minority language situations, especially where there is language erosion, has yet to be fully tested. *Sixth* and finally, these two motives are not necessarily opposites or alternatives. Both are capable of existing within an individual at the same time. A person may be motivated in different strengths by both orientations. It is possible to be both instrumentally and integratively motivated, with different contexts and expectations affecting the balance of the relative power of the motivations. Siguán & Mackey (1987) give the example of "somebody who learns a language for the main purpose of becoming integrated in the group which speaks it may also believe that integration in the new group will have personal advantages for him and will even help him to rise in society" (p. 80).

Further directions in research

Since the seminal early study by Gardner & Lambert (1959), there has been a variety of research which examines the role of integrative and instrumental motivation in language learning and the achievement of bilingualism. This is surveyed in detail by Robert Gardner (1982, 1985a). Three important themes will be considered here.

1. Replication and consolidation. Since the early research, one focus has been on establishing the validity and power, particularly of the integrative motive. Gardner (1985a) in a review of these studies concludes that the integrative motive often, but not always, comes out of a factor analytical study as a separate, unitary variable. That is, there is some evidence to suggest that the motive is a well-defined and important component in explanations of language learning and bilingualism.

Another focus since the early research has found that the relationship between the integrative motive and second language achievement is well replicated. Such a motive does appear to be an important contributory factor in success in learning a second language. Yet as Gardner (1985a) and Oller *et al.* (1977) have pointed out, the degree of relationship between the integrative motive and achievement in second language learning is small. Only about 5% of the variance in language achievement is usually accounted for by this motive. The percentage sounds small, but the variables accounting for achievement are likely to be many and complex. Allowing for error of measurement plus unaccounted variance due to variables not entered into the research, 5%, by tradition, is small but definitely not negligible. The integrative motive is one ingredient amongst many in the recipe for second language success.

2. Dissension and extension.   A series of studies by Oller and his associates has seemingly found conflicting evidence to the tradition of research stemming from Robert Gardner and colleagues. Oller's research does not find a link between motivation and proficiency in a second language. Oller, Perkins & Murakami (1980), for example, found among students learning English as a second language in Southern Illinois that "the degree of integrativeness of subjects is inconsistently related to scores on the language proficiency tests. In one case it appears to be negatively related" (p. 239). Oller *et al.* (1977) found that a Chinese student's positive beliefs about his or her own cultural group rather than a target "second language" group were the best predictors of second language proficiency. This research is complemented and contrasted by Genesee, Rogers & Holobow (1983) who found that a student's expectation of motivational support from the target "second language" group was a powerful predictor of second language proficiency. The research shows that motives do not exist within the individual in a vacuum. Intergroup factors provide one context where motives may be inhibited or promoted (Schumann, 1986).

Gardner (1985a) has attempted to reply to the findings of Oller and associates by pinpointing weaknesses in their type of research: invalidity and unreliability in measurement, different operational definition of motivations, using students from differing sources and creating one group which is not homogeneous, the nature of residualized predictors and the interpretation of beta coefficients in multiple regression analysis. On balance, the integrative motive does seem a valuable variable in analysing second language achievement, but its relative effect must not be overemphasized. Also, the motive must be viewed in a group and cultural context. Where a pupil is required or encouraged to learn a minority language (e.g. Welsh, Irish or Scottish Gaelic), cultural sanctions, perceived economic demands, religious affiliation and the target language group's expected reactions are all potentially important. That is, the presence of an integrative motive may be kept latent and unfulfilled if perceptions of reactions to the enactment of that motive are negative. The best of intentions can be thwarted by the worst of conditions.

3. Motivation and education.   Although the majority of the large number of researches on bilingualism and motivation would be regarded by their authors, at least, as having educational applications, the hope may too often be more pious than real. Much of the research gathers together knowledge of psychological importance, without attempting to make direct observations about real educational practice. Indeed, much of the research, although using pupils and students, does not require the investigation to enter a school or a classroom. The research is essentially "black-box". The classroom realities are hidden from view. The research is very much that of the input–output variety (Baker, 1985). The real life of the classroom, the process of motivation revealing itself in actual behaviour, is absent from most research on bilingualism and motivation.

Two important studies preferred the "glass box" tradition. Here, the classroom is opened up for viewing. The real-life drama of motive and language is studied. The process rather than presage and product are analysed. Thus Gliksman (1976, 1981) observed teenagers in school. In the first study observation was throughout the first term, and in the second study, 14- to 16-year-olds were observed once every two weeks for four months. These pupils were classified by motivation tests as being integratively motivated or not. Gliksman (1976) hypothesized that the integrative motive influenced the type of participation of individuals in second language learning. Systematic observations were made of the number of times a pupil:

(a) volunteered information by raising a hand
(b) was asked by teachers without volunteering
(c) answered correctly or incorrectly
(d) asked questions
(e) received positive, negative or no feedback from the teacher.

In both the studies, integratively motivated students volunteered more frequently, gave more correct answers and received more positive reinforcement from the teacher than the non-integratively motivated students. The two groups did not differ significantly on the number of questions they asked in class. These relationships were not a primacy effect. They continued throughout the term, indicating consistent behavioural patterns.

In the second study, Gliksman (1981) also obtained ratings on a 7-point scale of how interested the teenagers appeared during class. Integratively motivated pupils were rated as more interested in their lessons than the non-integratively motivated group, this being consistent over the whole term.

Naiman et al. (1978) also concentrated on pupil behaviour in class, differing from Gliksman (1981) in centring on the good language learner. The research issue was "Do good learners tackle the language learning task differently from poor learners, and do learners have certain characteristics which predispose them to good or poor learning?" (p. 2). Seventy-two pupils aged 13–17 were observed; close to half of these pupils were "good learners" and the remainder were among the less proficient. An integrative orientation was positively related to the number of times pupils volunteered to answer questions (r = 0.37). An instrumental orientation was positively correlated to volunteering to answer questions (r = 0.33) and inversely to giving incorrect responses (r = −0.23).

These two studies are important in showing that integrative and instrumental motivation are not just static variables measured like a snapshot by psychologists in abstraction of context. The studies show that in the classroom, motives enter into the film of everyday life, a film that is dynamic and interactive. Instrumental and integrative motives may affect the crucial behaviour that aids or detracts from becoming bilingual.

Research in Wales on bilingualism and motivation

Introduction

Three studies will be introduced to assess the role of motivation in a context different from that presupposed by most research on this topic. The research considered in this chapter has mostly been from Canada and a little from the USA. There is always a danger of generalizing results from one bilingual country to another. This is especially dangerous when there are differences in power and status of the two or more languages both in and between countries. The Canadian context often inspires research where the two languages (French and English) are majority languages and the possibility of additive bilingualism exists. In the USA, the dominance of English and the existence of many lower status languages in a "melting-pot" assimilatory philosophy leads to the possibility, but not necessity, of subtractive bilingualism. Multicultural groups in England provide a similar context. There is also the danger of confusing results from second language learning researches with results from immersion situations. The motivations associated with learning French or German for half an hour a day need analysing separately from motivations when a second language is the medium of much or all the curriculum. Different teaching contexts and different educational aims require initial separate consideration.

The Celtic situation is very different from that in Canada and the United States, with the heritage, indigenous languages being the minority languages under threat, and with English as the dominant language amongst the majority of population. Thus in comparison with Canada

from where much of the "motivation" and "bilingualism" research ema-
nates, the nature of "integrative" and "instrumental" motivations may
change with the difference in language status and context. One perspective
is that the likelihood of holding integrative and instrumental motives to
facilitate second language learning may be higher in majority language
than minority language situations. A Canadian may, for example, be more
motivated towards the economic advantages of learning a world-wide
language like French compared with a person learning a minority language
like Welsh or Irish or Gaelic. A language has a currency value, not only
in economic terms, but also in social and cultural terms. In this respect,
minority compared with majority language contexts differently affect the
establishment and invocation of motives to become bilingual.

In Britain, there are movements towards the retention and restoration of minority languages. The Linguistic Minorities Project (1985) has
lent credence to the possibility of ethnic minorities in parts of England
maintaining their mother tongues in the school situation. In Ireland,
Scotland and Wales, there are movements to encourage both children in
school, and adults continuing their education, to learn the minority language. Such movements depend on the motivation of children and adults to
join and continue minority language classes. Davies (1986) has shown the
strong and growing movement in Wales for adults to learn Welsh. What
are their motivations? Baker (1985) detailed the growing number of
bilingual units and schools in Wales since the 1960s. What are the motivations of parents who elect to send their children to these schools? When
pupils elect to continue studying Welsh in the secondary school, what
motivates the choice? Three researches from Wales attempt to provide
some answers.

The motivation of school choice

Since the establishment of the first bilingual primary school in Aberystwyth in 1939 (Isaac, 1972), the growth of such schools in Wales has
been a very significant part of the language revival movement. By 1950
there were seven designated bilingual primary schools; by 1960, twenty-
eight existed and today there are over sixty of these Ysgolion Cymraeg
catering for over 11,000 pupils. In addition, there are 16 designated
bilingual secondary schools containing over 10,000 pupils. Such schools
are mostly in anglicized areas and are in addition to the schools in
predominantly Welsh-speaking areas where the natural medium of much
communication is Welsh.

Not only were parents often instrumental in the establishment of such Ysgolion Cymraeg, but parents also have the choice of sending their children to such schools or the alternative English medium schools in most, but not all parts of Wales. Eluned Bush (1979) examined the motivation of parents who elected to send their children to such units in Gwent, the least Welsh county in Wales. One popular view in Wales is that the motivation of such parents is essentially instrumental. It is sometimes perceived that the motivation is economic and academic: economic in that bilingualism may make a pupil both more marketable and more qualified for the "up-market" white collar jobs in Wales; academic in that such schools tend to have good reputations in examinations which have currency in the rest of Britain and abroad.

Bush (1979) gave a questionnaire to all parents (N = 149) from four primary bilingual units in Gwent. Seventy per cent of parents responded and of these, in nine out of every ten homes, English was the main language of communication. Having considered and rejected the idea that motivation is élitist or dominated solely by middle-class educational and vocational aspirations, Bush found that many parents in the survey showed commitment or goodwill towards the Welsh language, even though many such parents did not foster the Welsh language and culture in the home. Parents' motives were, in rank order (Bush, Atkinson & Read, 1984):

1. Wanted child to be fluent in Welsh
2. Felt teachers more interested in children
3. Felt academic achievement higher
4. Closer parent–teacher relationships
5. Because classes are smaller
6. Better teaching methods
7. More emphasis on basics
8. More attention to cultural activities
9. Child would be at a disadvantage in future if not bilingual
10. Wanted child to be educated in the home language
11. Dissatisfied with local primary school.

Bush et al. (1984) find in this ordering a desire in bilingual education for academic values. Such schools are thought to be superior in general attainment and organization. Also, these authors argue that the Bush (1979) data also show a strong integrative motive. "Strong evidence of a strong, general positive attitude towards the Welsh language and ethnic identity was provided in the comments added to the Likert-scale items by the parents" (Bush et al., 1984:F1). As Williams, Roberts & Isaac (1978) found in similar research, the motives towards bilingual education in Wales tend to be mixed. Integrative and instrumental reasons combine and interact:

"it is the *combination* of a positive attitude towards the language in identity terms, a belief in the superiority of the bilingual educational institution and the *possibility* that the Welsh-language ability might help to widen the job market which underlie the preference for Welsh medium education" (Williams, Roberts & Isaac, 1978:201).

The motivation towards Welsh secondary schooling

In an important piece of research, Catrin Roberts (1985) found evidence that designated bilingual secondary schools in Wales tend to have superior examination performance than the national average. If this result is added to the finding that, with exceptions, the social class composition of these secondary Ysgolion Cymraeg tends to be, on average, more "middle-class" than general population trends, then one result might seem to explain the other. The relatively more "middle-class" composition of bilingual secondary schools may explain their relatively good examination results. However, Roberts' analysis showed that social class could only be a partial explanation and that "achievement in the bilingual schools is related to factors additional to social class" (p. 291).

Catrin Roberts' (1985) research suggested that the achievement of the Ysgolion Cymraeg is explained by the following further two factors:

1. There existed a greater sense of commitment and motivation of *teachers* in such bilingual schools, evidenced in their strong belief in bilingual education, greater participation in Welsh language and cultural activities outside the school, and more involvement in the provision of extra-curricular activity for the pupils. The teachers were relatively united in these endeavours in comparison with a "control" English medium school where such activity was more fragmented and diverse.

    Teachers with strong commitment to the indigenous language and culture, and therefore to bilingual education, appeared to provide integrative activities for children and inspired integrative motivation within their pupils. Such schools may be relatively successful because they provide the conditions that promote integrative motivation and behaviour.

2. There existed a difference in pupil motivation between the two schools studied. Pupils in the designated bilingual school were more motivated with regard to the Welsh language, the culture of the school and school norms and expectations. The integrative conditions provided by the teachers were reflected in the greater commitment of pupils to their bilingual schooling, the relationships being mutually reciprocating in an upward spiral fashion.

Roberts' (1985) research is important in that it reveals the importance of teachers in providing conditions for pupils' integrative motivation to be both fostered and activated. The research also portrays the sequencing and reciprocal interactions that occur between teachers, pupils, bilingual education and motivation.

The motivation of subject choice

Around 14 years of age, pupils in many parts of Wales can choose to carry on learning Welsh (as a language or as an interdisciplinary topic called Welsh Studies) or drop Welsh altogether. The reasons given for choosing a Welsh option or dropping the subject should reveal the kind of motivation that exists at this crucial examination stage in a secondary pupil's career.

Davies' (1980) research, reported in Baker (1985), while not directly measuring instrumental and integrative motivation, nevertheless provides results which allow suggestions of underlying motivations.

From a group of 431 pupils, 176 chose to carry on with a Welsh option. Those who opted to carry on with Welsh gave as their main reasons:

Learning Welsh due to residence in Wales (64.6%)
Wanting a job in Wales (43.3%)
To pass an exam in Welsh (43.3%)

Close to two-thirds of the "opters-in" chose Welsh/Welsh Studies believing that in response to living in Wales, they should learn the indigenous language. In this sense, the major reason appears an integrative one. Two subsidiary reasons given by a little less than half the sample were instrumental: employment and examination success. Classification of individuals shows that integrative motives were more prominent than instrumental motives, although in close to 25% of the pupils, multiple motivation existed. That is, both integrative and instrumental motives appeared to co-exist.

The motivation of adults learning Welsh

One of the outstanding movements in the struggle for the survival of the Welsh language concerns adult Welsh classes and courses. A variety of courses exists for non-Welsh-speaking Welsh people and other English speakers living in Wales to learn the Welsh language. Books, records, cassette tapes, radio and TV programmes are joined by a variety of day and evening classes in making the means of learning the indigenous language widely available. A report by Her Majesty's Inspectors of Schools revealed the existence of some 344 adult courses in 168 centres in Wales catering for over 4,000 students in one term (Welsh Office, 1984). Philip Davies (1986) conducted one of the first pieces of research to look, amongst other things, at the motivations of adult Welsh learners. Why do adults spend their leisure time in learning Welsh? Are the motives economic, cultural, social, vocational, affiliative or purely for self-actualization?

A questionnaire was given to 190 adults in beginners' classes, 162 (85%) of whom responded. Such respondents were, in the main, learning Welsh by evening classes and day classes. A grid provided 24 reasons why each adult may have been motivated to join the class. Table 7 provides the results.

Table 7 reveals four major reasons why adults attend classes: learning Welsh as a response to living in Wales, wanting to keep the language alive, a liking for the Welsh language and a knowledge of Welsh coming in useful. These reasons suggest integrative motives as being more influential than instrumental motives. This is confirmed by the smaller number of people who saw earning money, job prospects and present working conditions as their goals.

A factor analysis of the data confirmed the separate existence of an integrative and instrumental motive. The first extracted factor was labelled by Davies (1986) as an integrative motivational factor. The following statements obtained high loadings on the first factor (and these and other statements are indicated by an (A) in Table 7).

Factor
loading

2   A knowledge of Welsh makes me a more   (0.61)
    complete Welsh person
18 I want to keep the language alive   (0.56)
12 I wish to follow Welsh cultural events   (0.56)
22 I want to follow Welsh language programmes on   (0.43)
    TV/Radio

The second factor, indicated by (B) in Table 7, was regarded by Davies (1986) as indicating instrumental motivation. It loaded highly on three statements:

15 Job prospects improve with a knowledge of   (0.70)
    Welsh
5   A knowledge of Welsh may be necessary in my   (0.68)
    work
1   A knowledge of Welsh may help me earn more   (0.53)
    money

Two further factors were extracted (C and D in Table 7), and focused on parents helping their children with Welsh and children attending a Welsh school, with factor C having some sentimental values attached to it.

A second questionnaire was completed by 65 adults in "advanced learner" classes. The results replicate and strengthen the findings from beginners' classes. Davies (1986) again found that the first extracted factor was an integrative motive and the second factor an instrumental motive. Seven individual reasons were given by 40% or more of the advanced learners for their class attendance.

I live in Wales and I ought to learn Welsh   (83.1%)
To speak to Welsh friends   (63.1%)
I like the Welsh language   (55.4%)
To keep the language alive   (53.8%)
To follow Welsh TV/Radio   (50.8%)
To attend Welsh cultural events   (46.2%)
I'll be a more complete Welsh person   (40.0%)

Despite the inclusion of a number of instrumental items in the questionnaire, the integrative items were seen by adults as best fitting their motives.

TABLE 7. *Motivation of Adults Learning Welsh*

		% of N
1	A knowledge of Welsh may help me earn more money	14.8 (B)
2	A knowledge of Welsh makes me a more complete Welsh person	40.7 (A)
3	A knowledge of Welsh may come in useful	60.5 (D)
4	I live in Wales and I ought to learn Welsh	80.2 (unique)
5	A knowledge of Welsh may be necessary in my work	41.4 (B)
6	My parents used to speak Welsh	13.6 (A)
7	My children go to a Welsh school	20.4 (D)
8	I want to find my roots	9.9 (A)
9	My children are learning Welsh in an English school	17.3 (D)
10	I used to be good at Welsh in school	9.9 (C)
11	I like Welsh	63.6 (A)
12	I wish to follow Welsh cultural events	45.1 (A)
13	I want to sing in a Welsh choir	5.6 (C)
14	I want to help my children to learn Welsh	32.7 (B & C)
15	Job prospects improve with a knowledge of Welsh	31.5 (B)
16	I wish to read Welsh literature in the original language	22.8 (A)
17	I have many friends who speak Welsh	34.0 (A)
18	I want to keep the language alive	65.4 (A)
19	Welsh is my spouse/boy friend/girl friend's mother tongue	11.7 (unique)
20	I spend my holidays in Wales	14.8 (D)
21	I want to live in Wales	11.7 (D)
22	I want to follow Welsh language programmes on TV/ Radio	47.5 (A)
23	To fulfil a dream	14.8 (A)
24	To attend a Welsh chapel	4.9 (A)

Conclusions

The theme of motivation and bilingualism is important because it relates to a widespread public question. Why do people become bilingual, stay bilingual or lose their bilingual ability? Rather than just comment on behaviour, we speculate as to the pulls and pushes that initiate such behaviour.

Two concepts have dominated answers to the question. Integrative motivation in particular, and instrumental motivation have provided the main focus of research. Learning a second language successfully would appear to depend in part on a wish to affiliate with members of that second language group, and sometimes on having vocational or economic reasons. Different contexts will foster or inhibit the activation of both integrative and instrumental motivations. Where a person or society values vocational mobility and economic prosperity, then instrumental motivation may be more active. However, research has indicated that in the majority language situation of Canada and the minority language situation of Wales, the integrative motive appears more influential. Canadians learn French and people in Wales learn Welsh predominantly for friendship, for social and cultural reasons.

For the Welsh language, and other indigenous minority languages, this is a positive sign. To want to learn the indigenous language "to belong" may create an enduring lifeline thrown by Welsh language teachers to their students, who reciprocally throw that lifeline to a future for the language.

7 Theory into Practice

Introduction

The final chapter attempts to bring together the diverse findings concerning bilingualism and cognitive functioning, bilingual education, attitudes and motivation. Each chapter has examined the pertinent research in terms of basic questions that underlie the psychology of bilingualism and bilingual education. These basic questions tend to be the ones asked by parents, teachers, administrators and politicians. It has been a premise of the book that such fundamental questions, however imprecisely or simplistically phrased, require answers in the light of available research and knowledge.

Research does not, however, tend to be directed by the questions, issues and problems raised by parents, teachers and educational administrators. Research into bilingualism and IQ, cognitive functioning, attitudes and motivation has evolved due partly to the production of psychological concepts and tools of measurement. Research into bilingual education is slightly different. While it is impossible to deny that this research is constrained by measurement and valued outputs, the path of bilingual education evaluation, in Canada particularly, was partly inspired and partly informed by parental wishes and administrators' concerns.

At some point research is directed by theoretical questions. Many would argue that all research starts with theory. Such theory may be a researcher's "theory of practice", that is, an intuitive guess at the mechanisms operating inside an individual or classroom or educational system. Such a "theory of practice" may be held at a latent or tacit level. Each teacher, for example, has a "theory of practice" which guides classroom behaviour. Such a theory may not be conscious and well articulated, but nevertheless is the personal reference map that guides practice. In the same way, researchers have theories, often latent and not conscious, which may motivate and guide research.

When research has developed and evolved, a variety of findings exist. The findings upon first reading may not always seem to knit together.

169

The introduction of different variables or different tests, the use of a different type of sample of children or research in a different country or context, may produce findings which seem to be contradictory or idiosyncratic. Ideally, a well worked out theory, it is said, should be present at the outset of all good research. In practice, theory often enters when there is a need to explain findings and this includes the need to accommodate apparently contradictory results. A theory is not supposed to be a *post hoc* attempt to bring wholeness and sense to disparate research findings. Often that is what happens. Theory informs future research. A theory needs to be tested for its stability across time, place and person. A theory requires further testing to establish its power and veracity. Theory then informs the future path of research. Rather than a researcher testing a variety of variables, hoping that a statistical analysis will throw up interesting relationships, but failing to connect with previous research, a theory provides a tradition so that research can be systematic, progressive and evolutionary.

From the three major areas studied, cognitive functioning, bilingual education and attitudes/motivation, various overlapping theories have been expounded to explain, interpret, make coherent and to effect generalization. It is these theories that are now considered.

The Balance Theory

The balance theory of bilingualism needs comment for two reasons. First, it is the theory of bilingualism that is held intuitively by many people: parents, teachers, politicians, administrators. A first reaction to the topic of bilingualism is an assumption that increasing one language will automatically cause a decrease in the second language. Second, early research on IQ and school attainment often found bilinguals inferior to monoglots. That is, early research tended to support the balance theory.

To think of bilingualism as weighing scales, with a second language increasing at the expense of the first language, requires two assumptions. First, there is the assumption that the brain has only so much room for language skills. If a second language comes to stay, it decreases the amount of living quarters for the first language. The consequence is lower proficiency in both languages, in thinking, reading, vocabulary and knowledge. Cummins (1981a) uses the analogy of balloons. If balloons are being inflated "in the head" by the entrance of knowledge and skill, a bilingual has two half-filled balloons with the monolingual having one better filled balloon. This idea is further developed by Cummins (1980a) in terms of the Separate Underlying Proficiency model of bilingualism (SUP).

The second assumption of the balance theory is that the first language and second language are kept separate in the brain. The two balloons are apart and not interactive. When knowledge is blown into the balloon, the language of transmission of that knowledge determines which balloon is increased in size. According to balance theory, lessons in Welsh will inflate the Welsh language part of the brain; lessons in English will inflate the English part of the brain, with little or no transfer between the two parts. Stimulating one area will have no effect on the other.

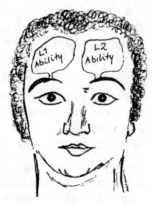

The balance effect theory is plausible, even logical. Pouring in a second language would seem to leave less space for other learning. Separate languages would seem to require separate storage. Children's cognitive skills and academic achievement would then seem to suffer. Bilinguals would be expected to have lower IQs and be behind at school.

Despite popular belief in the balance theory, the theory is unsubstantiated. Indeed, research shows the theory is misconceived. What is logically conceivable is not psychologically correct. Chapters 1 and 2 have shown that balanced bilinguals do not suffer cognitively. Intellectual ability and capacity are not affected by becoming a balanced bilingual. Indeed, the tentative suggestion is that balanced bilingualism is linked to certain cognitive benefits. Similarly, Chapters 3 and 4 revealed that bilingual education which fostered both languages to a good level of proficiency had no negative effects on first language skills or on general achievement throughout the school curriculum. The balance theory does not fit research. The weight of the evidence is firmly against balance theory.

Think Tank model

While, as will be considered later, there are theories and models to explain the results of the bilingualism and cognitive functioning and bilingual education research, Cummins (1981a) has presented an appealing analogy. In place of a balance model or the two bilingual balloons, Cummins suggests a picture of the head as a Think Tank. In the Think Tank, Cummins finds an illustration which fits the various research findings on bilingualism. The Think Tank is summarized by Cummins (1981a:30) as follows:

> "although the linguistic contents of the Think Tank often retain specific L1 or L2 characteristics (that is, they do not become linguistically homogenized), the same mental expertise underlies performance (namely, processing of input and output) in both languages. The quantity and quality of the linguistic input and of the feedback received from linguistic output in both languages is an important stimulus for the growth of the *total* Think Tank".

In other words, while two languages do not merge and are necessarily separated, the Think Tank works in a unitary way. Feeding that Tank richly and well results in a well developed engine. Bilingualism can stimulate a well tuned engine and not create an engine working on half throttle.

Cummins (1981a) outlines three assumptions for the Think Tank which further elucidate its nature. First, whichever language a bilingual uses, the thoughts that accompany talking, reading, writing and listening come from the same "place". Underlying two languages is one integrated source of thought. The two cylinders are powered by the same engine. Irrespective of the language of production or reception, cognitive activity is centralized and integrated. Second, although the same ability underlies the two languages, precise connotations of words may be different in different languages. The Welsh "hiraeth" translates into "a longing for something". Yet in translation the word loses much of its affective expression. Two languages can result in an increased richness of meaning and cultural connotations. Third, all language contributes to the growth of the Think Tank. Speaking, listening, reading or writing in the first or second language helps the whole Tank to develop. However, the operation and development of the Think Tank may be negatively affected if children are forced to operate in a second language where they have little proficiency. If children are made to use a poorly developed second language in school, for example, the quality and quantity of what they take in from the teacher's curriculum materials and produce by oral and written means will be relatively impoverished. This is the experience of Finns in schools in Sweden who are forced to operate in Swedish (Skutnabb-Kangas & Toukomaa, 1976). Such children tend to perform comparatively badly in both Finnish and Swedish. This is the reason why in immersion education, pupils are usually allowed to talk to peers and teachers in their first language until able and willing to use their second language.

Most analogies and pictures can paint only a partial picture and may be extended too far to maintain veracity and validity. However, Cummins (1981a), with some humour, extends the Think Tank analogy to envelop the duties of the Think Tank Manager. The Think Tank Manager is allotted three control and regulation functions. The Manager of the bilingual Tank must *first* inspect and monitor. The two languages must be contrasted, so that sentence order, grammar, meanings for each language are neatly stored, able to be correctly summoned from store and, if necessary, corrected. Inspecting and monitoring the two languages is one reason why bilinguals may have a subtle advantage over monoglots in word meanings and language awareness (see Chapter 2). The Manager must *secondly* operate a switch control. Bilinguals need to be sensitive to switching to the appropriate language. For example, a telephone call may start in English, and, by detecting accent or phraseology, the bilingual may switch to Welsh for a mutually more worthwhile and natural exchange. *Third*, the Manager of the Think Tank may consciously operate a valve control. Here the valve is knowingly opened and shut to regulate the language of communication. A child may keep the second language valve partially closed in school, only speaking or responding in the second language if absolutely necessary. On the other hand, a child or adult who is very keen to learn to operate well in the second language may seek opportunities to open the second language valve. Minority language pupils disparaging their home language may deliberately shut down the first language valve and open the second language valve as much as possible (Cummins, 1981a).

There is good utility in the idea of the Think Tank model. It paints a picture that helps to explain the results of various areas of research on bilingualism. The Think Tank is capable of accommodating two languages. Thinking both stimulates and is stimulated by two languages. Such stimulation may produce possible small cognitive advantages for balanced bilinguals. Performance in school is determined not only by language available, but by the Think Tank. The Think Tank is fed by the totality of a child's experience in both first and second language. Thus, with the immersion experience of bilingual education, a child's Think Tank is being as adequately developed as in monolingual education, with an extra language in the Tank and the potential of wider bicultural experience.

This idea is further developed by Cummins (1980a) in terms of the Common Underlying Proficiency model of bilingualism (CUP).

To summarize the basic nature of the Think Tank model:

(i) Bilingualism is viable because people have the capacity to store adequately two or more languages.

(ii) Conceptual and academic skills (cognitive functioning and educational attainment) may be developed equally well through the use of two languages as through one language. Cognitive functioning and educational attainment may be fed through one monolingual channel or equally successfully through two language channels. Both channels feed the same "Tank".

(iii) To the extent that bilingual education successfully fosters conceptual and academic development, full bilingualism is a viable and valuable outcome of such education.

(iv) When one or both language channels are externally or internally stopped from functioning fully (e.g. through low motivation to learn a language, or pressure to replace the home language with the majority language), cognitive functioning and academic development may be impeded.

The Think Tank model provides a picture model to conceive of the relationship between cognitive functioning, bilingual education and bilingualism. For many, this could be a valuable and fresh way of re-thinking the bilingual debate. That is, the tendency of many parents, teachers and educational administrators is to think of bilingualism as a weighing balance. The provision of a powerful, more valid analogy may more easily infiltrate and change prejudices and beliefs than the presentation of research reports, abstract theories and statistical models. Nevertheless, the Think Tank model does not fully express recent theoretical thinking about cognitive functioning, bilingual schooling and bilingualism. The chapter therefore continues to consider such theories and models.

The Thresholds Theory

In Chapter 2, it was tentatively concluded that balanced bilinguals show positive cognitive advantages. The implication is that where one or both of a person's languages are less well developed, alternative cognitive consequences may ensue. Thus Skutnabb-Kangas & Toukomaa (1976) and Tsushima & Hogan (1975) have provided evidence of possible negative cognitive consequences when one or both languages lack in proficiency. Cummins (1976) suggested that with studies which find a negative relationship between bilingualism and cognitive processes, one explanation is an inadequate level of language proficiency in the bilingual subjects.

In comparison, a number of studies suggest that the further a child progresses towards balanced and proficient bilingualism, the greater the probability of cognitive advantages (Cummins & Mulcahy, 1978; Duncan & De Avila, 1979; Kessler & Quinn, 1982). As Cummins (1976) has noted, the important issue is not what effect bilingualism has on cognitive processes. Rather, the crucial question is under what conditions does bilingualism facilitate or retard cognitive growth? As Fishman (1977) contended: "I would predict that every conceivable relationship between intelligence and bilingualism *could* obtain and that our task is not so much the determination of whether there is a relationship between the two but of *when*" (p. 38).

One theoretical proposition to explain the negative and positive findings is the Thresholds Theory (Toukomaa & Skutnabb-Kangas, 1977; Cummins, 1976). Two thresholds are posited. Each threshold is a level of linguistic competence that children must reach, firstly, to avoid the negative consequences of bilingualism, and secondly, to experience the possible positive consequences of bilingualism. The child may experience either positive, negative, or neither positive nor negative cognitive effects, according to whether that child has respectively limited, proficient or partial bilingualism. This may be conceived pictorially as simultaneously climbing two ladders which represent language competence or proficiency (Figure 2). If too few steps are climbed, the child stays somewhere in the lower level. At this level there are potential negative cognitive effects. Limited linguistic skills limit academic learning and cognitive growth. The first threshold is reached when a child has age-appropriate proficiency in one language. When a child can function effectively in one language, there are likely to be no negative or positive cognitive effects. Figuratively, the child is then somewhere in the middle level. The second threshold is reached when a child is relatively balanced and proficient in both languages. At this top level, there is the potential of cognitive benefits. Such children will exhibit age-appropriate ability in both languages.

The Thresholds Theory also helps explain why in early and late immersion education there are temporary lags in achievement when the curriculum is taught through the second language. Until the second language has been developed to a level sufficient to cope with conceptual learning, below average performance may be expected. Once the second language is proficient enough to comprehend and conceptualize curriculum

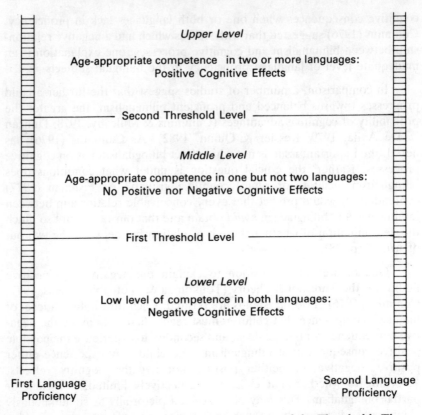

Upper Level

Age-appropriate competence in two or more languages:
Positive Cognitive Effects

——————— Second Threshold Level ———————

Middle Level

Age-appropriate competence in one but not two languages:
No Positive nor Negative Cognitive Effects

———— First Threshold Level ————————————

Lower Level
Low level of competence in both languages:
Negative Cognitive Effects

First Language
Proficiency

Second Language
Proficiency

FIGURE 2.   *Bilingualism, Cognitive Functioning and the Thresholds Theory*

content, immersion experience is unlikely to have detrimental consequences, and may have additional cognitive benefits.

While the Thresholds Theory helps to express why immersion education is successful, the theory also indicates that minority children taught
through their second language (e.g. immigrants, subtractive contexts), and
who fail to develop sufficient competency in their second language, will
not benefit from second language instruction (Cummins, 1984b). "This
condition is cumulative and the children fall progressively further behind
in academic and cognitive skills because their low level of L2 proficiency
limits the scope of their interaction with the conceptual environment of
the school" (Cummins, 1984b:60).

The Thresholds Theory tends to fit much of the available data and
provides a neat and efficient encapsulation of the essential components

of bilingualism and cognitive functioning. Further refinements of the theory may be found in Cummins (1984b). While the theory is unable to specify precisely the level of proficiency required to reach a certain threshold level, and while research has yet to be precise as to the nature and boundaries of cognitive effects, Thresholds Theory provides an important idea to help parent, teacher, administrator and researcher. While there is the continuous danger that a picture theory such as the Think Tank or Thresholds Theory over-simplifies a complex pattern of interacting variables and makes appear "real" ideas and concepts that are often abstract and contentious, such picture theories are useful in correcting invalid images such as found in the balance theory. It may be better to paint an incomplete picture than allow the reproduction of false theories. Since not everyone can understand the most abstract or detailed of paintings, for the wider public to be better informed, picture theories such as Thresholds and the Think Tank may be of value.

The evolution of a theory concerning the language proficiency of bilinguals

The major theory of the relationship between bilingualism and academic progress is one that has evolved in the last decade. It started with the Thresholds Theory. Since the Thresholds Theory does not consider the relationship and interaction between a child's two languages, Cummins (1978d) suggested the developmental interdependence hypothesis. This hypothesis held that the level of second language competence a child acquires is partly dependent on the level of competence achieved in the first language. For example, older immigrants, whose academic ability in their first language is better established than younger immigrants, become academically more proficient in second language literacy as well as in their first language literacy (Skutnabb-Kangas & Toukomaa, 1976). This suggested a distinction between surface fluency and the ownership of more evolved language skills necessary to benefit from the educative process. Simple communciation skills may hide a child's relative lack of the language proficiency required to meet the cognitive and academic demands of schooling.

This initial distinction between a linguistic façade (surface fluency) and the more cognitive and academic aspects of language skills, developed into BICS and CALP (Cummins, 1980b). A distinction was made between basic interpersonal communication skills (BICS) and cognitive academic language proficiency (CALP), and was posed to explain the relative failure of many minority language pupils. For example, in the United States, transitional bilingual education programmes often enabled pupils to achieve English language skills sufficient for them to converse with peers and teachers. Having reached this level, they may be transferred to mainstream education, the teachers wrongly believing such pupils had the language competence to cope with the conceptual and academic demands of the curriculum. What Cummins (1980b) regards as essential in bilingual education is that "common underlying proficiency" is well developed. That is, to cope with the demands of the classroom, a child's general cognitive abilities and academic skills need to be developed. This underlying ability could be developed through the first or second language. When such "common underlying proficiency" is available, skills will transfer across languages. Teaching someone to read in Welsh, for example, develops cognitive and academic ability, such that the ability positively affects the development of reading in English.

The most recent evolution of this theory proposes two dimensions (Cummins, 1981b, 1983b and 1984c). Each dimension concerns communicative proficiency. The first dimension is the degree of contextual support available to a pupil. For example, in a "good" classroom, a pupil may be able to negotiate meaning with a teacher, ask questions and indicate to the teacher a lack of understanding. In such a "good" classroom, language may be supported by non-verbal communication: the use of eyes, head nods, hand gestures and intonation, for example. Cummins (1981b) refers to this as context embedded communication. At the other end of this dimension is context reduced communication where there are so few cues to meaning that gaining knowledge may not occur, as a linguistically under-developed child has to concentrate on meaning. A chat between two friends is likely to be context embedded, "whereas many of the linguistic demands of the classroom reflect communication that is closer to the context-reduced end of the continuum" (Cummins, 1981b:12).

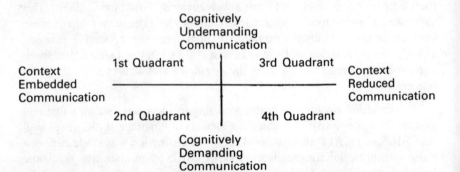

(Adapted from Cummins, 1981b)

The second dimension is the amount of cognitive demands required in communication. High cognitive demands may be exemplified in a classroom where much information needs processing quickly and where the pupil does not have mastery of the necessary skills. Cognitively undemanding communication is where a pupil has mastery of the language skills to enable efficient communication.

Surface fluency, or Basic Interpersonal Communication Skills, concerns the first quadrant (context embedded, cognitively undemanding use of language). Language which is cognitively and academically more advanced (CALP) concerns the fourth quadrant (context reduced, cognitively demanding). Cummins' (1981b) theory suggests that first language competence in the first quadrant (surface fluency) develops relatively independently of second language surface fluency. In comparison, context reduced, cognitively demanding communication develops inter-dependently.

This theory has evolved to conceptualize the relationship between bilingual education and school attainment in varying school and home contexts. The foundation of the theory is that this relationship must explain how the first language is related to the development of a second language. Although an over-simplification, the two extremes are: (a) language developed enough for conversation which is cognitively undemanding and where lots of clues and cues help understanding, and (b) the language skills required to operate successfully in an "academic" classroom which may be cognitively demanding and lack helpful cues and clues.

Bilingual education will begin to be successful when children have enough second language proficiency to work in context reduced, cognitively demanding situations. Children with some conversational ability in their second language may *appear* ready to be taught through their second language. The theory suggests that such children are not in fact ready. Such children may fail to understand meanings and be unable to engage in higher-order cognitive processes such as synthesis, discussion analysis, evaluation and interpretation. This explains a number of research findings:

1. In the United States, minority language children may be transferred from transitional bilingual programmes into English-only schooling when their conversational ability in English seems sufficient. Such pupils then frequently perform poorly in mainstream schooling. The theory suggests that this is due to their not having the developed ability in English (or their home language) to operate in an environment which is more cognitively and academically demanding.

2. Immersion students in Canada tend to lag behind their monolingual peers for a short period. Once they acquire second language proficiency sufficient to operate in a cognitively demanding and context reduced environment, they normally catch up with their peers.

3. Experiments in the United States, Canada and Europe with minority language children who are allowed to use their minority home language for part or much of their infant and junior schooling, show that such children do not experience retardation in school achievement or in majority language proficiency. Through their minority language, they develop the ability to be relatively successful in the cognitively demanding and context reduced classroom environment. This ability then transfers to the majority language when that language is well enough developed.

Children learning to read in their home language, be it Welsh, Gaelic, Irish, Spanish, Frisian or whatever, are not just developing home language skills. They are also developing higher order cognitive and linguistic skills which will help with the future development of reading in the majority language as well as with general intellectual development. As Cummins (1984a) notes, "Transfer is much more likely to occur from minority to majority language because of the greater exposure to literacy in the majority language and the strong social pressure to learn it" (p. 143).

As Cummins (1984a) has noted, the theory is congruent with various well known theoretical distinctions that explain the relationship between language proficiency and academic achievement. For example, Bruner's (1975) distinction between communicative and analytic competence, Donaldson's (1978) distinction between embedded and disembedded thought, and Bereiter & Scardamelia's (1981) distinction between conversation and composition, each add credence to Cummins' (1981b) explication of his L1/L2 theory. However, this theory has also received criticism (Edelsky et al., 1983; Martin-Jones & Romaine, 1986; Rivera (ed.), 1984). The major criticisms may be summarized as:

1. The theory is not expanded to acknowledge ethnic, cultural, social, political, community, teacher expectations, motivation, attitude and home factors, each of which may affect and explain school achievement. The relationship between language and social situation is not fully explicated. The high success of certain

Asian groups and lower success of working-class children needs an explanation not covered by the theory. "Social and cultural factors may be much more powerful than purely linguistic factors in influencing educational achievement" (Troike, 1984:49).

2. The definition of school success tends to be narrow, and centres on the dominant, traditional, middle-class indices of achievement (e.g. literacy). Alternative outcomes of schooling (e.g. self-esteem, employment, attitude to continued learning) are not highlighted.

3. The relationships between similar constructs and the relationships of constructs to valid and reliable measurement are questioned (e.g. the relationships between linguistic skills, cognitive competence, academic skills, learning and cognitive retardation).

4. The research data provide pooled, averaged results. Variation within a class or group is rarely examined and individual exceptions are rarely explored. The effect of individual personality factors, for example, is not included.

5. The theoretical framework still requires empirical confirmation. The theory provides hypotheses which need testing in a variety of contexts, although Martin-Jones & Romaine (1986) have doubts about the possibility of fully testing the theory (e.g. "the skills, involved in CALP are related to culture-specific types of literacy": p. 30).

6. Terms such as BICS and CALP tend to be vague, value-laden, in danger of acquiring credence beyond their empirical validity, and exist on a continuum and not as a dichotomy. Just as Basil Bernstein's restricted and elaborated codes became simplified and misused, so these BICS and CALP labels may create over-simplification and stereotyping.

Two attitude/motivation models·

Of the theories considered so far in this chapter, each tends to centre on individual psychological explanation. Consideration of attitude and motivation adds social factors, and moves into social psychological models. Two such theories will be considered, each being concerned with bilingual development and not just applicable to the sometimes more restricted notion of second language teaching.

(i) Lambert's model

Lambert's (1974) model commences with an individual's attitudes and aptitude. As has been expressed in Chapter 5, aptitude and attitude are regarded as two major and relatively separate influences on learning to be bilingual. Some cognitive ability is required as well as a positive attitude. For Lambert, attitude relates to motivation which may be instrumental and/or integrative. Bilingual proficiency is thus based on the extent of aptitude and the relationship between, and extent of, attitudes and motivation.

Lambert's (1974) model does not end with bilingual achievement. For Lambert, becoming bilingual has effects both on the self-concept and on the perception of bilingualism. Being able to communicate with a different language group may change one's self-picture. A Welsh speaker having mastered English may choose English speakers as a reference group and develop norms of behaviour that affect self-concept. Also, learning a second language may involve enculturation. A child or adult may become bicultural, and have new aspirations, world-views, values and beliefs. Active involvement in two cultures may affect the self-concept. An English speaker who learns Welsh may be involved in eisteddfodau, the Welsh chapel or Welsh rugby culture, causing modification to self-perception. When the second language and culture are acquired with little or no pressure to replace or reduce in importance the first language, an *additive* form of bilingualism may occur. Positive self-concept is likely to accompany additive bilingualism. For example, the English speaker learning Welsh is potentially gaining additive bilingualism and biculturalism. When the second language and culture are acquired with pressure to replace or demote the first language, a *subtractive* form of bilingualism may result. In situations where children are encouraged to learn the majority language, where education is solely through that majority language, and where cultural assimilation rather than cultural pluralism is intended, a subtractive bilingualism and a less positive self-concept may potentially result. The loss of cultural identity, the severing of one's roots in minority culture and traditions, and possible alienation from one's first reference group may result in a subtractive form of bilingualism. For example, the Welsh person learning English may sometimes become anglicized in culture and consciously or unconsciously speak less and less Welsh.

Lambert's (1974) model is simple but powerful. It appears to contain the central variables in acquiring bilingualism, whilst indicating that social milieu is both affected by and affects the path of bilingualism. Integrative

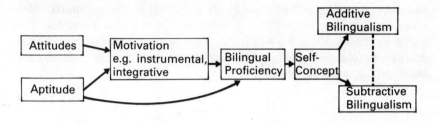

and instrumental motivation are social motivations, being conceived as inputs in the attainment of bilingualism. Subtractive and additive bilingualism are social effects or outputs concerning the status of languages in society and the educational system. Social and cultural factors and situational context are thus important variables in the passage of bilingualism at an individual and societal–political level.

(ii) Gardner's socio-educational model

R. C. Gardner (1979, 1983, 1985a), having examined a variety of social psychological models of second language learning, presents his own more universal and empirically tested model. There are four stages to Gardner's model. First, the model begins with the *social and cultural milieu*. The child grows up in a community which transmits beliefs about language and culture. In many white communities in England, the transmitted belief is that bilingualism is unnecessary, difficult to achieve and, if achieved, is at the expense of other areas of achievement. Such communities also tend to share the traditional United States philosophy of assimilation of minority cultures and languages. In some Canadian communities, opposite beliefs about French–English bilingualism and biculturalism exist, thus allowing the establishment, evolution and extension of bilingual schooling. The psychosocial influence of home, social group and type of language group (e.g. majority, minority) is further explored by Hamers & Blanc (1982, 1983) and Siguán & Mackey (1987).

The second stage of Gardner's (1979, 1983, 1985a) model is *individual differences*. This comprises four major variables: intelligence, language aptitude, motivation and situational anxiety. The child's social and cultural milieu affects individual differences which comprise four key individual variables. Attitudes and personality are not listed in this individual differences section, but are held to be subsumed in the four variables. This seems to confuse variables which may have negligible effects on language proficiency (e.g. personality traits) and concepts which have similarity and overlap (e.g. attitude and motives).

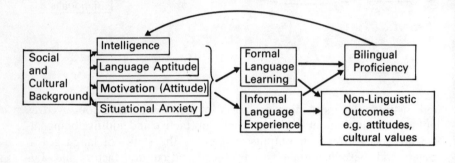

Gardner (1985a) lists these four variables because "intelligence is assumed to play a role because it determines how well or how quickly individuals understand the nature of any learning task or any explanations provided" (p. 147); language aptitude concerns the degree of talent specific to learning any language; motivation concerns effort, desire and affect; and situational anxiety is viewed as important "because it would have an inhibiting effect on the individual's performance, thus interfering with acquisition" (p. 148).

The third stage of Gardner's (1979, 1983, 1985a) model concerns the *context* where language is acquired. A distinction is made between formal and informal contexts of language acquisition. An example of a formal context is the classroom where a primary purpose is for pupils to learn to be linguistically competent and functionally bilingual. Drill and practice, audio-visual methods, translations and grammar exercises are examples of a formal, manifest and directed approach to language teaching. Informal contexts are where language learning is not the primary aim. Watching a French language film may be principally motivated by entertainment needs, and hence extending skills in French may be an unintended outcome. Talking to a friend or relative in Irish or Welsh may be for affiliative or social reasons. Practising skills and becoming more functionally competent may be a valuable incidental outcome but not a reason for such communication. However, formal and informal contexts may on occasions overlap. For example, talking to the teacher in the classroom at the end of a lesson, or listening to a radio programme for both learning and pleasure, are examples of where the formal merges with the informal. Gardner (1985a) suggests that all four individual difference variables, intelligence, motivation, language aptitude and situational anxiety, influence the formal learning context. In informal contexts, motivation and situational anxiety are the principal determinants of entry into that context. Intelligence and language aptitude play a secondary role, as they are said to be less likely causal variables. An example of the secondary role of intelligence is given by Gardner (1985a): "Once students enter into an informal context, their level of intelligence and aptitude will influence how much language material is learned" (p. 148). While this may certainly be the case, it is not impossible that intelligence and aptitude are causally linked with entry into informal language contexts. A high integrative motive and freedom from situational anxiety may not be enough to watch a second language film. Intelligence and aptitude may also influence entry into the experience of the informal context. Such an influence may be less than motivation and situational anxiety; nevertheless intelligence and aptitude could still be causal in a primary sense.

Finally, Gardner (1979, 1983, 1985a) suggests two final *outcomes* in the four-stage model. One outcome concerns bilingual proficiency (fluency, vocabulary and pronunciation, for example); the second outcome refers to non-linguistic outcomes such as attitudes, self-concept, cultural values and beliefs. The mention of attitudes suggests that the model is not static but dynamic and cyclical. Outcomes feed back into the model. The experience of the classroom or film affects attitude which affects motivation which, in a never-ending cyclical process, then affects continued experience in the classroom or other environments.

The value of Gardner's (1979, 1983, 1985a) model lies not only in its inclusiveness, but also in that it has been empirically tested using advanced, sophisticated causal modelling techniques (structural equation modelling via LISREL IV). Three studies have investigated whether Gardner's model is empirically valid. R. C. Gardner (1983), Gardner, Lalonde & Pierson (1983) and Lalonde (1982) generally found the model to be valid and powerful in explanation. The LISREL causal modelling technique cannot prove that links are always causal. Nevertheless, given that variables are interactive and that language development is cyclical, the model has been shown to summarize reasonably well important variables and their likely temporal order. The researches also suggested that the integrative motive was a well defined and important variable in second language proficiency, that personality traits influence attitude and motivation rather than being a separate and direct contributory cause of achievement, and that attitude causes motivation or, as Gardner (1985a) suggests, "attitude variables are important in that they serve to maintain levels of motivation and that they are not implicated directly in achievement" (p. 158). In one of the researches (Lalonde, 1982) motivation was found to be an indirect cause of achievement. Motivation affected self-confidence, with self-confidence directly affecting achievement.

The models considered thus far in the chapter have predominantly concerned psychological and social psychological theories. Although educational contexts (e.g. immersion education, transitional bilingual education, bilingual classrooms) and educational variables (e.g. language and literacy skills) have been part of these theories, models of bilingual schooling which focus on the educational aspects of bilingual education have yet to be considered. Four such bilingual education theories are now presented.

C. B. Paulston's bilingual education theories

Christina Bratt Paulston (1980) has examined in detail how eight theories of social and educational change may be used to examine and classify the aims and methods of different types of bilingual education. The eight theories fit into two major paradigms: the functional or equilibrium paradigm and the conflict paradigm. The functional theories of bilingual education (evolutionary, neo evolutionary, structural-functionalist and systems analysis) each concern the maintenance of society "in an equilibrium through the harmonious relationship of the social components, and they emphasize smooth, cumulative change" (Paulston, 1980:16). The conflict theories of bilingual education (Marxian, Group Conflict, Cultural Revitalization and Anarchistic Utopian) each concern the instability of society with conflicts over power, resources, beliefs and values, oppressive institutions and human nature. It is not possible to summarize these theories simply, as their power lies in their complex abstractionism and detailed analysis. For present purposes, two issues are well illustrated by Paulston (1980). First, her theoretical analysis adds a sociological and political viewpoint that is an important partner to the dominant psychometric tradition in bilingual research. Paulston's comment about Canadian research is generalizable across continents. She suggests that researchers have "tended to slight social factors in their research and to minimize the potential conflict situation between the English and French-speaking group" (p. 29). Second, Paulston demonstrates well that research into bilingualism and bilingual education is not value free. The assumptions of researchers, their values and motivations, their choice of variables and style of research each affect the conclusions of the research. No research is totally objective, unbiased and value free.

Spolsky's bilingual education evaluation model

Bernard Spolsky developed a model for bilingual education evaluation that seeks to ensure a comprehensive multi-faceted coverage of all aspects of such evaluation (Spolsky, Green & Read, 1974; Spolsky, 1978). The model is pictured as a multi-tiered wedding cake, with each tier of the same size. Each tier has the same basic parts, that is, the same factors which affect bilingual education. These factors, which Spolsky (1978) pictures as potential slices of the cake, are the psychological, sociological, economic, political, religious, cultural, geographical, demographic, historical and linguistic factors that affect bilingual education. The picture is of an uncut cake, so that the "factors overlap and interact with one another in a manner that cannot be adequately represented without sacrificing simplicity" (Spolsky, 1978:350). In the centre of each tier is education. The image is of the central importance of education in such evaluation, the other factors circumscribing and shaping it on all sides.

Spolsky (1978) suggests four tiers to the cake. The *first* tier is the total situation of a *community* in which bilingual education functions. The community could be an ethnic group (e.g. Asians), a country (e.g. Wales), a neighbourhood (e.g. St Lambert) or any size of unit. This first tier suggests that bilingual education is always enveloped in wider social, cultural, political and economic considerations. The classroom or school cannot be totally understood except in its relation to the community in which it exists.

The *second* tier concerns the *aims* or rationale of a bilingual education programme. Such aims may evolve from government, local administration, parents, or local interest groups, and involve stated and unstated goals. The hidden curriculum is as important as the given aims of the curriculum. There may be unanimity in aims or various degrees of disagreement and conflict.

The *third* tier concerns the actual *operation* of the bilingual classroom and school. The second by second, minute by minute, day by day practice of bilingual schooling may be evaluated. At times there may be a difference between intentions and outcomes, aims and practice.

The *fourth* tier is the *effects* of bilingual education. Linguistic proficiency, bicultural knowledge, self-esteem, vocational success, attitude to the two languages and biliteracy form a small subset of possible outcomes. Communities, politicians and teachers will differ as to their priorities in desired outcomes.

Spolsky (1978) provides a useful basic taxonomy of variables that could be examined in evaluation of bilingual education. The taxonomy suggests that present research has been narrow in its outlook, with only a small subset of questions being asked from a wide universe of potential issues.

The input–output–context–process bilingual education model

Dunkin & Biddle (1974), attempting to summarize research on teaching, suggested a four-part model. There are *inputs* or human ingredients into the classroom which may be thought of in terms of varying teacher and pupil characteristics. Much research examines how different inputs (e.g. teacher personality, pupil ability) affect *outputs*. Outputs or outcomes may be short-term (e.g. exam success) or longer-term (e.g. attitude to learning). The relationship between inputs and outputs can be modified by the *context* or environment in which schooling occurs. At a macro level, context could be, for example, ethnic group or local community effects on education. At a micro level, context may refer to the classroom environment (e.g. a classroom poor or rich in audio-visual resource material). The final part of the model is *process*, where the second by second life of actual classroom practice may be examined.

Baker (1985) extended this model to bilingual education. The suggestion is that bilingual education has inputs, outputs, contexts and processes over and above that of "normal" schooling as detailed by Dunkin & Biddle (1974). The model is illustrated in Figure 3.

The linguistic and cultural knowledge of bilingual teachers, their competency to operate in two languages and transmit two or more cultures are examples of teacher *inputs*. Pupil *inputs* include aptitude and skill in the two languages, their attitudes and motivations. *Outputs* could be many and are likely to be contentious, but are likely to include proficiency in the two languages, biliteracy, attitudes towards the languages and cultures, initial and subsequent integration into linguistically and culturally different groups, and self-esteem.

FIGURE 3.   *A Bilingual Education Model[1]*

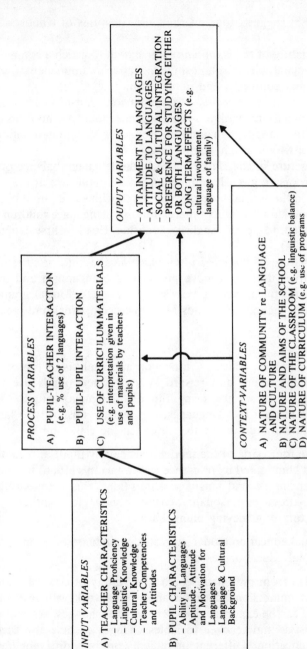

Note 1. This model may be extended to include attributes not specific to bilingual education
by reference to Dunkin & Biddle, (1974).

2. Arrows show the most usual connections made by research in relating elements of the
model.

Baker (1985) suggests four overlapping categories of *context*:

1. The nature of the *community*: the extent to which a community is bilingual, bicultural, positive, negative or ambivalent towards bilingual education and bilingualism.
2. The nature of the *school*: e.g. immersion, transitional bilingual, a bilingual unit within a mainstream school, a school inside a minority language heartland area or a designated bilingual school within an anglicized area.
3. The nature of the *classroom*: e.g. the language balance of the classroom (e.g. early immersion where pupils are at the same level in the second language compared with some United States "submersion" schools where minority language children are expected to learn English alongside English first language speakers).
4. The nature of the *curriculum material*: the kind of curriculum resources used to achieve progress in bilingualism and biculturalism, the use of audio-visual techniques, formal grammar lessons, technological aids (e.g. microcomputer) and creative activity.

Finally, the *process* concerns inspection and analysis of topics such as teacher's reinforcement and reward systems when pupils use their second language, criticism for using the first language, pupils' work involvement rate in their two languages, and teacher's use of two languages, in a qualitative and quantitative sense, in the classroom.

Each of the four parts of the model, particularly input and context, is illustrated and illuminated by reference to Schumann's (1986) taxonomy of factors influencing second language acquisition. This taxonomy considers the social, affective, personality, cognitive, biological, aptitude, and instructional factors in achieving bilingualism.

The bilingual education model suggests certain limitations and possibilities in bilingual education research.

(i) Generalization from present research to a variety of contexts can be dangerous. That immersion education appears to work well in Canada does not mean it can be exported elsewhere without changes. As contexts, pupil characteristics and teacher variables change, so may the success of immersion education. Different ingredients produce different meals. Occasionally the change of just one ingredient can change the taste of the whole product. Recipes for success need testing in a variety of contexts to assess their generalization potential. Research on bilingual education needs to be replicated in as many different contexts as possible, both across and inside countries. Such research also needs replication with the inputs varied. For example, using samples of working-class children, or schools where teachers have varying levels of commitment to bilingual education. Recipes for success are likely to be varied, complex and not necessarily stable over time. The model suggests the dangers of theologies and *ex cathedra* statements which abound in writings on bilingualism and bilingual education.

(ii) Outputs need to be thought of in a relative, contentious and pluralistic manner. Different interest groups expect different outcomes from bilingual schooling. Researchers have tended to focus narrowly on traditional skills which can be quantitatively measured. There may be alternative outcomes of bilingual education, sometimes contentious, which need investigating (e.g. self-concept, vocational success and adjustment, integration into society). Too much emphasis has hitherto been placed on end-of-year, end-of-school outcomes. Arguably, the more important effects of bilingual schooling are longer-term. For example, attitude to both languages and cultures after five, ten, twenty years of schooling; commitment and participatory activity in the two languages and cultures; raising children bilingually or not, and sending such children to bilingual schools are all investigatable long-term effects. Does bilingual education have a short-term effect that dies after leaving school? Does bilingual schooling have long-term, cumulative effects that are beneficial or otherwise to society? The critics of bilingual education can rarely be answered, as longitudinal studies are so rare.

(iii) Research studies in education occasionally examine all four parts of the model (e.g. Rutter et al., 1979). More often research looks at relationships between pairs of variables: context–process, process–output, input–process, input–output, process–output and input–context. In the research considered in this book it is apparent that much research is of the input–output (e.g. bilingualism–IQ) and context–output (e.g. immersion education–attainment) variety. Too little effort appears to have been given to process–output research in bilingual education. While second language teaching is well covered by process–output research, studies that examine the manifest and hidden curriculum of bilingual schooling are lacking. There are exceptions (e.g. Cleghorn & Genesee, 1984). The way teachers and pupils behave and interact, think, feel, talk, write, move and relate to one another are vital issues for teachers, parents and school administrators. Bilingual classrooms are, at times, different from mainstream classrooms and therefore need different process–output research.

Cummins' theoretical framework for minority student intervention and empowerment

A recent development in bilingual education theories is important and valuable. Although the theory represents an evolution rather than a revolution from previous theoretical ideas, it moves towards the practical and the possible. While necessarily containing some abstractions, it moves towards some direct implications for educational policy, provision and practice.

Cummins' (1986) theoretical framework concerns minority student failure, whether such students are in compensatory education or bilingual education. Only the latter focus will be considered here. There are three fundamental statements to Cummins' (1986) theory. First, "language minority students instructed through the minority language (for example, Spanish) for all or part of the school day perform as well in English academic skills as comparable students instructed totally through English" (p. 20). The proposition that language minority students need maximum exposure to English to boost their English achievement is logically possible but not supported by research. What seems logically possible is not always psychologically correct. Canadian immersion pupils develop English language skills comparable to mainstream English pupils. Teaching children through a second or minority language can lead to no loss in the development of English academic skills.

The second statement is the "interdependence hypothesis". This proposed that "to the extent that instruction through a minority language is effective in developing academic proficiency in the minority language, transfer of this proficiency to the majority language will occur given adequate exposure and motivation to learn the language" (Cummins, 1986:20). This idea has already been presented. Underlying the surface characteristics of both languages is one common core of developed ability or "academic proficiency". Beneath two tips on the water lies the one iceberg. The third statement concerns context. Community and school liaison, power and status relationships all need to be considered in a proper bilingual education theory.

Cummins' (1986) theory argues that minority language pupils are "empowered" or "disabled" by four major characteristics of schools.

1. *The extent to which minority language pupils' home language and culture are incorporated into the school curriculum.* If minority language children's home language and culture are excluded, minimized or successively reduced, the likelihood is there of that child being academically disabled.

Where the school incorporates, encourages and gives status to the minority language, the chances of empowerment are increased. Apart from potential positive and negative cognitive effects, the inclusion of minority language and culture into the curriculum may have effects on personality (e.g. self-esteem), attitudes, social and emotional well-being. This point is important because it raises an unanswered question about why bilingual education which emphasizes the minority language is successful. Is it due to such education fostering cognitive and academic proficiency, as the interdependence hypothesis suggests? Or is it also due, or more due, to pupils' cultural identity being secured and reinforced, thus enhancing self-confidence and self-esteem?

Cummins (1986) sees the incorporation of minority students' language and culture existing on an *additive–subtractive dimension*. "Educators who see their role as adding a second language and cultural affiliation to their students' repertoire are likely to empower students more than those who see their role as replacing or subtracting students' primary language and culture" (p. 25).

2. *The extent to which minority communities are encouraged to participate in their children's education.* Where parents are given power and status in the partial determination of their children's schooling, the empowerment of minority communities and children may result. When such communities and parents are kept relatively powerless, inferiority and lack of school progress may result. Parents may need help to help their children. If such co-operation is absent, parents may be blamed for their perceived lack of interest. The growth of the paired reading schemes in Britain is evidence of the power of a parent–teacher partnership. Parents listening to their children reading on a systematic basis tend to be effective agents of increased literacy.

As an illustration of the importance of community participation, Cummins (1986) cites the Haringey Project in England. Parental involvement in children's reading, even when parents were non-English-speaking and non-literate, had an important effect on children's reading progress.

Teachers are seen as being locatable on a dimension ranging from the *collaborative* to the *exclusionary*. Teachers at the collaborative end encourage parents of minority languages to participate in their offspring's academic progress through home activities or the involvement of parents in the classroom. Teachers at the exclusionary end maintain tight boundaries between themselves as professionals and parents. Collaboration with parents may be seen as irrelevant, unnecessary, unprofessional, even detrimental to children's progress.

3. *The extent to which education promotes the inner desire for children to become active seekers of knowledge and not just passive receptacles.* Learning can be active, independent and internally motivated or passive, dependent and requiring external pulls and pushes. Cummins (1986) suggests a dimension of pedagogy with two models at the extremes, namely the *transmission model* and the *reciprocal interaction model.* The transmission model views children as a bucket into which knowledge is willingly or unwillingly poured. The teacher controls the nature of the fluid being poured and the speed of pouring. Disabled students may be rendered relatively powerless as the transmission model tends to focus on the formal structure of curriculum areas. Highly structured drill and practice, for example, may teach only the surface features of language. The hidden curriculum of the transmission model may also reinforce and symbolize the powerlessness of language minority pupils. There are those in control and those controlled.

The alternative model, reciprocal interaction,

"requires a genuine dialogue between student and teacher in both oral and written modalities, guidance and facilitation rather than control of student learning by the teacher, and the encouragement of student/student talk in a collaborative learning context. This model emphasizes the development of higher level cognitive skills rather than just factual recall, and meaningful language use by students rather than the correction of surface forms. Language use and development are consciously integrated with all curricular content rather than taught as isolated subjects, and tasks are presented to students in ways that generate intrinsic rather than extrinsic motivation" (Cummins, 1986:28).

If the transmission model is allied to the disablement of minority language pupils, then the reciprocal interaction model is related to the empowerment of pupils. This latter model aims to give pupils more control over their own learning, with consequent potential positive effects for self-esteem, co-operation and motivation.

4. *The extent to which assessment of minority language pupils avoids locating problems in the pupil and seeks to find the root of the problem in the social and educational system or curriculum wherever possible.* Psychological and educational tests tend by their very nature to locate problems in the. individual pupil (e.g. low IQ, low motivation, backwardness in reading). At worst, educational psychologists and teachers may test and observe a child until a disability can be found in that child to explain poor academic attainment. Such a testing ideology and procedure may fail to

locate the root of the problem in the social, economic or educational system. The subtractive nature of transitional bilingual education, the transmission model used in the curriculum, the exclusionary orientation of the teacher towards parents and the community, the relative economic deprivation of minority children and their socio-economic background could each or jointly be the real origin of a minority language child's problem. Therefore assessment and diagnostic activity need to be *Advocacy rather than Legitimization oriented*. Advocacy means the assessor or diagnostician advocating for the child, by critically inspecting the social and educational context in which the child operates. This may involve comments about the power and status relationships between the dominant and dominated groups, at national, community, school and classroom level.

The theoretical framework can be summarized as follows:

	Empowered Minority Language Children	Disabled Minority Language Children
Dimension 1:	*Additive*: Incorporation of Home Language and Culture in the School	*Subtractive*: Home Language and Culture excluded from the school
Dimension 2:	*Collaborative*: Community Participation	*Exclusionary*: Community non-participation
Dimension 3:	*Reciprocal Interaction Curriculum*	*Transmission Oriented Curriculum*
Dimension 4:	*Advocacy* Oriented Assessment and Diagnosis	*Legitimization* Oriented Assessment and Diagnosis

Cummins' (1986) theoretical framework may be, in educational terms, a most important theory. It moves away from theories which explain one set of results or concentrate on the purely individual level of psychological functioning. It is a theory which incorporates psychological functioning and educational attainment, and gives some cognizance to the social, economic and political background that is so often crucial to fully understanding bilingualism and bilingual education. The theory covers research on cognitive functioning, motivation (although not very fully), educational success or failure in different forms of bilingual education, and takes on board the context of education in terms of power relationships, culture, community and parental involvement. The theory will require thorough testing in a variety of contexts and thus provides researchers with an agenda for future research.

The theory is not only important in that it is inter-disciplinary, attempting comprehensive if outline coverage of key issues and integrating a variety of research. It is almost important in that it suggests action and change. Many theories provide neat summaries or good explanations of data, but are static, and leave much guessing and filling in before they relate to the practical perspectives of educational administrators and teachers. Cummins' (1986) theory is an educational theory. It relates to possible practical progress in bilingual education and the achievement of bilingualism and biculturalism in minority groups. The theory has practical utility in that it directly suggests policy inspection and policy reformulation.

Conclusion

A chapter on diverse theories and models demonstrates that researchers on bilingualism and bilingual education speak different languages. There is multilingualism and multiculturalism in bilingual research methodologies. Some authors prefer the language of complex statistics, others the culture of grand theorizing. To summarize or synthesize the theories and models would be like describing an elaborate collage by listing the colours. A realistic and optimistic conclusion is given by Gardner (1985a:166) talking about his own model.

"There is no intention here to convince others that the model is a true or final one. I personally don't believe it is. I do feel, however, that it contains many elements which must be considered in future developments. A true test of any theoretical formulation is not only its ability to explain and account for phenomena which have been demonstrated, but also its ability to provide suggestions for further investigations, to raise new questions, to promote further developments and open new horizons".

Bibliography

AMERICAN PSYCHOLOGICAL ASSOCIATION, 1982, Review of Department of Education Report entitled "Effectiveness of Bilingual Education: A Review of Literature". Letter to the Congressional Hispanic Caucus, April 22nd.

ANISFELD, E., 1964, A comparison of the cognitive functioning of monolinguals and bilinguals. Unpublished Ph.D. thesis, McGill University.

ARGYLE, M., 1964, *Psychology and Social Problems.* London: Methuen.

ARNBERG, L., 1981, Bilingual education of young children in England and Wales. University of Linköping, Sweden: Department of Education.

ATKINSON, J.W., 1958, The thematic apperception measurement of motives within the context of a theory of motivation. In J. W. ATKINSON (ed.), *Motives in Fantasy, Action and Society.* London: Van Nostrand.

ATKINSON, J. W., 1964, *An Introduction to Motivation.* New York: Van Nostrand.

BAIN, B. C., 1975, Toward an integration of Piaget and Vygotsky: Bilingual considerations. *Linguistics* 160, 7–19.

BAIN, B. and YU, A., 1980, Cognitive consequences of raising children bilingually; 'One parent, one language'. *Canadian Journal of Psychology* 34 (4), 304–313.

—— 1984, The development of the body percept among working- and middle-class unilinguals and bilinguals. In M. PARADIS & Y. LEBRUN (eds), *Early Bilingualism and Child Development.* Lisse, Holland: Swets and Zeitlinger.

BAKER, C., 1976, Affiliation motivation; A psychological examination of some aspects of its origins, nature and effects. Unpublished Ph.D. thesis, University of Wales.

—— 1985, *Aspects of Bilingualism in Wales.* Clevedon: Multilingual Matters.

BAKER, K. A. and DE KANTER, A. A., 1981, *Effectiveness of Bilingual Education: A Review of Literature.* Washington D.C.: Office of Planning, Budget and Evaluation, U.S. Department of Education.

—— 1983, *Bilingual Education.* Lexington, Mass.: Lexington Books.

BALKAN, L., 1970, *Les Effets du Bilingualisme Français–Anglais sur les*

Aptitudes Intellectuelles. Brussels: Aimav.

BANNISTER, D. and FRANSELLA, F., 1971, *Inquiring Man. The Theory of Personal Constructs*. Harmondsworth, Middlesex: Penguin.

BARKE, E. M., 1933, A study of the comparative intelligence of children in certain bilingual and monoglot schools in South Wales. *British Journal of Educational Psychology* 3, 237–250.

BARKE, E. M. and PARRY-WILLIAMS, D.E., 1938, A further study of comparative intelligence of children in certain bilingual and monoglot schools in South Wales. *British Journal of Educational Psychology* 8, 63–67.

BARRIK, H. C. and SWAIN, M., 1976, A longitudinal study of bilingual and cognitive development. *International Journal of Psychology* 11, 251–263.

BEATY, S., 1985, Post-secondary bilingual education in British Columbia: To be or not to be. *Canadian Modern Language Review* 41 (5), 816–818.

BEN-ZEEV, S., 1977a, The influence of bilingualism on cognitive strategy and cognitive development. *Child Development* 48, 1009–1018.

—— 1977b, The effect of bilingualism in children from Spanish–English low economic neighbourhoods on cognitive development and cognitive strategy. *Working Papers on Bilingualism* 14, 83–122.

—— 1984, Bilingualism and cognitive development. In N. MILLER (ed.), *Bilingualism and Language Disability. Assessment and Remediation*. London: Croom Helm.

BEREITER, C., and SCARDAMELIA, M., 1981, From conversation to composition: The role of instruction in a development process. In R. GLASER (ed.), *Advances in Instructional Psychology* Volume 2. Hillsdale, New Jersey: Erlbaum.

BOURHIS, R. Y. and GILES, H., 1977, The language of intergroup distinctiveness. In H. GILES (ed.), *Language, Ethnicity and Intergroup Relations*. London: Academic Press.

BROOK, M. R. M., 1980, The 'mother-tongue' issue in Britain: Cultural diversity or control? *British Journal of Sociology of Education* 1 (3), 237–256.

BRUCK, M., 1978, The suitability of early French immersion programs for the language-disabled child. *Canadian Journal of Education* 3, 51–72.

—— 1985a, Predictors of transfer out of early French immersion programs. *Applied Psycholinguistics* 6, 39–61.

—— 1985b, Consequences of transfer out of early French immersion programs. *Applied Psycholinguistics* 6, 101–120.

BRUCK, M., LAMBERT, W.E. and TUCKER, G.R., 1976, Cognitive consequences of bilingual schooling: The St. Lambert Project through grade 6. Unpublished manuscript. Department of Psychology, McGill University.

BRUNER, J. S., 1975, Language as an Instrument of Thought. In A. DAVIES (ed.), *Problems of Language and Learning*. London: Heinemann.

BULLOCK REPORT, 1975, see under DEPARTMENT OF EDUCATION AND SCIENCE.

BURSTALL, C., JAMIESON, M., COHEN, S., and HARGREAVES, M., 1974, *Primary French in the Balance*. Windsor: NFER/Nelson.

BUSH, E., 1979, Bilingual Education in Gwent: Parental Attitudes and Aspirations. Unpublished M.Ed. thesis, University of Wales.

BUSH, E., ATKINSON, P. and READ, M., 1984, A Minority Choice: Welsh Medium Education in an Anglicised Area — Parents' Characteristics and Motives. *Polyglot* 5, Fiche 1 (April).

CACIOPPO, J. T., and PETTY, R. E., 1982, Language Variables, Attitudes and Persuasion. In E. B. RYAN and H. GILES (eds), *Attitudes Towards Language Variation*. London: Edward Arnold.

CALIFORNIA STATE DEPARTMENT OF EDUCATION, 1984, *Studies on Immersion Education. A Collection for United States Educators*. Sacramento, California: California State Department of Education.

CARRINGER, D. C., 1974, Creative Thinking Abilities of Mexican Youth. The Relationship of Bilingualism. *Journal of Cross Cultural Psychology* 5 (4), 492–504.

CATTELL, R. B., 1971, *Abilities: Their Structure, Growth and Action*. Boston: Houghton Mifflin.

CHÁVEZ, L. C., 1980, Jean Piaget's Theory of Equilibration Applied to Dual Language Development. In R. V. PADILLA (ed.), *Ethnoperspectives in Bilingual Education Research, Volume II: Theory in Bilingual Education*. Michigan: Eastern Michigan University.

CILAR (Committee on Irish Language Attitudes Research), 1975, *Report of the Committee on Irish Language Attitudes Research*. Dublin: Government Stationery Office.

CLEGHORN, A. and GENESEE, F., 1984, Languages in Contact: An Ethnographic Study of Interaction in an Immersion School. *TESOL Quarterly* 18 (4), 595–625.

CLEMENT, R., GARDNER, R.C., and SMYTHE, P.C., 1977, Motivational Variables in Second Language Acquisition: A Study of Francophones Learning English. *Canadian Journal of Behavioural Science* 9, 123–133.

—— 1980, Social and Individual Factors in Second Language Acquisition. *Canadian Journal of Behavioural Science* 12, 293–302.

COHEN, G., 1984, The Politics of Bilingual Education. *Oxford Review of Education* 10 (2), 225–241.

CROLL, P., 1986, *Systematic Classroom Observation*. London: Falmer.

CUMMINS, J., 1975, Cognitive Factors Associated with Intermediate Levels of Bilingual Skills. Unpublished manuscript, Educational Research Centre, St. Patrick's College, Dublin.

—— 1976, The Influence of Bilingualism on Cognitive Growth: A Synthesis of Research Findings and Explanatory Hypotheses. *Working Papers on Bilingualism* 9, 1–43.

—— 1977a, Cognitive Factors Associated with the Attainment of Intermediate Levels of Bilingual Skills. *Modern Language Journal* 61, 3–12.

—— 1977b, Immersion Education in Ireland: A Critical Review of Mac-Namara's Findings (with replies). *Working Papers in Bilingualism*, 1977, 13, 121–129.

—— 1977c, A Comparison of Reading Achievement in Irish and English Medium Schools. In V. GREANEY (ed.), *Studies in Reading*. Dublin: Education Co. of Ireland.

—— 1978a, Bilingualism and the Development of Metalinguistic Awareness. *Journal of Cross Cultural Psychology*, 1978, 9, 131–149.

—— 1978b, Metalinguistic Development of Children in Bilingual Education Programs: Data from Irish and Canadian Ukrainian–English Programs. In M. PARADIS (ed.), *Aspects of Bilingualism*. Columbia: Hornbeam Press.

—— 1978c, Immersion Programs: The Irish Experience. *International Review of Education* 24, 273–282.

—— 1978d, The Cognitive Development of Children in Immersion Programs. *Canadian Modern Language Review* 34, 855–883.

—— 1980a, The Construct of Language Proficiency in Bilingual Education. In J. E. ALATIS (ed.), *Georgetown University Round Table on Languages and Linguistics 1980*. Washington D. C.: Georgetown University Press.

—— 1980b, The Entry and Exit Fallacy in Bilingual Education. *NABE Journal* IV (3), 25–59.

—— 1981a, *Bilingualism and Minority-Language Children*. Ontario: Ontario Institute for Studies in Education.

—— 1981b, The Role of Primary Language Development in Promoting Educational Success for Language Minority Students. In CALIFORNIA STATE DEPARTMENT OF EDUCATION (ed.), *Schooling and Language Minority Students. A Theoretical Framework*. Los Angeles, California: Evaluation, Dissemination and Assessment Center. California State University.

—— 1983a, *Heritage Language Education. A Literature Review*. Ontario: Ministry of Education.

—— 1983b, Language Proficiency, Biliteracy and French Immersion. *Canadian Journal of Education* 8 (2), 117–138.

—— 1984a, *Bilingualism and Special Education: Issues in Assessment and Pedagogy*. Clevedon: Multilingual Matters.

—— 1984b, Bilingualism and Cognitive Functioning. In S. SHAPSON and V. D'OYLEY (eds), *Bilingual and Multicultural Education: Canadian Perspectives*. Clevedon: Multilingual Matters.

—— 1984c, Wanted: A Theoretical Framework for Relating Language Proficiency to Academic Achievement Among Bilingual Students. In C. RIVERA (ed.), *Language Proficiency and Academic Achievement*. Clevedon: Multilingual Matters.

—— 1986, Empowering Minority Students: A Framework for Intervention. *Harvard Educational Review* 56 (1), 18–36.

CUMMINS, J. and GENESEE, F., 1985. Bilingual Education Programmes in Wales and Canada. In C. J. DODSON (ed.), *Bilingual Education: Evaluation, Assessment and Methodology*. Cardiff: University of Wales Press.

CUMMINS, J. and GULUTSAN, M., 1974, Some Effects of Bilingualism on Cognitive Functioning. In S. CAREY (ed.), *Bilingualism, Biculturalism and Education*. Edmonton: University of Alberta Press.

CUMMINS, J., and MULCAHY, R., 1978, Orientation to Language in Ukrainian–English Bilingual Children. *Child Development* 49, 1239–1242.

CURRICULUM AND EXAMINATIONS BOARD, 1985, *Language in the Curriculum*. Dublin: Curriculum and Examinations Board.

DANOFF, M. N., COLES, G. J., McLAUGHLIN, D. H. and REYNOLDS, D. J., 1977, *Evaluation of the Impact of ESEA Title VII Spanish/English Bilingual Education Programs*. Volume 1. Palo Alto, California: American Institutes for Research.

—— 1978, *Evaluation of the Impact of ESEA Title VII Spanish/English Bilingual Education Programs*. Volume 3. Palo Alto, California, American Institutes for Research.

DARCY, N. T., 1953, A Review of the Literature on the Effects of Bilingualism upon the Measurement of Intelligence. *Journal of Genetic Psychology* 82, 21–57.

DAVIES, J. P., 1980, Ymagweddiad Disgyblion Trydydd Dosbarth Ysgolion Uwchradd yng Nghlwyd tuag at y Gymraeg. Unpublished M.Ed. thesis, University of Wales.

—— 1986, Dadansoddiad O Nodau Graddedig Ar Gyfer Oedolion Sy'n Dysgu'r Gymraeg Fel Ail Iaith. Unpublished Ph.D. thesis, University of Wales.

DAY, R. R., 1982, Children's Attitudes Towards Language. In E. B. RYAN and H. GILES (eds), *Attitudes Towards Language Variation: Social and Applied Contexts*. London: Edward Arnold.

DEPARTMENT OF EDUCATION AND SCIENCE, 1975, *A Language for Life* (Bullock Report). London: HMSO.

—— 1985, *Education for All* (Swann Report). London: HMSO.

DODSON, C. J., 1978, Evaluation Report. In *Bilingual Education in Wales, 5–11*. London: Evans/Methuen.

—— 1981, A Reappraisal of Bilingual Development and Education: Some Theoretical and Practical Considerations. In H. BAETENS BEARDSMORE (ed.), *Elements of Bilingual Theory*. Brussels: Vrije Universiteit Brussel.

—— 1983, Bilingualism, Language Teaching and Learning. *British Journal of Language Teaching* 1983, 21, 3–8.

—— 1985a, Second Language Acquisition and Bilingual Development: A Theoretical Framework. *Journal of Multilingual and Multicultural Development* 6 (5), 325–346.

—— 1985b, Schools Council Project on Bilingual Education (Secondary Schools) 1974–1978: Methodology. In C. J. DODSON (ed.), *Bilingual Education: Evaluation, Assessment and Methodology*. Cardiff: University of Wales Press.

—— 1985c, Schools Council Bilingual Education Project (Primary Schools) 1968–1977: An Independent Evaluation. In C. J. DODSON (ed.), *Bilingual Education: Evaluation, Assessment and Methodology*. Cardiff: University of Wales Press.

DONALDSON, M., 1978, *Children's Minds*. Glasgow: Collins.

DULAY, H.C. and BURT, M.K., 1978, *Why Bilingual Education? A Summary of Research Findings*. San Francisco: Bloomsbury West. (2nd Edition.)

—— 1979. Bilingual Education: A Close Look at Its Effects. *Focus*, no. 1.

DUNCAN, S.E. and DE AVILA, E. A., 1979, Bilingualism and Cognition: Some Recent Findings. *NABE Journal* 4 (1), 15–50.

DUNKIN, M. and BIDDLE, B.J., 1974, *The Study of Teaching*. New York: Holt, Rinehart and Winston.

EDELSKY, C. *et al.*, 1983, Semilingualism and Language Deficit. *Applied Linguistics*, 1983, 4 (1), 1–22.

EDWARDS, J.R., 1981, The Context of Bilingual Education. *Journal of Multilingual and Multicultural Development* 2 (1), 25–44.

—— 1984a, The Social and Political Context of Bilingual Education. In R. J. SAMUDA, J. W. BERRY and M. LAFERRIÈRE (eds), *Multiculturalism in Canada. Social and Educational Perspectives*. London: Allyn and Bacon.

—— 1984b, Irish: Planning and Preservation. *Journal of Multilingual and*

Multicultural Development 5 (3 & 4), 267–275.

—— 1984c, Irish and English in Ireland. In P. TRUDGILL (ed.), *Language in the British Isles*. Cambridge: Cambridge University Press.

EDWARDS PERSONAL PREFERENCE SCHEDULE, 1959, *Manual for the Edwards Personal Preference Schedule* (Revised Edition). New York: Psychological Corporation.

EDWARDS, V., 1984, *Language Policy in Multicultural Britain*. London: Academic Press.

EVANS, B. and WAITES, B., 1981, *IQ and Mental Testing. An Unnatural Science and Its Social History*. London: Macmillan.

EVANS, D.J., 1960, *Language Survey Report*. Dolgellau: Meirioneth Education Authority.

FELDMAN, C. and SHEN, M., 1971, Some Language-Related Cognitive Advantages of Bilingual Five-Year-Olds. *Journal of Genetic Psychology* 118, 235–244.

FESTINGER, L., 1957, *A Theory of Cognitive Dissonance*. Stanford: Stanford University Press.

FESTINGER, L. and CARLSMITH, J. M., 1959, Cognitive Consequences of Forced Compliance. *Journal of Abnormal and Social Psychology* 54, 369–374.

FIGUEROA, P., 1984, Minority Pupil Progress. In M. CRAFT (ed.), *Education and Cultural Pluralism*. London: Falmer Press.

FINDLING, J., 1969, Bilingual Need Affiliation and Future Orientation in Extragroup and Intragroup Domains. *Modern Language Journal*, 1969, 53, 227–231.

FISHMAN, J. A., 1965, Who Speaks What Language to Whom and When? *La Linguistique*, 67–68.

—— 1975, Review of CILAR, *Irish Times*, 15th August.

—— 1977, The Social Science Perspective. In Centre for Applied Linguistics (ed.), *Bilingual Education: Current Perspectives*. Arlington, Virginia: CAL.

FITZPATRICK, F. 1987, *The Open Door: The Bradford Bilingual Project*. Clevedon, Avon: Multilingual Matters Ltd.

GAARDER, A. B., 1976, Linkages between Foreign Language Teaching and Bilingual Education. In J. E. ALATIS and K. TWADDELL (eds), *English as a Second Language in Bilingual Education*. Washington, D. C.: TESOL.

GARDNER, H., 1983, *Frames of Mind. The Theory of Multiple Intelligences*. New York: Basic Books.

GARDNER, R. C., 1979, Social Psychological Aspects of Second Language Acquisition. In H. GILES and R. ST. CLAIR (eds), *Language and Social Psychology*. Oxford: Blackwell.

—— 1982, Language Attitudes and Language Learning. In E. B. RYAN and H. GILES (eds), *Attitudes Towards Language Variation*. London: Edward Arnold.

—— 1983, Learning Another Language: A True Social Psychological Experiment. *Journal of Language and Social Psychology* 2, 219–239.

—— 1985a, *Social Psychology and Second Language Learning*. London: Edward Arnold.

—— 1985b, The Attitude/Motivation Test Battery. Technical Report. University of Western Ontario, Canada.

GARDNER, R. C., LALONDE, R. N., and MACPHERSON, J., 1986, Social Factors in Second Language Attrition. *Language Learning* 35 (4), 519–540.

GARDNER, R. C., LALONDE, R. N. and PIERSON, R., 1983, The socio-educational model of second language acquisition: an investigation using LISREL causal modeling. *Journal of Language and Social Psychology* 2, 51–65.

GARDNER, R. C. and LAMBERT, W. E., 1959, Motivational Variables in Second Language Acquisition. *Canadian Journal of Psychology* 13, 266–272.

—— 1972, *Attitudes and Motivation in Second Language Learning*. Rowley, Mass.: Newbury House.

GARDNER, R. C. and SMYTHE, P. C., 1975, Second Language Acquisition: A Social Psychological Approach. Research Bulletin 332, University of Western Ontario.

—— 1981, On The Development of the Attitude/Motivation Test Battery. *Canadian Modern Language Review* 37, 510–525.

GENESEE, F., 1978, Second Language Learning and Language Attitudes. *Working Papers on Bilingualism* 16, 19–42.

—— 1983, Bilingual Education of Majority-language Children: The Immersion Experiments in Review. *Applied Psycholinguistics* 4, 1–46.

—— 1984, Historical and Theoretical Foundations of Immersion Education. In CALIFORNIA STATE DEPARTMENT OF EDUCATION (ed.), *Studies on Immersion Education. A Collection for United States Educators*. California: California State Department of Education.

—— 1985, Second Language Learning Through Immersion: A Review of U.S. Programs. *Review of Educational Research* 55 (4), 541–561.

GENESEE, F. and HAMAYAN, E., 1980, Individual Differences in Young Second Language Learners. *Applied Psycholinguistics*, 1, 95–110.

GENESEE, F., ROGERS, P. and HOLOBOW, N., 1983, The Social Psychology of Second Language Learning: Another Point of View. *Language Learning*, 1983, 33 (2), 209–224.

GENESEE, F., TUCKER, G.R. and LAMBERT, W. E., 1975, Communication Skills in Bilingual Children. *Child Development* 46, 1010–1014.
—— 1978a, An Experiment in Trilingual Education. *Language Learning* 28, 343–365.
—— 1978b, An Experiment in Trilingual Education. *Canadian Modern Language Review* 34, 621–643.
GILES, H., HEWSTONE, M. and BALL, P., 1983. Language Attitudes in Multilingual Settings: Prologue with Priorities. *Journal of Multilingual and Multicultural Development* 4 (2 & 3), 81–100.
GITTINS REPORT, 1967, *Primary Education in Wales*. Central Advisory Council for Education Report. London: HMSO.
GLASS, G. V., McGAW, B., and SMITH, M. L., 1981, *Meta-analysis in Social Research*. Beverley Hills: Sage.
GLIKSMAN, L., 1976. Second Language Acquisition: The Effects of Student Attitudes on Classroom Behaviour. Unpublished M.A. thesis, University of Western Ontario.
—— 1981, Improving the Prediction of Behaviours Associated with Second Language Acquisition. Unpublished Ph.D. thesis, University of Western Ontario.
GONZÁLEZ, J. M., 1979, Coming of Age in Bilingual/Bicultural Education: A Historical Perspective. In H. T. TRUEBA and C. BARNETT-MIZRAHI, (eds), *Bilingual Multicultural Education and the Professional. From Theory to Practice*. Rowley, Mass.: Newbury House.
GORDON, M. E., 1980, Attitudes and motivation in second language achievement. Unpublished Ph.D. thesis, University of Toronto.
GOWAN, J. C. and TORRANCE, E. P., 1965, An Intercultural Study of Nonverbal Ideational Fluency. *Gifted Child Quarterly* 9, 13–15.
GRANT, J. H., 1983, An Investigation into the Feasibility of Establishing Gaelic/English Bilingual Primary Schools on the Mainland of Scotland. Unpublished Master's thesis, University of Glasgow.
GRANT, N., 1984, Cultural Diversity and Education in Scotland. *European Journal of Education* 19 (1), 53–64.
GREENE, D., 1981, The Atlantic Group: Neo Celtic and Faroese. In E. HAUGEN, J. D. McCLURE and D. THOMSON (eds), *Minority Languages Today*. Edinburgh: Edinburgh University Press.
GRIFFITHS, M., 1986, The Growth of Welsh-Medium Schools. In M. GRIFFITHS (ed.), *The Welsh Language in Education*. Cardiff: Welsh Joint Education Committee.
GROSJEAN, F., 1985, The Bilingual as a Competent But Specific Speaker-Hearer. *Journal of Multilingual and Multicultural Development* 6 (6), 467–477.
GUILFORD, J. P., 1982, Cognitive Psychology's Ambiguities: Some sug-

gested Remedies. *Psychological Review* 89, 48–59.

HAKUTA, K., 1986, *Mirror of Language. The Debate on Bilingualism.* New York: Basic Books.

HAMERS, J. F. and BLANC, M., 1982, Towards a Social-Psychological Model of Bilingual Development. *Journal of Language and Social Psychology* 1 (1), 29–49.

—— 1983, Bilinguality in the Young Child: A Social Psychological Model. In P. H. NELDE (ed.), *Theory, Methods and Models of Contact Linguistics.* Bonn: Dümmler.

HARRIS, J., 1984, *Spoken Irish in Primary Schools. An Analysis of Achievement.* Dublin: Institiúid Teangeolaíochta Éireann.

HEARNSHAW, L. S., 1979, *Cyril Burt: Psychologist.* London: Hodder and Stoughton.

HEIDER, F., 1958, *The Psychology of Interpersonal Relations.* New York: Wiley.

HER MAJESTY'S STATIONERY OFFICE, 1965, *Immigration from the Commonwealth.* London: HMSO.

HERMAN, S. R., 1968, Explorations in the Social Psychology of Language Choice. In J. A. FISHMAN (ed.), *Readings in the Sociology of Language.* The Hague: Mouton.

HERNÁNDEZ-CHÁVEZ, E., 1984, The Inadequacy of English Immersion Education as an Educational Approach for Language Minority Students in the United States. In CALIFORNIA STATE DEPARTMENT OF EDUCATION (ed.), *Studies on Immersion Education. A Collection for United States Educators.* California: California State Department of Education.

HIGHAM, J., 1975, *Send These To Me.* New York: Atheneum.

HOULTON, D. and WILLEY, R., 1983, *Supporting Children's Bilingualism. Some Policy Issues for Primary Schools and Local Education Authorities.* York: Longman/Schools Council.

HUDSON, L., 1966, *Contrary Imaginations. A Psychological Study of the English Schoolboy.* Harmondsworth, Middlesex: Penguin.

IANCO-WORRALL, A. D., 1972, Bilingualism and Cognitive Development. *Child Development* 43, 1390–1400.

INNER LONDON EDUCATION AUTHORITY, 1979, *Report on the 1978 Census of those ILEA Pupils for whom English was not a First Language.* London: ILEA.

—— 1982, *Bilingualism in the ILEA: The Educational Implications of the 1981 Language Census.* London: ILEA.

INSKO, C. A., 1965, Verbal Reinforcement of Attitudes. *Journal of Personality and Social Psychology* 2, 621–623.

ISAAC, N., 1972, *Ifan ab Owen Edwards: 1895–1970.* Cardiff: University of Wales Press.

JAMES, C. B.E., 1947, A Comparative Study of General Performance Between Bilingual and Monoglot Children in South Wales. Unpublished B.Ed. thesis, University of Edinburgh.

JENKINS, G. H., 1986, The Welsh Language in Education: An Historical Survey. In M. GRIFFITHS (ed.), *The Welsh Language in Education*. Cardiff: Welsh Joint Education Committee.

JENSEN, J. V., 1962, Effects of Childhood Bilingualism. *Elementary English* 39, 132–143.

JONES, G. E., 1982, *Controls and Conflicts in Welsh Secondary Education, 1889–1944*. Cardiff: University of Wales Press.

JONES, T. P., 1987, Thirty Years of Success: A Brief Outline of the Development of Welsh Language Teaching Materials. *Education for Development*, in press.

JONES, W. R., 1933, Tests for the Examination of The Effect of Bilingualism on Intelligence. Unpublished M.A. thesis, University of Wales.

—— 1949, Attitude Towards Welsh as a Second Language. A Preliminary Investigation. *British Journal of Educational Psychology* 19 (1), 44–52.

—— 1950, Attitudes Towards Welsh as a Second Language. A Further Investigation. *British Journal of Educational Psychology* 20 (2), 117–132.

—— 1953, The Influence of Reading Ability in English on Intelligence Test Scores of Welsh-Speaking Children. *British Journal of Educational Psychology* 23, 114–120.

—— 1955, *Bilingualism and Reading Ability in English*. Cardiff: University of Wales Press.

—— 1959, *Bilingualism and Intelligence*. Cardiff: University of Wales Press.

—— 1960a, Replies to Comments by J. L. Williams. *British Journal of Educational Psychology* 30, 272–273.

—— 1960b, Ymchwil Addysgol yng Nghymru. *Y Faner*, May 12th.

—— 1966, *Bilingualism in Welsh Education*. Cardiff: University of Wales Press.

JONES, W. R., MORRISON, J. R., ROGERS, J. and SAER, H., 1957, *The Educational Attainment of Bilingual Children in Relation to Their Intelligence and Linguistic Background*. Cardiff: University of Wales Press.

KAGAN, J., 1971, *Understanding Children*. New York: Harcourt, Brace and Javanovich.

—— 1972, Motives and Development. *Journal of Personality and Social Psychology* 22, 51–66.

KAHLE, L. R., 1984, *Attitudes and Social Adaptation*. Oxford: Pergamon.

KATZ, D., 1960. The Functional Approach to the Study of Attitude. *Public Opinion Quarterly* 24, 163–204.

KELLY, A., 1986, A Method to the Madness? Quantitative Research Reviewing. *Research in Education* 35, (May), 25–41.

KELLY, G. A., 1955, *A Theory of Personality. The Psychology of Personal Constructs*. New York: Norton.

KESSLER, C. and QUINN, M.E., 1982, Cognitive Development in Bilingual Environments. In B. HARTFORD, A. VALDMAN and C. R. FOSTER (eds), *Issues in International Bilingual Education. The Role of the Vernacular*. New York: Plenum Press.

KLINE, P., 1983, *Personality Measurement and Theory*. London: Hutchinson.

KRASHEN, S. D., 1981, Bilingual Education and Second Language Acquisition Theory. In CALIFORNIA STATE DEPARTMENT OF EDUCATION (ed.), *Schooling and Language Minority Students. A Theoretical Framework*. Los Angeles, California: Evaluation, Dissemination and Assessment Center. California State University.

LALONDE, R. N., 1982, Second Language Acquisition: A Causal Analysis. Unpublished M.A. thesis, University of Western Ontario.

LAMBERT, W. E., 1974, Culture and Language as Factors in Learning and Education. In F. E. ABOUD and R. D. MEADE (eds), *Cultural Factors in Learning and Education*. Bellingham, Washington: 5th Western Washington Symposium on Learning.

—— 1977, Culture and Language as Factors in Learning and Education. In F. E. ECKMAN (ed.), *Current Themes in Linguistics. Bilingualism, Experimental Linguistics and Language Typologies*. New York: Wiley.

LAMBERT, W. E. and ANISFELD, E., 1969, A Note on the Relationship of Bilingualism and Intelligence. *Canadian Journal of Behavioural Science* 1 (2), 123–128.

LAMBERT, W. E. and TUCKER, G. R., 1972, *Bilingual Education of Children. The St. Lambert Experiment*. Rowley, Mass.: Newbury House.

LAMBOURNE, R., and WHELDALL, K., 1979, The Use of the Analysis of Co-variance in Educational Research: Panacea or Pitfall for the Unwary? *Educational Studies* 5 (1), 43–51.

LANDRY, R. G., 1974, A Comparison of Second Language Learners and Monolinguals on Divergent Thinking Tasks at the Elementary School Level. *Modern Language Journal* 58, 10–15.

LAPIERE, R. T., 1934, Attitudes Versus Actions. *Social Forces* 14, 230–237.

LAPKIN, S. and CUMMINS, J., 1984, Canadian French Immersion Education: Current Administrative and Instructional Practices. In CALI-

FORNIA STATE DEPARTMENT OF EDUCATION (ed.), *Studies on Immersion Education. A Collection for United States Educators*. California: California State Department of Education.

LAURIE, S. S., 1890, *Lectures on Language and Linguistic Method in the School*. Cambridge: Cambridge University Press.

LEOPOLD, W. F., 1939–1949, *Speech Development of a Bilingual Child. A Linguist's Record*. Evanston, Illinois: Northwestern University Press (4 volumes).

LEWIS, D. G., 1960, Differences in Attainment Between Primary Schools in Mixed-Language Areas. *British Journal of Educational Psychology* 30, 63–70.

LEWIS, E. G., 1975, Attitude to Language Among Bilingual Children and Adults in Wales. *International Journal of the Sociology of Language* 4, 103–121.

—— 1977, Bilingualism and Bilingual Education: The Ancient World to the Renaissance. In B. SPOLSKY and R. L. COOPER (eds), *Frontiers of Bilingual Education*. Rowley, Mass.: Newbury House.

—— 1981, *Bilingualism and Bilingual Education*. Oxford: Pergamon.

LIEDTKE, W. W. and NELSON, L. D., 1968, Concept Formation and Bilingualism. *Alberta Journal of Educational Research* 14 (4), 225–232.

LIKERT, R., 1932, A Technique for the Measurement of Attitude. *Archives of Psychology*, No. 140.

LINGUISTIC MINORITIES PROJECT, 1984, Linguistic Minorities in England: A Short Report on the Linguistic Minorities Project. *Journal of Multilingual and Multicultural Development* 5 (5), 351–366.

—— 1985, *The Other Languages of England*. London: Routledge and Kegan Paul.

LUKMANI, Y. M., 1972, Motivation to Learn and Learning Proficiency. *Language Learning* 22, 261–273.

MCCLELLAND, D. C., 1958, The Importance of Early Learning in the Formation of Motives. In J. W. ATKINSON (ed.), *Motives in Fantasy, Action and Society*. London: Van Nostrand.

—— 1961, *The Achieving Society*. London: Free Press.

MCCONNELL, B., 1980, Effectiveness of Individualized Bilingual Instruction for Migrant Students. Unpublished Ph.D. dissertation, Washington State University.

MACDONALD, B., ADELMAN, C., KUSHNER, S. and WALKER, R., 1982, *Bread and Dreams. A Case Study of Bilingual Schooling in the U.S.A.* Norwich: CARE Occasional Publications, No. 12.

MCGUIRE, W. J., 1981, The Probabilogical Model of Cognitive Structure and Attitude Change. In R. E. PETTY, T. M. OSTROM and

T. C. BROCK (eds), *Cognitive Responses in Persuasion*. Hillsdale, N.J.: Lawrence Erlbaum.

McKEACHIE, W. J. and DOYLE, C. L., 1966, *Psychology*. New York: Addison and Wesley.

MACKEY, W. F., 1962, The Description of Bilingualism. *Canadian Journal of Linguistics*, 7, 51–85.

—— 1970, A Typology of Bilingual Education. *Foreign Language Annals* 3, 596–608.

—— 1977, The Evaluation of Bilingual Education. In B. SPOLSKY and R. COOPER (eds), *Frontiers of Bilingual Education*. Rowley, Mass.: Newbury House.

MacKINNON, K., 1981, Scottish Opinion on Gaelic. *A Report on a National Attitude Survey for An Comunn Gaidhealach*. Hatfield Polytechnic, Social Science Research Publication No. SS14.

—— 1984a, Power at the Periphery: The Language Dimension and the Case of Gaelic Scotland. *Journal of Multilingual and Multicultural Development* 5 (6), 491–510.

—— 1984b, Scottish Gaelic and English in the Highlands. In P. TRUDGILL (ed.), *Language in the British Isles*. Cambridge: University of Cambridge Press.

—— 1986, *Gaelic Language Regeneration amongst Young People in Scotland 1971–1981 from Census Data*. Hatfield Polytechnic, Social Science Series No. SSR15.

McLAUGHLIN, B., 1984, Early Bilingualism: Methodological and Theoretical Issues. In M. PARADIS and Y. LEBRUN (eds), *Early Bilingualism and Child Development*. Lisse, Holland: Swets and Zeitlinger.

MacNAB, G. L., 1979, Cognition and Bilingualism: A Reanalysis of Studies. *Linguistics* 17, 231–255.

MacNAMARA, J., 1966, *Bilingualism and Primary Education. A Study of Irish Experience*. Edinburgh: University Press.

—— 1970, Bilingualism and Thought. In J. E. ALATIS (ed.), *Report of the Twenty-First Annual Round Table Meeting on Linguistics and Language Studies*. Georgetown: Georgetown University Press.

MALHERBE, E. C., 1946, *The Bilingual School*. London: Longmans.

MARTIN-JONES, M., 1984, The Newer Minorities: Literacy and Educational Issues. In P. TRUDGILL (ed.), *Language in the British Isles*. Cambridge: Cambridge University Press.

MARTIN-JONES, M. and ROMAINE, S., 1986, Semilingualism: A Half Baked Theory of Communicative Competence. *Applied Linguistics* 7 (1), 26–38.

MASLOW, A. H., 1954, *Motivation and Personality*. New York: Harper.

MATTHEWS, T., 1979, *An Investigation into the Effects of Background*

Characteristics and Special Language Services on the Reading Achievement and English Fluency of Bilingual Students. Seattle, Washington: Seattle Public Schools, Department of Planning, Research and Evaluation.

MERCER, J., 1978/1979, Test "Validity", "Bias", and "Fairness": An Analysis from the Perspective of the Sociology of Knowledge. *Interchange* 9 (1), 1–16.

MINISTRY FOR EDUCATION, 1963, *English for Immigrants.* Pamphlet No. 43. London: HMSO.

MORRISON, J. R., 1958, Bilingualism: Some Psychological Aspects. *The Advancement of Science* 56, 287–290.

MOTET (Mother Tongue and English Teaching Project), 1981, *Summary of the Reports* (2 volumes). Bradford: School of Education, University of Bradford.

MURRAY, H. A., 1938, *Explorations in Personality.* New York: Oxford University Press.

MURRAY, J. and MORRISON, C., 1984, *Bilingual Primary Education in the Western Isles, Scotland.* Stornoway, Isle of Lewis: Acair.

NAIMAN, N., FRÖHLICH, M., STERN, H. H. and TODESCO, A., 1978, The Good Language Learner. *Research in Education Series/7.* Ontario Institute for Studies in Education.

NCMTT (National Council for Mother Tongue Teaching), 1985, The Swann Report: Education for All? *Journal of Multilingual and Multicultural Development*, 1985, 6 (6), 497–508.

NEUFELD, G. G., 1974, A Theoretical Perspective on the Relationship of Bilingualism and Thought: Revisited. *Working Papers on Bilingualism*, No., 2, 125–129.

NFER/WJEC (National Foundation for Educational Research/Welsh Joint Education Council), 1969, *A Report on the 1960 National Survey.* Cowbridge, Glamorgan: D. Brown & Sons.

NOBLE, G., and DALTON, G., 1976, "Some Cognitive Implications of Bilingualism", *Oideas* 16, 42–52.

Ó BUACHALLA, S., 1984, Educational Policy and the Role of the Irish Language from 1831 to 1981. *European Journal of Education* 19 (1), 75–92.

O'DOHERTY, E. F., 1958a, Bilingualism: Educational Aspects. *Advancement of Science* 56, 282–290.

—— 1958b, Bilingual School Policy. *Studies* 47, 259–268.

OLLER, J. W., HUDSON, A. and LIU, P., 1977, Attitudes and Attained Proficiency in ESL: A Sociolinguistic Study of Native Speakers of Chinese in the United States. *Language Learning* 27, 1–27.

OLLER, J. W., PERKINS, K. and MURAKAMI, M., 1980, Seven Types of

Learner Variables in Relation to ESL Learning. In J. W. OLLER and K. PERKINS (eds), *Research in Language Testing*. Rowley, Mass.: Newbury House.

Ó RIAGÁIN, P. and Ó GLIASÁIN, M., 1984, *The Irish Language in the Republic of Ireland 1983: Preliminary Report of a National Survey*. Dublin: Institiúid Teangeolaíochta Éireann.

PAULSTON, C. B., 1980, *Bilingual Education. Theories and Issues*. Rowley, Mass.: Newbury House.

PAWLEY, C., 1985, How Bilingual are French Immersion Students? *Canadian Modern Language Review* 41 (5), 865–876.

PEAL, E. and LAMBERT, W. E., 1962, The Relationship of Bilingualism to Intelligence. *Psychological Monographs* 76, 27, 1–23.

PETERS, R. S., 1958, *The Concept of Motivation*. London: Routledge and Kegan Paul.

PIAGET, J., 1952, *The Child's Conception of Number*. London: Routledge and Kegan Paul.

—— 1955, *The Language and Thought of the Child*. New York: World Press.

PINTNER, R. and ARSENIAN, S., 1937, The Relation of Bilingualism to Verbal Intelligence and School Adjustment. *Journal of Educational Research*, 31, 255–263.

PRICE, E., 1978, Evaluation Report. In *Bilingual Education in Wales, 5–11*. London: Evans/Methuen.

—— 1983, Assessing the Listening and Speaking Skills of Welsh Learners — Lessons for Syllabus Design. In P. H. NELDE (ed.), *Theory, Methods and Models of Contact Linguistics*. Bonn: Dümmler.

—— 1985, Schools Council Bilingual Education Project (Primary Schools) 1968–1977: An Assessment. In C. J. DODSON (ed.), *Bilingual Education: Evaluation, Assessment and Methodology*. Cardiff: University of Wales Press.

PRICE, E., POWELL, R. and JONES, A., 1981, *Report on the Survey of Speaking Skills Among 10–11 Year Old Welsh Learners, 1981*. Cardiff: Welsh Office.

PRICE-JONES, E., 1982, A Study of Some of the Factors which Determine the Degree of Bilingualism of a Welsh Child between 10 and 13 Years of Age. Unpublished Ph.D. thesis, University of Wales.

RIVERA, C. (ed.), 1984, *Language Proficiency and Academic Achievement*. Clevedon: Multilingual Matters.

ROBERTS, C., 1985, Teaching and Learning Commitment in Bilingual Schools. Unpublished Ph.D. thesis, University of Wales.

ROSEN, H. and BURGESS, T., 1980, *Languages and Dialects of London School Children: an Investigation*. London: Ward Lock.

ROSENTHAL, R., 1966, *Experimenter Effects in Behavioural Research*. New

York: Appleton–Century–Crofts.

—— 1984, *Meta-Analytic Procedures for Social Research*. London: Sage.

RUEDA, R., 1983, Metalinguistic Awareness in Monolingual and Bilingual Mildly Retarded Children. *NABE Journal* 8, 55–68.

RUTTER, M. *et al.*, 1979, *Fifteen Thousand Hours*. London: Open Books.

RYAN, E. B., 1979, Why Do Low-Prestige Language Varieties Persist? In H. GILES and R. N. ST. CLAIR (eds), *Language and Social Psychology*. Oxford: Blackwell.

SAER, D. J., 1922, An Inquiry into the Effect of Bilingualism upon the Intelligence of Young Children. *Journal of Experimental Pedagogy* 6, 232–240 and 266–274.

—— 1923, The Effects of Bilingualism on Intelligence. *British Journal of Psychology* 14, 25–38.

SAER, D. J., SMITH, F. and HUGHES, J., 1924, *The Bilingual Problem*. Wrexham: Hughes and Son.

SCHUMANN, J. H., 1986, Research on the Acculturation Model for Second Language Acquisition. *Journal of Multilingual and Multicultural Development* 7 (5), 379–392.

SCOTT, S., 1973, The Relation of Divergent Thinking to Bilingualism: Cause or Effect? Unpublished Research Report, McGill University.

SHARP, D., THOMAS, B., PRICE, E., FRANCIS, G. and DAVIES, I., 1973, *Attitudes to Welsh and English in the Schools of Wales*. Basingstoke/ Cardiff: Macmillan/University of Wales Press.

SIGUÁN, M. and MACKEY, W. F., 1987, *Education and Bilingualism*. London: Kogan Page.

SIMONS, H., 1979, Mother Tongue and Culture in Bedfordshire. First External Evaluation Report. Cambridge: Cambridge Institute of Education.

SINGH, R., 1986, Immersion: Problems and Principles. *Canadian Modern Language Review* 42 (3), 559–571.

SKUTNABB-KANGAS, T., 1981, *Bilingualism or Not: The Education of Minorities*. Clevedon: Multilingual Matters.

SKUTNABB-KANGAS, T. and TOUKOMAA, P., 1976, *Teaching Migrant Children Mother Tongue and Learning the Language of the Host Country in the Context of the Socio-Cultural Situation of the Migrant Family*. Tampere, Finland: Tukimuksia Research Reports.

SMITH, F., 1923, Bilingualism and Mental Development. *British Journal of Psychology* 13, 271–282.

SPEARMAN, C., 1927, *The Abilities of Man*. New York: Macmillan.

SPOLSKY, B., 1978, A Model for the Evaluation of Bilingual Education. *International Review of Education*, 24 (3), 347–360.

SPOLSKY, B., GREEN, J. B. and READ, J., 1974, *A Model for the Description, Analysis and Perhaps Evaluation of Bilingual Education*. University of New Mexico: Navajo Reading Study Progress Report No. 23.

STAATS, A. and STAATS, C., 1958, Attitudes Established By Classical Conditioning. *Journal of Abnormal and Social Psychology* 57, 37–40.

STEBBINS, L. B., ST. PIERRE, R. G., PROPER, E. C., ANDERSON, R. B. and CERVA, T. R., 1977, *Education as Experimentation: A Planned Variation Model.* Volume 4. Cambridge, Mass.: ABT Associates.

STEPHENS, M., 1976, *Linguistic Minorities in Western Europe.* Llandysul: Gomer Press.

STERN, H. H., 1984, A Quiet Language Revolution: Second Language Teaching in Canadian Contexts — Achievements and New Directions. *Canadian Modern Language Review* 40 (5), 506–524.

STERNBERG, R. J., 1983, How Much Gall Is Too Much Gall? A Review of Frames of Mind: The Theory of Multiple Intelligences. *Contemporary Education Review* 2 (3), 215–224.

—— 1985, *Human Abilities. An Information-Processing Approach.* New York: Freeman.

STRONG, M., 1984, Integrative Motivation: Cause or Result of Successful Second Language Acquisition? *Language Learning* 34 (3), 1–14.

SWAIN, M. and CUMMINS, J., 1979, Bilingualism, Cognitive Functioning and Education. *Language Teaching and Linguistics: Abstracts,* 12 (1), 4–18.

SWAIN, M. and LAPKIN, S., 1982, *Evaluating Bilingual Education: A Canadian Case Study.* Clevedon: Multilingual Matters.

SWANN REPORT, 1985, see under DEPARTMENT OF EDUCATION AND SCIENCE.

TANSLEY, P. and CRAFT, A., 1984, Mother Tongue Teaching and Support: A Schools Council Enquiry. *Journal of Multilingual and Multicultural Development* 5 (5), 367–384.

TEITELBAUM, H. and HILLER, R. J., 1979, Bilingual Education: The Legal Mandate. In H. T. TRUEBA and C. BARNETT-MIZRAHI (eds), *Bilingual Multicultural Education and the Professional. From Theory to Practice.* Rowley, Mass.: Newbury House.

THOMAS, B., 1986, Schools in Ethnic Minorities: Wales. *Journal of Multilingual and Multicultural Development* 7 (2 & 3), 169–186.

THORNTON, G., 1986, *APU Language Testing 1979–1983. An Independent Appraisal of the Findings.* London: Department of Education and Science.

THURSTONE, L. L., 1938, *Primary Mental Abilities.* Chicago: University of Chicago Press.

THURSTONE, L. L. and CHAVE, E. J., 1929, *The Measurement of Attitudes.* Chicago: University of Chicago Press.

TOMLINSON, S., 1986, Ethnicity and Educational Achievement. In S. MODGIL, G. VERMA, K. MALLICK and C. MODGIL (eds), *Multicul-*

tural Education. The Interminable Debate. London: Falmer.

TORRANCE, E. P., 1974a, *Torrance Tests of Creative Thinking. Directions Manual and Scoring Guide, Verbal Test B*. Lexington, Mass.: Ginn.

—— 1974b, *Torrance Tests of Creative Thinking. Norms-Technical Manual*. Lexington, Mass.: Ginn.

TORRANCE, E. P., GOWAN, J. C., WU, J. J. and ALIOTTI, N. C., 1970, Creative Functioning of Monolingual and Bilingual Children in Singapore. *Journal of Educational Psychology* 61, 72–75.

TOSI, A., 1984, *Immigration and Bilingual Education*. Oxford: Pergamon.

TOUKOMAA, P. and SKUTNABB-KANGAS, T., 1977, *The Intensive Teaching of the Mother Tongue to Migrant Children at Pre-School Age*. Research Report No. 26. Department of Sociology and Social Psychology, University of Tampere.

TRIANDIS, H. C., 1971, *Attitude and Attitude Change*. New York: Wiley.

TRITES, R. L., 1981, *Primary French Immersion: Disabilities and Prediction of Success*. Ontario: Ministry of Education.

TROIKE, R. C., 1978, Research Evidence for the Effectiveness of Bilingual Education. *NABE Journal* III (1), 13–24.

—— 1984, SCALP: Social and Cultural Aspects of Language Proficiency. In C. RIVERA (ed.), *Language Proficiency and Academic Achievement*. Clevedon: Multilingual Matters.

TRUEBA, H. T., 1979, Bilingual Education Models: Types and Designs. In H. T. TRUEBA and C. BARNETT-MIZRAHI (eds), *Bilingual Multicultural Education and the Professional. From Theory to Practice*. Rowley, Mass.: Newbury House.

TSUSHIMA, W.. T. and HOGAN, T. P., 1975, Verbal Ability and School Achievement of Bilingual and Monolingual Children of Different Ages. *Journal of Educational Research* 68, 349–353.

TUCKER, G. R. and D'ANGLEJAN, A., 1972, An Approach to Bilingual Education: The St. Lambert Experiment. In M. SWAIN (ed.), *Bilingual Schooling. Some Experiences in Canada and the United States*. Ontario: Ontario Institute for Studies in Education. Symposium Series/1.

USSHER, A., 1949, *The Face and Mind of Ireland*. London: Gollancz.

VAN DEN BERGHE, P. L., 1967, *Race and Racism: A Comparative Perspective*. New York: Wiley.

VANIKAR, R. and DALAL, K. P., 1986, Bilingual Education: Education for All? *Journal of Multilingual and Multicultural Development* 7 (5), 423–427.

VERNON, M. D., 1969, *Human Motivation*. Cambridge: Cambridge University Press.

VERNON, P. E., 1963, *Personality Assessment. A Critical Survey*. London: Methuen.

—— 1979, *Intelligence: Heredity and Environment*. San Francisco: Freeman.

VYGOTSKY, L. S., 1962, *Thought and Language*. Cambridge, Mass.: MIT Press.

WAGNER, D. A., 1980, Cognitive Perspectives on Bilingualism in Children. *International Review of Applied Psychology* 29, 31–41.

WELSH OFFICE, 1984, *The Teaching of Welsh as a Second Language to Adults*. Cardiff: Welsh Office/Her Majesty's Stationery Office.

WIJNSTRA, J. M., 1980a, Attainment in English in the Schools of Wales. *International Review of Applied Psychology* 29, 61–74.

—— 1980b, Education of Children with Frisian Home Language. *International Review of Applied Psychology* 29 (1–2), 43–60.

WILLIAMS, G., ROBERTS, E. and ISAAC, R., 1978, Language and Aspirations for Upward Social Mobility. In G. WILLIAMS (ed.), *Social and Cultural Change in Contemporary Wales*. London: Routledge and Kegan Paul.

WILLIAMS, I. W., 1987, Mathematics and Science: The Final Frontier for Bilingual Education. *Education for Development*, in press.

WILLIAMS, J. G., 1915, *Mother-Tongue and Other-Tongue. A Study in Bilingual Teaching*. Bangor: Jarvis and Foster.

WILLLIAMS, J. L., 1960a, Comments on Articles by Mr. D. G. Lewis and Mr. W. R. Jones. *British Journal of Educational Psychology* 30, 271–272.

—— 1960b, Y Ddwy Iaith yn Arfon. *Y Faner*, April 20th.

—— 1974, Bilingualism in Wales. *System* 2 (3), 60–66.

WILLIAMS, M. W., 1953, Bilingualism in Welsh Schools. Unpublished thesis, University of Birmingham.

WILLIAMS, P., 1984, Overview. In P. WILLIAMS (ed.), *Special Education in Minority Communities*. Milton Keynes: Open University Press.

WILLIG, A. C., 1981/1982. The Effectiveness of Bilingual Education: Review of a Report. *NABE Journal* 6 (2 & 3), 1–19.

—— 1985, A Meta-Analysis of Selected Studies on the Effectiveness of Bilingual Education. *Review of Educational Research* 55 (3), 269–317.

WITHERS, C. W. J., 1984, *Gaelic in Scotland 1698–1981*. Edinburgh: John Donald.

WITKIN, H. A., DYK, R. *et al.*, 1962, *Psychological Differentiation*. New York: John Wiley.

WITKIN, H. A., OLTMAN, P. K. *et al.*, 1971, *A Manual for the Embedded Figures Tests*. Palo Alto, California: Consulting Psychologists Press.

ZAPPERT, L. T. and CRUZ, B. R., 1977, *Bilingual Education: An Appraisal of Empirical Research*. Berkeley, California: Bay Area Bilingual Education League.

Author Index

Subject Index